MW00484701

INDIA
STILL A SHACKLED
GIANT

INDIA
STILL A SHACKLED
GIANT

DEV KAR

PORTFOLIO
PENGUIN

An imprint of Penguin Random House

PORTFOLIO

USA | Canada | UK | Ireland | Australia
New Zealand | India | South Africa | China

Portfolio is part of the Penguin Random House group of companies
whose addresses can be found at global.penguinrandomhouse.com

Published by Penguin Random House India Pvt. Ltd
7th Floor, Infinity Tower C, DLF Cyber City,
Gurgaon 122 002, Haryana, India

Penguin
Random House
India

First published in Portfolio by Penguin Random House India 2019

10 9 8 7 6 5 4 3 2 1

ISBN 9780670091966

Typeset in Adobe Garamond Pro by Manipal Technologies Limited, Manipal
Printed at Thomson Press India Ltd, New Delhi

www.penguin.co.in

But for the love of India, this book could not have been written. I dedicate it to the memory of my parents who loved me unconditionally, to my family whose love supported me through the pages, and to the millions of Indians whose struggles against the odds made the retelling necessary. I do not expect everyone to agree with all that I say but I fervently hope that the book inspires some improvements in governance, however small, much like the first streaks of dawn that finally conquer the night.

Contents

Part 4: The Long and Winding Road to Redemption

Preface

It was an unusual confluence of factors that led me to write this book. My long career at the International Monetary Fund (IMF) took me to many countries where I had the privilege of working with senior government officials on some of the most pressing economic and statistical issues of the day. However, except in the case of a few countries, I seldom got to work directly on governance-related issues.

Speaking of governance, I vividly recall an incident that took place while on an official visit to undivided Sudan in early 1988. I ran into a gentleman in the lobby of the hotel in Khartoum where I was staying and we struck up a conversation. He introduced himself as a 'personal wealth manager' working at a large multinational bank based in London. I asked him how business was going and whether he expected to drum up much business here. Privately, I was surprised to see a 'personal wealth manager' in a poverty-stricken country that has had a history of coming to the IMF for subsidized loans.

He said, 'Oh, you would be surprised. There are a lot of wealthy businessmen and generals here who are interested in investing abroad. They routinely seek my advice on how to maximize the return on their investments.' It became clear that he often travelled from London to seek new clienteles and cultivate the old. But he seemed blissfully unaware that the country was almost bankrupt, struggling to repay its loans. Yet, the rich and famous not only had enough money to stash abroad, they were seeking his advice on how to further increase their wealth!

From the languid pace of life in Khartoum, you could not have guessed that large parts of the country had descended into civil war. Eventually, that civil war would lead to the breakaway nation of South Sudan.

While that was a classic case of weak governance feeding economic and social instability, I noticed telltale signs of such weakness in some of the other countries I visited as well (such as Ghana, Liberia, and Sierra Leone). However, I could not pursue those interests in earnest as they fell outside my responsibilities. In those days, the IMF typically did not get involved in such matters unless corruption had so drained the country that it was unable to repay the institution.

Lately, the IMF has increasingly started looking more closely into the governance problems of member countries. This new approach entails an examination of its various aspects which go well beyond those related to debt repayment difficulties. The expanded analysis is driven by the realization that poor governance can lead to economy-wide instability, which is the foremost concern of the IMF.

The labyrinthine path to economic instability is often marked by massive bank loan defaults, poor tax collection due to widespread tax evasion, very large transfers of scarce capital abroad, and endemic corruption amidst a general lack of law and order. Such symptoms of state failure must be addressed in order to pre-empt economic and social crisis.

After retiring from the IMF, I headed the economics department of Global Financial Integrity (GFI), a leading think tank based in Washington DC. There I was able to renew my interest in the subject. Funding from donor countries and foundations allowed GFI to carry out in-depth studies on the major adverse implications of poor governance. These studies showed that governance has a far greater impact on the quality of life than economic growth itself. Often the poor suffer more under the brunt of corruption and fragility than do the rich who can better insulate themselves from both.

The national animal of India is the tiger. This book discusses how the tethers of corruption and fragility have prevented it from becoming another Asian Tiger. The term represents Hong Kong, Singapore, South Korea and Taiwan, which developed so rapidly between the 1960s and the 1990s that they essentially transformed themselves into industrial economies. Attaining rapid economic growth is only part of their success story which entailed many other initiatives to improve the lives of their people.

There are a number of good books on India's governance conundrum, most of which have been written either by former senior government officials or by academics working in the field of governance. They present useful insiders' perspectives on how things went wrong, when and why, and what could be done about them. This book is a departure from that body of work in that it presents an Indian economist's 'outsider's perspective looking in'. Where possible or relevant, I will be comparing a specific issue in governance with the current situation in the US. In doing so, it is not my intention to portray US governance as some sort of a benchmark that other countries should strive for. Rather, having lived in the United States for the last forty-six years, I am familiar with the system here. But, more importantly, under the current Trump administration, the United States serves as a useful example of what to do as well as what not to do. Inasmuch as certain institutions and personalities maintain their independence against unprecedented attempts to politicize them, they underscore the importance of strong institutions for good governance.

We begin by raising a number of important questions. For example, what is India's standing in the world today based on widely cited international indicators? How has this standing evolved over time? How does governance impact the quality of life, which in turn determines happiness? Through these I discuss important aspects of governance focusing on major failures in post-Independence India when it comes to corruption, government effectiveness, political stability and peace, law and order and so forth.

Left unchecked, corruption and poor governance will not only further erode the quality of life of an average Indian, they are likely to hamper economic growth itself. India, the giant, fed on a steady diet of dirty money, is sick and getting sicker. It will become clear to the reader how poor governance diminishes the quality of life of far more Indians in far more ways than growth alone could ever improve their condition.

Each issue or even sub-issue dealt with in this book presents a serious challenge which experts have written on and discussed extensively. It is not possible for a relatively short book to deal exhaustively with all the factors that adversely impact the quality of life of the average Indian. Instead, this book presents a collection of free-standing essays on important issues of governance.

Most people in India think that high rates of economic growth will ultimately solve all their problems. While it is true that economic growth has helped to lift millions of Indians out of poverty, poor governance has continued to erode their quality of life.

Ever since the economic liberalization of the early 1990s, India has achieved rapid rates of economic growth, which have surpassed China's in recent years. It is likely that India will continue to register impressive rates of growth, barring some severe and unforeseen adverse economic developments. Yet, it will become amply clear that, for the vast majority of India's poor, growth will be meaningless without good governance. That was why the 2004 Bharatiya Janata Party (BJP) campaign slogan 'India Shining' failed to resonate with them, and the party lost that election.

The book also seeks to raise awareness about the consequences of poor governance and the price that society has had to pay. Policies to redress the situation are long overdue because even after seventy years of Independence, India has failed to clean up its politics, curtail rampant corruption, and improve law and order to name a few. But if the government were to implement a few of the important remedial measures, the quality of life would improve markedly for the average citizen.

I make liberal use of anecdotes in highlighting serious governance issues. Thus, while it can be a practitioner's book on governance, it has been mainly written for the general public. That said, I hope it will also be helpful to government officials interested in a quick review of the issues on which remedial actions are urgently needed.

One final note. I am grateful to my editor, Lohit Jagwani of Penguin India, for providing me the opportunity to write this book and giving me helpful feedback along the way. I also owe a debt of gratitude to numerous people in and out of the government, in universities and think tanks in both India and the US, and in international organizations such as the IMF, World Bank and United Nations for insightful discussions and comments on India's governance issues. Finally, I am thankful to Roshan Kumar Mogali and Joseph Antony of Penguin for their excellent editorial suggestions. However, the views expressed are my own and I take responsibility for any remaining errors.

PART 1

THE SLIDE

1

What Is Governance and Why Should We Care?

Poor governance, of which corruption is a defining feature, undermines government funding as well as the efficiency of investment allocation. For instance, countries that are weakly governed tend to invest far less in health, education and other key sectors that strengthen the nation state and the development process itself. Take, for example, the question of national security.

The movie *Hotel Mumbai* (2018) depicts the horrific 26 November 2008 terrorist attacks on Mumbai's Taj Mahal Palace Hotel, the railway terminus, and a Jewish outreach centre. The movie accurately captures the abject state of India's national security when it comes to dealing with terrorist attacks. Poorly trained police, many wielding sticks, were shown chasing heavily armed terrorists. While innocent men, women and children were being killed, India's elite commandos, the National Security Guard (NSG), took nine hours to arrive on the scene. The Delhi-based NSG lacked a dedicated aircraft to fly them to Mumbai.[1]

While there have been some improvements in the security apparatus, serious gaps remain in many areas.[2] I feel that India is

---

[1] Sumit Ganguly, 'India's Not as Safe as You Think It Is', *Foreign Policy*, 26 April 2019, https://bit.ly/2Z7Sgyz

[2] 'A decade after the Mumbai attacks, India remains vulnerable', *The Economist*, 1 December 2018, https://econ.st/33AePzf

ill-prepared to deal with the next terror threat. For instance, the various agencies involved in ensuring security lack adequate equipment for surveillance and to take offensive action against terrorists. The NSG still does not have a dedicated aircraft to transport them in the event of a terrorist strike. Meanwhile, the various national and state security agencies continue to squabble among themselves over turf. To make matters worse, India's long coastlines remain vulnerable to terrorist infiltration.

Apart from weaknesses in counterterrorism measures, there are other failures of the state. One of the main reasons why the recent 'Make in India' proposal failed to take off is that successive governments since Independence did not invest adequately in education and vocational training. As a result, India's pool of skilled manpower is rather shallow, providing little support for investments in manufacturing and high-technology industries.

As we shall see later, healthcare in India, particularly for the poor, leaves much to be desired. Public hospitals are few and far between, and the quality of care is abysmal. Private hospitals and nursing homes are better but the cost of care is well out of reach of the poor or even many middle-class Indians. Health insurance schemes tend not to provide adequate coverage for serious illnesses at a reasonable cost.

Governance not only represents the quantity and quality of goods and services provided by the government such as security, education, and healthcare, but also the extent to which law and order underpins all contracts, actions, transactions and behaviour. The law applies to everyone including citizens, politicians and the government itself.

We all pay the price when there is poor law and order. For example, thousands have perished in riots in India since Independence. Yet, many of the perpetrators have not been brought to book. Moreover, the verdicts take decades to be handed down by clogged courts. These are some of the many facets of fragility and poor governance.

What sets apart the rich (or advanced) countries from poor developing ones besides income? Rich countries typically have a huge lead over developing ones when it comes to the state of overall governance. Daily life is so much easier when everything works as expected. While corruption in advanced countries may be hiding in high places, there is no corruption at the grass-roots level where we have to bribe others just to get basic services. This is because there is a healthy respect for law and order. Private transgressions, which are thankfully few and far between, attract sure and swift punishment.

Nevertheless, advanced countries have also experienced colossal failures in governance. The cases that follow show that when institutions relax their oversight or are infected with corruption, those lapses could lead to serious political and economic instability.

The larger point is that if advanced countries with stronger governance can experience serious crisis, the risks are much higher for a developing country like India. Often, these risks are hidden until a crisis strikes. The crisis can take any shape or form such as a terrorist strike or a mega scam that takes advantage of weak institutions and regulatory oversight. Politicians cannot afford to neglect the poor state of affairs. Yet, apart from paying lip service at election time, nothing significant has been done by successive governments since Independence to curb corruption, strengthen institutions, or improve law and order to name a few.

Many Indians may wonder why they should be concerned about governance when India has been among the world's fastest growing economies for quite some time. After all, today there are more than a hundred billionaires, millions of millionaires, and a middle-class that is larger than the population of some developing countries. Besides, millions more have been lifted out of poverty as a result of rapid economic growth. So what is there to worry?

The short answer is 'plenty'. High rates of growth provide no insurance against a failure to govern. In fact there may be more ways to make black money in a rapidly growing economy that is poorly governed. One simply needs to know how to exploit the existing weaknesses in the system in order to do that. We have been reminded time and again about the costs of corruption but our attention span seems too short.

Governance Failure: United States of America

Weak governance not only caused the financial crisis of 2008 that originated in the US, but was also responsible for the surprise election of President Donald Trump. The financial crisis was brought on by weak regulatory oversight of banks, mortgage companies and the agencies which rated them. If lax oversight can cause a crisis in an advanced country, imagine the economic damage that regulatory weaknesses can cause in India. The benign neglect of governance issues is sorely misplaced; we have been told that those who do not learn from history are condemned to repeat it.

It is widely known that dissatisfaction with mainstream politicians led to the election of Trump. But most political pundits did not see the huge backlash by disgruntled voters that put Trump in the White House. He had been loudly complaining for years that many countries had taken advantage of America. In his view, globalization had harmed the US economy. However, Trump's assertions and complaints were not taken seriously.

One of Trump's major complaints was that China was cheating in international trade. It restricted the entry of US goods, stole American company secrets and resorted to unfair practices in order to gain a competitive edge. Moreover, he argued that while the US maintains low tariffs on its imports of foreign goods, other countries impose much higher duties on its goods. This makes it very difficult for US firms to compete and create jobs in the country. Indeed, a record number of US firms have shifted their production abroad. This has displaced millions of workers from their jobs. Most of the unemployed have still not found work that pays anywhere close to what they used to make.

J.D. Vance, a former US marine and a graduate of Yale Law School, wrote a haunting book on poor, white Americans. It is based on his own personal experience of growing up in Ohio and the Appalachian town of Jackson, Kentucky.[3] Jennifer Senior of the *New York Times* called the book 'a civilized guide for an uncivilized election', adding 'and he's done so in a vocabulary intelligible to both Democrats and Republicans. Imagine that.' I wasn't aware that such depths of despair, poverty and hopelessness exist in the US. The book opened my eyes.

There is truth to the charge that China resorts to unfair trade practices. However, the collapse of certain US industries and the resulting loss of jobs cannot simply be attributed to higher tariffs on US products imposed by other countries. Even if all duty rates imposed by China and other developing countries were set to equal US rates, the US would still not be able to compete with them. The lack of competitiveness is particularly pronounced in the manufacturing of low-end products such as clothing, furniture and shoes. The average wages and benefits of US workers are too high relative to those offered in developing countries for the US to be able to produce and sell those goods at a competitive price.

The truth of the matter is that globalization is a double-edged sword. It has its benefits and its costs. As far as the United States of America is concerned, few economists would question that the cost of globalization pales in comparison to the enormous benefits the country has enjoyed.

Professor Jagdish Bhagwati of Columbia University is an ardent defender of globalization and free trade.[4] But he also points out that while the overall effect of globalization on a country is beneficial, it has its downsides which need to be managed by governments in order to make globalization work better. For instance, he advocates unemployment insurance for workers displaced by plant closures and retraining programmes to help them find employment. In addition

---

3   J.D. Vance, *Hillbilly Elegy: A Memoir of a Family and Culture in Crisis* (New York: HarperCollins, 2016).
4   Jagdish Bhagwati, *In Defense of Globalization* (New Delhi: Oxford University Press, 2004).

to helping at an individual level, Bhagwati also recommends policy initiatives to reduce volatility in agricultural production and incomes.

Dani Rodrik of Harvard University has been at the other end of the ideological spectrum when it comes to globalization. Rodrik was quite prescient about globalization's downsides. In his 1997 book, Rodrik argued that globalization can lead to social tensions within a country as some groups of workers gain while others lose.

The determination as to who gains and who loses depends upon the industry that is subject to global competition and the skill sets of the workers. Globalization works best for those adaptable to changes in technology and competition. He also warned of a political backlash against trade if governments do not address these tensions.[5] They would need to manage the consequences of globalization in order to maximize its benefits and minimize its costs.

This is precisely what happened in the US. While successive governments, both Democrat and Republican, took the benefits of globalization for granted, they failed to mitigate its costs. Globalization led to the displacement of millions of workers through plant shutdowns and the collapse of entire industries. These losses are highly visible while the gains are not. Nevertheless, the fact remains that neither Democrats nor Republicans have tried to mitigate the cost of globalization in any meaningful way.

No wonder then that a large part of white working-class America is angry. The anger in the steel mill, coal and other once-vibrant industrial towns of America continues to fester even today. Trump sensed the anger and played to the gallery all the way to the White House. His opponent, Hillary Clinton, never saw it coming.

But the jobs are not coming back regardless of Trump's promises to bring back coal and other industries. The jobs are gone and are extremely unlikely to return. Other countries are better placed to produce those goods at a much lower cost and ship them to the US.

---

[5]   Dani Rodrik, *Has Globalization Gone Too Far?* (Washington DC: Institute for International Economics, 1997).

Higher duty rates on those imported goods are hardly the solution. They would simply rob consumers by imposing higher taxes on them and lowering their consumption. Such a high-tariff regime will hit the poor especially hard. Moreover, the US trade deficit with China may not improve if China finds ways to skirt the tariffs by routing their exports to the United States through other countries in Asia such as Vietnam.[6]

By that same token, unfair trade practices against US goods cannot be overlooked. The recent trade war underscores the fact that China needs to level the playing field when it comes to how it carries out its trade policy. Pursuing unbridled export expansion while placing all kinds of restrictions on imports is not a policy that can be sustained in the long run.

That said, as both Bhagwati and Rodrik point out, it is the job of the government to try and mitigate the costs of globalization. It could be through adequate worker education and training, help with worker relocation, or by providing generous family support through social security during the transition period. Yet, nothing much has been done to extend meaningful support to those adversely impacted by globalization. In fact, Trump has also done little to address the root cause of anger among less-educated unemployed whites. Political stump speeches are one thing but delivery on promises is quite another.

Governance Failure: Greece

There are other cases of advanced countries failing at governance. Take the case of Greece where wholesale tax evasion became a national sport. The tax administration knew what was going on but did nothing due to apathy and corruption among the ranks. Tax evasion became rampant even among highly educated professionals.

---

[6] 'Chinese Exports to the U.S. Sidestep Tariffs', *The Wall Street Journal*, 27 June 2019.

For instance, some 150 top doctors in posh localities of Athens with luxury stores such as Prada and Chanel claimed that their annual incomes were less than USD 40,000 in 2010! Thirty-four of them were even bolder and claimed that they owed no taxes as their incomes were less than the minimum (USD 13,300).[7]

On the other hand, Greeks had always enjoyed generous retirement and other government benefits. The party was good as long as it lasted. Poor tax collection, combined with rising government expenditures, created massive fiscal deficits. The deficits were deliberately understated by inflating government revenues to include tax revenues not yet collected. This was done so that Greece could obtain financing from foreign creditors at lower rates of interest than would have been the case had reported revenues reflected actual tax collections. The practice was clearly fraudulent. That was how endemic corruption led to cooked official data as well.

Such entrenched corruption and other weaknesses in governance plunged Greece into a financial crisis. The IMF, Germany, and the European Union (known as the troika) together had to rescue the country from the verge of bankruptcy through a massive bailout. The amount needed to rescue Greece from its creditors was so huge that no single member of the troika could afford to pay. The country is still trying to recover from the painful dose of austerity imposed by the troika as a necessary step towards self-sufficiency and solvency.

Governance As a Force

It is useful to look upon governance as a force. A significant worsening in a country's fragility and governance can produce a potent force—a force that neither governments nor citizens can ignore. The force acts both ways—in strongly governed countries, it works by retaining their deeply vested citizens while in poorly

---

7   Suzanne Daley, 'Greek Wealth Is Everywhere but Tax Forms', *The New York Times*, 1 May 2010, https://nyti.ms/2OWV5ma

governed countries, that same force tends to uproot families in search of a better life elsewhere.

Human migration takes place when the force of governance pushes people from poorly governed countries to strongly governed ones. The world is witness to the fact that when poor governance slides into anarchy, the force is enough to devolve emigration into an exodus. History is replete with sporadic episodes of mass migration and exodus. In fact, the widely dispersed Indian diaspora of today had itself been compelled into migration and exodus in the not too distant past. I can take a page from my own childhood.

Like many thousands of Indians in the 1960s, my parents saw compelling reasons to leave Burma and emigrate to India just before the military junta seized power from a democratically elected government. The junta expropriated the assets of all non-Burmese, who were mainly Indians, declaring that Burma is for the Burmese. Thousands of Indians who had cultivated deep roots in Burma over decades, were forced to uproot their families and leave the country. Later, such insular, nationalistic policies also led to the emigration of many Indians from Uganda.

The force of governance continues to act today. As in the past, the present humanitarian crisis is due to the abject failures of governance in the countries of origin of the refugees. Thus, the unprecedented influx of refugees from the Middle East to Europe or from Mexico and other Latin American countries to the US can be understood as a force compelling people to escape poor governance in search of better economic opportunities and greater personal security. The specific cause of these exoduses may be different but the force is the same—poor governance.

Border walls can perhaps temporarily deter illegal cross-border migration but they cannot stop the flow of illegals into a country. Because the force of governance acts both ways, we do not see an outflow of refugees from the US into Mexico or from India into Bangladesh. The present Trump administration seems oblivious to these basic forces and propensities at work. Fundamentally, Trump's trade policy is at odds with its immigration policy. But no one seems to have pointed this out to him. Not that Trump would care. In fact, I don't think either Trump or his millions of supporters care. But the truth never goes away just because we don't care about it! The truth comes in layers.

First, presidencies have limited terms. Even if Trump wins in 2020, his time as president would be up in another four years. That's not even a drop in the bucket, considering the lives of nations. The United States will continue to exist as a beacon of hope for all the despairing Mexicans, Hondurans, Colombians and Venezuelans, to name a few. The incoming president would like to leave his or her own mark on policy—a policy that would not only be fair but also perceived as such. Such an immigration policy has a much better chance of working in the long run compared to a border wall that can be likened to a Band-Aid over a hemorrhage.

Second, any immigration policy that wants to discourage the mass migration of illegal immigrants would need to facilitate those countries' trade with the US. The US trade deficits vis-à-vis many developing countries are a far more effective policy than aid ever was, or could be, in generating jobs and reducing poverty in those countries, thereby limiting illegal immigration into the US.

Therefore, US import restrictions and tariffs under the Trump administration is a penny wise and pound foolish policy that is choking business in those countries, further impoverishing poor people, and encouraging their illegal migration into the US. All the jingoism, brutality and downright racism backed by the best wall there is cannot stand up to the twin forces of fragility and poor governance.

That said, deterrence of illegal immigration must have an important and rightful place because there is little tolerance around the world for absorbing an exodus of refugees. Thus, the interdiction and deterrence of illegal immigration not only needs to be dovetailed with trade and aid, but there also need to be concrete efforts to improve governance in fragile states.

The time has come for strongly governed countries to turn up the heat on fragile states to seek the assistance of international organizations to improve governance. Unless economic opportunities and governance are strengthened in fragile states, the impetus of mass migration will continue regardless of any nationalistic president, wall or other deterrents. Policies of physical deterrence need to work in tandem with soft policies such as trade, aid, security collaboration, and technical assistance to improve governance.

Given that India is halfway around the world from the US, it comes as a surprise that Indians themselves are now the fastest-growing new illegal immigrants to the US.[8] Whereas the vast majority of Indians in the US are legal immigrants based on highly specialized skills in software development, computer or other engineering, medicine, and business management, the growing number of illegal immigrants from India are mostly unskilled.

According to Pew Research Center, between 2009 and 2014, some 500,000 illegal immigrants from India sneaked into the US even as the number of illegal immigrants from Mexico fell by 8 per cent to 5.85 million. Indians are now the fourth-largest group of illegal immigrants in the US after those from Mexico, El Salvador and Guatemala.

What does all this mean? Well, it seems all the drum-beating about 8 per cent growth and 10 per cent growth was not good enough for those who felt compelled to leave. Their lives obviously failed to improve and there are countless millions who are eking out such a living in India. They would also leave if they could.

It is not necessary that poor governance should always lead to cross-border migration of people. Indeed, poor governance can also lead to internal migration, displacement and fragmentation. The internal displacement of thousands of Kashmiri Pandits from

---

8   Karan Deep Singh, 'India Is the Fastest-Growing Source of New Illegal Immigrants to the U.S.', *Wall Street Journal*, 22 September 2016, https://on.wsj.com/2siwGdR

Kashmir is also a result of poor governance. When poor governance deteriorates into increasing fragility, it can separate or divide parts of the country. Thus, governance has serious implications for national security.

The abrogation of Article 370 on 5 August 2019 was a bold move by the Modi government. That article should never have been promulgated anyway. The righting of this wrong has the potential to vastly improve the governance of Kashmir as well as its economic and political integration into India.

2

India: Assessing Trends in Fragility and Governance

Fragility is a state of affairs, consisting of many economic, social, demographic, political, environmental, and security-related pressure points that either strengthen or weaken a nation state. Countries around the world have been subject to various pressures over time which have led to changes in their fragility. If fragility is left unchecked, the nation can slide towards civil war and break up.

The overall fragile states index (FSI) is derived from twelve sub-indices which are: demographic pressures, economic inequality, economy, external intervention, factionalized elites, group grievance, human flight and brain drain, human rights, public services, security apparatus, state legitimacy, and refugees and internally displaced persons (IDPs). Readers are referred to the appendix for further details on some of these indicators. Many of these sub-indices mimic the conditions captured by the six indices of the worldwide governance indicators (WGI) as detailed in the appendix. Inevitably, some of the discussions below will overlap with those under other chapters in this book.

According to the 2018 FSI, the five most fragile countries are South Sudan, Somalia, Yemen, Syria and the Central African Republic in decreasing order of fragility. At the other end of the spectrum we have strong democracies such as the Nordic countries, Singapore and other advanced countries (see table at the end of the appendix).

For our purposes, it will suffice to note that these indices not only capture the 'normal' pressures which all states experience, but also the latent ones that may be building up to a point where the state loses control over them. In highlighting these latent vulnerabilities, the FSI seeks to draw the attention of state leaders and policymakers to adopt remedial action before things get out of hand. A common caveat underlying all of them is that they are meant to track trends and patterns over the long run.

India's overall fragility increased from the ninety-third rank in 2006 to the seventy-second rank in 2018. India's slide by twenty-one ranks over this period was mainly driven by uneven development (such as rising income inequality), human flight and brain drain, state legitimacy, demographic pressures and security apparatus. These are explained below:

Uneven development considers inequality of income distribution regardless of the rate of economic growth. As we shall see in Chapter 14, India has one of the most unequal distributions of income in the world.[9] The uneven development indicator not only considers actual inequality but makes qualitative assessment on perceptions of inequality that can feed group grievance or reinforce tensions between groups. The indicator also measures economic opportunity such as the extent of free education, equal education opportunity, fair housing for the poor, job training, etc.

Research shows that income inequality in India has increased significantly since the mid-1980s. When income inequality worsens at such a pace, it is bound to lead to an increase in fragility. Income inequality is typically measured based on income data collected through official surveys of households. Where governance is weak and black money income is high, official surveys understate the income of the upper income groups because they do not report

---

9   Facundo Alvaredo, Lucas Chancel, Thomas Piketty, Emmanuel Saez and Gabriel Zucman (eds), *World Inequality Report 2018*, (Cambridge: The Belknap Press of Harvard University Press, 2018).

their actual income (including the black money component). In other words, actual income inequality which takes account of black money incomes is significantly worse than income inequality based on official surveys of household incomes. This, in turn, understates the uneven development component of the FSI.

Human flight and brain drain is partially evidenced by the rising number of applicants for US H1-B visas, the increasing number of illegal Indians trying to enter the US from Mexico, and the rising tide of Indians seeking to emigrate. The illegal immigrants are mostly poor Indians with little or no skills. In contrast, recorded immigration involves skilled and educated workers looking for better opportunities abroad. These immigrants are mostly located in India's larger cities. In fact, human flight and brain drain are happening in spite of the higher economic growth rates in the post-liberalization era.

State legitimacy considers the extent of openness of the government (i.e., transparency of operations). How open are the elites, who are close to power (called ruling elites), to transparency with regard to their business operations and taxes? Are they held accountable for their actions, for corruption, profiteering and marginalizing, persecuting, or otherwise excluding opposition groups? Other aspects of state legitimacy consider the population's level of confidence in state institutions, whether riots and uprisings occur and with what frequency, and whether people consider elections to be free and fair. State legitimacy also assesses the scope and frequency of political violence, armed insurgencies, and terrorism. India has had a long history of various armed insurgencies, political violence and riots. A very low score on the political stability and absence of violence component of the WGI is entirely consistent with a worsening score on the state legitimacy sub-indicator of the FSI.

When I was attending college in Calcutta in the early 1970s, the city was racked by violence perpetuated by the Naxalites. Prominent signs and wall paintings of Mao Zedong were appearing all over the city proclaiming 'Lal Salaam' (Red Salute) or 'Chairman Mao is our chairman'. Even at the ripe old age of eighteen, I could not figure out why Chairman Mao should be our chairman! This was shortly followed by some other communist group marching down the streets shouting in Bengali 'Amar Naam, Tomar Naam, Vietnam' (literally, my name and your name is Vietnam, implying there is solidarity between the common man and the revolution in Vietnam).

Although these ridiculous sound bites failed to resonate with the masses, it would not be wise of the government to ignore the reasons why these kinds of grievances exist in our society. So, even after systematically destroying the Naxalite movement, there are still pockets of Naxal activity in some states in India. This is true for other insurgent movements as well. The government has tried to address the legitimate causes for grievance with some degree of success. However, there are other reasons or demands which simply cannot be accepted by any democratically elected government under the Constitution of India.

Today, West Bengal's reputation for dirty politics has sunk to a new low after Mamata Banerjee came to power in 2011. The police are used to shield the party's street thugs and file charges against political opponents which are dropped when they pledge allegiance to her party (the All India Trinamool Congress). When the Central Reserve Police Force (CRPF) tried to ensure law and order at the local council elections in 2018 which had turned violent, their barracks were flooded with prostitutes. I am not sure how prostitutes were able to prevent the CRPF from taking action but I guess seeing is believing.[10]

Demographic pressures capture population pressures in relation to food supply, access to safe drinking water, energy requirements and other life-sustaining resources. This indicator also considers

---

[10]   'India's election campaign is racked by dirty tricks: Intimidating voters, bullying rivals, buying defections—you name it', *The Economist*, 21 March 2019, https://econ.st/2YTPvpr

demographic characteristics such as pressures from high population growth rates or skewed population distributions. For example, more than half of India's population is under the age of twenty-five.[11] A high proportion of young population is known as a youth bulge or a demographic dividend (discussed in Chapter 17). But a youth bulge, or sharply divergent rates of population growth among competing communal groups, can have profound social, economic and political effects. Moreover, while a youthful population can be more productive, the youths need to first find employment. If government policies are not able to encourage the private sector to create more jobs, that demographic dividend can easily turn into a demographic curse. Beyond the population, the indicator also takes into account pressures stemming from natural disasters (hurricanes, earthquakes, floods or drought), and pressures upon the population from environmental hazards.

Security apparatus considers the security threats to the country, the presence of serious criminal elements such as organized crime and homicides, and perceived trust of citizens in domestic security. The indicator would also be based on information related to the perceived professionalism of the police force, the prevalence or extent of armed insurgency groups that challenge the authority of the state, the extent and frequency of politically motivated violence, and other security-related factors.

The main findings for India are that there has been an increase in fragility since the BJP came to power. India was ranked seventy-ninth among 178 countries in overall fragility in 2013, the last full year when the Congress was in power, increasing thereafter to the seventy-second rank in 2018. However, India's fragility increased even more under the Congress from a rank of ninety-third in 2006 to a rank of seventy-ninth in 2013.

---

[11]   Ian Jack, 'India has 600 million young people—and they're set to change our world', *The Guardian*, 13 January 2018.

Yascha Mounk, a lecturer on government at Harvard University and Roberto Foa, a lecturer in political science at the University of Melbourne, find that only the rich democracies, with per capita incomes above USD 14,000 per annum, are reliably secure.[12] What to speak of India with a per capita income way below that threshold and where democracy is subject to much more internal competition for scarce resources, unequal distribution of income, grinding poverty, and corruption?

There is evidence that poor democracies tend to become increasingly fragile over time as they are unable to address these stresses and tensions among various groups.[13] For example, in a country such as India with a diverse population along the lines of caste, class, language, religion, race and tribes, fault lines can emerge between them if they identify along one or more of these lines rather than as citizens of the country. Tensions and grievances can arise when these groups compete for limited resources such as land, water and food, and limited opportunities such as education, healthcare and jobs.

These group grievances, which can remain hidden even as they are unresolved, can ignite like a powder keg. Politicians play an outsized role in managing these group tensions and stresses through appropriate, fair, and non-discriminatory policies, or exacerbating them through vote-bank politics for personal or political gain. Many countries in Africa with a diverse population along tribal or religious lines suffer from political instability as a result of divisive politics and corruption of all hues.

I am not suggesting that India is in imminent danger of sliding into widespread chaos or civil war. Rather, I am pointing out that given a low per capita income, wide diversity, demographic pressures, poor government services in the face of endemic corruption, lack

---

[12]   Yascha Mounk and Roberto Stefan Foa, 'The End of the Democratic Century: Autocracy's Global Ascendance', *Foreign Affairs*, Vol. 97, No. 3, May/June 2018.

[13]   Ibid., pp. 29–36.

of jobs, etc., a country such as India faces a much higher risk of increasing fragility than richer democracies. The fact that data show a worsening of fragility ought to raise the government's concern. It cannot afford to drag its feet on governance issues given the increase in fragility. Instead, as we shall shortly see, except for a few measures which are being implemented in a haphazard manner in recent years (Chapter 26), India has neglected to strengthen good governance. At a minimum, vote-bank politics of all hues need to be called out by the Election Commission, the Supreme Court and other watchdogs, and the most egregious practices outlawed.

Trends in Governance

The entire worldwide governance indicators exercise is based on perceptions and judgements of survey respondents in each country. The World Bank makes it quite clear that it simply compiles the information provided by them. Governance, as I mentioned earlier, is a complex subject and it is not possible to study it with scientific precision. Judgements will always be involved. These indicators are extremely useful to understand the nature of governance issues facing a country, whether the state of governance is getting better or worse, and how the country is faring vis-à-vis all the other countries in the world.

Good governance is not the exclusive preserve of rich countries. Over a dozen developing countries such as Botswana, Chile, Costa Rica, Czech Republic, Estonia, Hungary, Latvia, Lithuania, Mauritius, Slovenia and Uruguay had better governance scores for many years than advanced countries such as Italy or Greece. Readers interested in the methodological details on how the six indicators are compiled are referred to the World Bank's worldwide governance indicators (WGI) website.[14] The indicators themselves are described in more detail in the appendix.

---

[14]   Refer 'The Worldwide Governance Indicators (WGI) project', https://bit.ly/2cHS3d8

To recapitulate, the numbers refer to percentile ranks. For instance, an average percentile rank of 14.11 which India scores on political stability and absence of violence/terrorism for the period 1996–2017, means that 85.89 per cent (100 per cent minus 14.11 per cent) of countries in the world are better than India when it comes to this aspect of governance.

Table 1. India: Percentile Ranks in Worldwide Governance Indicators, 1996–2017

Year	Political Stability and Absence of Violence	Voice and Accountability	Rule of Law	Regulatory Quality	Government Effectiveness	Control of Corruption
1996	19.15	64.00	61.31	26.09	54.10	43.01
1998	12.77	61.69	64.00	30.57	55.44	48.45
2000	17.46	59.20	62.38	44.10	51.28	44.16
2002	15.87	61.19	53.96	42.35	53.06	35.86
2003	9.05	63.18	58.91	42.35	56.12	41.41
2004	13.11	61.54	55.02	38.42	52.22	40.98
2005	17.48	61.54	56.94	45.10	52.45	44.39
2006	16.91	59.13	58.37	45.10	53.66	46.83
2007	13.53	59.62	56.46	42.23	57.28	40.29
2008	13.94	60.10	57.69	40.29	54.85	44.17
2009	10.43	59.72	54.98	41.63	56.46	38.76
2010	11.37	60.19	54.03	38.76	56.94	38.57
2011	10.90	61.03	52.58	40.76	54.98	35.55
2012	10.90	61.03	52.58	35.07	48.82	36.97
2013	12.32	61.50	53.05	35.07	47.87	36.97
2014	13.81	60.10	54.81	34.62	45.19	41.83
2015	17.14	60.59	55.77	39.90	56.25	44.71
2016	14.76	61.58	53.37	41.35	55.77	47.60
2017	17.14	60.10	52.88	42.31	56.73	48.56
Avg. 96–2017	14.11	60.90	56.27	39.27	53.66	42.06
Avg. 02–2017	13.67	60.76	55.09	40.33	53.67	41.47
Grade	**F**	**C**	**D**	**F**	**D**	**F**

Grade Criteria: Average percentile ranks over period shown are assigned the following grades: F for percentile ranks from 0–50; D for percentile ranks from 51–59; C for percentile ranks from 60–69; B for percentile ranks from 70–89; and A for percentile ranks from 90–100.

The table above illustrates India's abject failure at governance as shown by these indicators. Each score reflects the perceptions of Indians about a particular aspect of governance (e.g., corruption) vis-à-vis how other people feel about the same issue in their countries.

Note that the governance scores for 1996–2017 do not form a continuous series because the World Bank carried out this expensive exercise only on a biannual basis until 2002. Average for both the discontinuous and continuous periods are shown to underscore the fact that no matter which period we chose, the message is the same—India scores poorly on governance rankings.

We can assign grades based on the scores attained. It is useful to look at the world as a class of countries in order to interpret the grades. The grades are assigned based on a country's performance. For example, if India scores less than 50 per cent of what other countries have attained on that particular aspect of governance, an 'F', for Fail, grade is assigned; India gets a 'D' grade for percentile ranks between 51–59; a 'C' grade for ranks between 60–69; 'B' for ranks ranging from 70–89; and 'A' for ranks between 90–100. Some grading systems are not as generous and actually deem a 'D' grade as a failing grade.

Long-term average percentile scores (or grades assigned here based on these average scores) are much more robust than small changes in the ranks themselves over that length of time. In fact, none of the changes in any of the six aspects of governance are statistically significant over the period 1996–2017 or between the continuous period 2002–2017. While the changes are not statistically significant, the deteriorations from already low scores need to be arrested first before the government can think of improving upon them. With that purpose in mind, we make the following points:

Among all the six WGIs, India registers a particularly low score on political stability and absence of violence/terrorism (PV). Not only that, India's PV dropped from the percentile rank of 19.15 in 1996 (the earliest year for which data are available) to the percentile rank of 17.14 in 2017 (the latest year of data availability). In other words, while 80.85 per cent (100 minus 19.15) of countries did better than India on PV in 1996, 82.86 per cent of countries did better on that score in 2017.

Although the decline in India's PV score is not large, India has always been one of the most violence-prone and politically unstable countries in the world! This increase in political instability and violence is fully consistent with the increase in fragility registered by the FSI. This is because increasing political instability and violence typically leads to increasing fragility of the nation state. So we should be more concerned about the low average score or grade over this period rather than the small drop in the rank itself.

Over the same period 1996–2017, there is also a slide in Voice and accountability (from sixty-fourth percentile rank to 60.10 percentile rank) and in the rule of law (from the percentile rank of 61.31 to the percentile rank of 52.88). Percentile-wise, the slide in the rule of law is the sharpest (more than an eight percentile drop), followed by voice and accountability (nearly a four percentile drop).

Measures to improve voice and accountability include ensuring greater press and media freedom, more participation by civic groups and NGOs (non-governmental organizations), and wide latitude granted to dissension. However, recent moves to curtail the activities of civic organizations and NGOs, as well as attacks on journalists, do not augur well for improving voice and accountability in India.

Regulatory quality (RQ) showed a rather consistent improvement over the period from 1996 to 2017. RQ improved from a 26.09 percentile rank in 1996 to a 42.31 rank in 2017.

However, the improvement in control of corruption (CC) is small and uneven. For instance, although CC improved from the 43.01 percentile rank in 1996 to the 48.56 percentile rank in 2017, the 2017 rank is almost the same as what India attained almost twenty years ago in 1998. While the 'improvement' in the control of corruption is not statistically significant, at least it is in the right direction.

By this grading criteria, India gets an 'F' grade in political stability and absence of violence/terrorism, regulatory quality, and control of corruption, a 'D' grade in government effectiveness and rule of law, and a 'C' grade (barely) in voice and accountability.

While few will disagree that India deserves an 'F' grade for political stability and absence of violence/terrorism, one can argue that scores in the 40–41 percentile ranks that India scores on regulatory quality and control of corruption should deserve a 'D' and not an 'F'.

The grading depends upon your perception. If you feel that periodic bank scams and massive amounts of non-performing loans of public sector banks are a serious form of regulatory failure, you would not hesitate to give regulatory quality an 'F' grade.

Similarly, when we recollect that corruption and black money were two of the main issues on which the BJP came to power and that the Congress lost massively because the party failed to curtail them, we should also assign scores in the 40–41 percentile range an 'F' grade. After all, those kinds of grades on corruption amounted to a force that changed the government at the Centre. The flip side of this argument is that unless the BJP is able to curtail corruption and black money, it can also suffer the same fate at the hands of the electorate in future elections at the national, state and local levels.

In sum, India scores three 'F's, two 'D's, and a 'C' (barely). Given the shrinking space for dissension and criticism of the government; restrictions on NGOs, freedom of the press and media in general, the BJP government needs to pay close attention to the voice and accountability score so that it does not drop to a 'D' in the long run!

Implications of Fragility and Poor Governance

While growth is necessary for improving living standards, it is likely to falter at some point if governance is weak and has been neglected for a long time. Threats to growth and economic stability can arise from any direction. For example, if regulatory and enforcement institutions are weak, the country may face serious risks of economic and financial crisis due to poor oversight of financial institutions.

Another aspect of weak governance is ineffective government policy. For example, if tax and subsidy policies are subject to corruption and other weaknesses due to weak governance, the major share of growth's benefits would continue to accrue to the top income groups and the rising income inequality could well derail growth in the long run.

Weak governance also restricts investments in the education and health of poor sections because of vested interests. Those without a voice have no means of representing their case for better healthcare and education. Their elected representatives, who came to them with folded hands for votes, cannot be held accountable once in power.

That is how fragile and weakly governed countries tend to invest much less in healthcare and education for the poor. Politicians would rather invest in prestigious mega projects to curry favour with the elite who often support them financially during elections. The result is a shallow pool of educated and skilled manpower from which investors are hard-pressed to draw upon. Consequently, the country again faces difficulties attracting investments into, say, export-oriented or technology-intensive manufacturing.

'Make in India' is a great objective but has had a hard time taking off given the long-standing neglect of healthcare and education. In that case, the country may be unable to sustain the high rates of growth due to the shortage of skilled labour in the long run.

Finally, weak governance could very well allow the unbridled exploitation of the environment by private and public enterprises in the pursuit of economic growth. But, sooner or later, environmental degradation can pose a serious constraint to economic growth or the attainment of the country's growth potential.

Adverse developments in fragility and governance over the long run, apart from seriously reducing the quality of life, can come with significant economic consequences. For instance, a country steeped in corruption is simply unlikely to be a good investment destination. Why should foreign investors looking to invest profitably, choose a country where corruption is rampant, law and order is weak, protections for private property are flimsy, or where there is no political stability or peace? After all, investors have a wide choice of countries where investment conditions are much better and they can make a decent return on their investment.

Governance under the BJP

Americans, as well as my Indian friends and relatives, often ask me whether governance in India has improved since the BJP came to power. This question can only be answered with reference to data on the six dimensions of governance. The change in the governance scores since the BJP came to power must also pass a 'test of significance'. Otherwise, the answer will be an opinion which may be biased due to the person's political views.

The test of significance is a statistical technique that allows one to determine whether changes in a variable measure genuine developments or whether the changes could be due to errors in the data themselves. Economists and statisticians typically use a 90 or 95 per cent confidence mark to say whether a change can be deemed to be a genuine improvement (or a deterioration) and not due to spurious errors in the data themselves. For example, if the rule of law indicator shows sufficient improvement over the period 1996 to 2016 and this improvement passes the 90 or 95 per cent confidence mark, we can say that this was not due to data errors but represents a genuine improvement in law and order. The World Bank recommends a 90 per cent confidence interval for a test of significance involving their governance data. In our cases, none of the changes in the six governance indicators met the required confidence mark. Therefore, we cannot say whether the deteriorations or the improvements are genuine or whether they were caused by measurement errors in the underlying data.

A simple method to check for significance is afforded by the World Bank's interactive database on governance. Interested readers could visit the website,[15] select some or all the governance indicators,

---

15   Refer 'Worldwide Governance Indicators', https://bit.ly/2ypLMlj

select India (or any country), select the time period for comparison, to generate the graph view.

We found that the changes in all six indicators for the period that the BJP has been in power were too small and failed to pass the test of significance. In fact, the World Bank deems even a decade to be a 'relatively short period' for estimating changes in governance.[16] While the 'improvements' did not turn out to be statistically significant, at least they are headed in the right direction. This is how improvements in governance take hold in the long run, provided the policies sustaining them are supported at the highest levels of government.

Going Forward

Various international indicators show that the responsibility for increasing fragility and weaknesses in governance must lie with the Congress. After all, the BJP has been in power at the Centre for a far shorter period of time than the Congress. However, the BJP government needs to implement policies that consolidate and solidify these gains and take measures to improve the other aspects as well. These are dealt with in more detail in the chapters that follow. Each of the six dimensions entails taking a range of measures which need to be sustained over the long run. That is why the transition from weak to strong governance is so challenging.

In fact, making sustained improvements in just one crucial aspect such as the control of corruption has been difficult for most countries. India scores the highest in voice and accountability, a 'C' grade. What is involved in making further improvements there? As the World Bank notes, voice and accountability aspect captures the extent to which there is freedom of expression, freedom of association, and a free media that is pluralistic and independent in expressing

---

[16] *Governance Matters 2009: Worldwide Governance Indicators 1996-2008* (Washington DC: World Bank Institute, 2009).

their viewpoints. The measure also includes holding public officials accountable, strengthening human rights and civil liberties, and encouraging rather than restricting civil societies such as NGOs and think tanks. Moreover, strengthening voice and accountability would also involve improving the electoral process, and promoting transparency in government policymaking.

So, there is a lot of work to be done in order to improve just this aspect of governance. Part II takes stock of matters as they stand while Part III explores the consequences of weak governance. Part IV provides an outline of recent initiatives by the government to address some of these concerns and concludes with an agenda for reform.

PART 2

THE GATHERING DARKNESS

3

Dirty Politics

There is no doubt that the source of corruption in India is its rotten politics. If politicians can use black money to get elected, criminals can contest elections and win, and if they can all play vote-bank politics, what kind of example do they set for the rest of the country? These days, it seems every political party needs criminals to intimidate the opposition, suppress dissent, and extract rent in order to ensure its hold over power. Under the circumstances, there can be neither raj (rule) nor neeti (ethics) left in rajneeti (politics). Another way of looking at this sad state of affairs is that many voters perceive the criminal politicians to be more effective in delivering government services. I think, either way, from the supply of criminal politicians to the demand for them, they pose a huge problem for any democracy and its governance.

There is a popular TV serial called *Crime Patrol* which is based on the dramatization of real-life criminal cases. It often ends with the message 'Crime never pays'. We wish. Crime pays and pays big when it comes to Indian politics!

If past elections are any guide, criminals tend to have a much better chance of winning elections in India than do politicians with a clean slate. Sometimes, as happens with sickening regularity, there are no good candidates on the ballot—they are all tainted by a corrupt or criminal past. When that happens, a small portion of the electorate (around 2 per cent in the Rajasthan state elections in 2018) express their frustration by opting for none of the above (NOTA) candidates. As the *Economist* put it recently, one could walk all the way from Mumbai to Kolkata without stepping outside a constituency whose member of Parliament isn't facing a criminal charge.[17]

Power and Corruption

By the end of their first elected term, most politicians (as well as their heirs) typically rack up assets far in excess of what their declared incomes could afford. Publicly available information obtained under the Right to Information Act show that there is a significant return to getting elected to public office in India. Rent extraction is higher for senior politicians such as ministers and incumbents. This means as politicians move up the political hierarchy, rent extractions also increase.[18]

But politicians are neither fearful nor embarrassed about the grotesque imbalance between the wealth they have accumulated illegally and their actual income. The nonchalance is understandable. It has been hard to make corruption charges stick in court as the following two cases show.

Jayalalithaa, the late erstwhile chief minister of Tamil Nadu, had a notional salary of Re 1. Yet, during the first period of her power in the early 1990s, she accumulated assets from virtually nothing to around Rs 53 crore. Her popularity and influence seemed to increase along with her wealth. People garlanded her, and both male and female colleagues prostrated before her in public. While being

---

[17] 'Why many Indian politicians have a criminal record: A penchant for criminality is an electoral asset in India, the world's biggest democracy', review of *When Crime Pays*, by Milan Vaishnav, *The Economist*, 4 February 2017, https://econ.st/2yZklNY

[18] Raymond Fisman et al., 'The Private Returns to Public Office', *Journal of Political Economy*, Vol. 122, No. 4, August 2014, pp. 806–62.

autocratic, she demanded and got a servile bureaucracy and secured voter loyalty through a steady stream of freebies and handouts.[19]

One would think that the successful investigation of her disproportionate assets would be a simple affair. As it turned out, she was found guilty of corruption and jailed for four years in 2014. Her sentencing sent shockwaves through the Indian political establishment. But shortly thereafter, her conviction was overturned on a technicality. She was out of prison in less than a month.[20]

Adulation for Amma, as Jayalalithaa was affectionately known, reached a cult-like status in Tamil Nadu. When I visited Chennai shortly before she passed away, I found her smiling down from giant billboards at different parts of the city as if bestowing her blessings.

Attempts to convict Mayawati for corruption met with more spectacular failure. Between 2003 and 2007, her self-reported financial assets increased fifty times.[21] In April 2016, the Supreme Court agreed to hear a petition from a former Bahujan Samaj Party (BSP) member against her. But, thus far the evidence collected has not been sufficient to convict her.

Governance in Uttar Pradesh (UP), India's largest state, is widely recognized as a 'goonda raj'—a rule by goondas or criminals. In fact, vast swaths of the eastern parts of the state are controlled by criminals with a penchant for brutal patronage politics, caste favouritism and crony capitalism—all backed by ruthless violence.[22]

Mulayam Singh Yadav, the erstwhile stalwart of the Samajwadi Party, was a master at playing caste-based politics. Under his tutelage and political brinkmanship, the Yadavs became UP's dominant caste force which ensured Mulayam's continued influence until his own

---

[19] James Crabtree, *The Billionaire Raj: A Journey through India's New Gilded Age* (New York: Tim Duggan Books, 2018), pp. 189–217.
[20] Victor Mallet, 'Indian politician jailed for lavish corruption', *Financial Times*, 28 September 2014, https://on.ft.com/2MkCi2c
[21] Milan Vaishnav, *When Crime Pays: Money and Muscle in Indian Politics* (New Haven: Yale University Press, 2017), p. 206.
[22] Crabtree, *The Billionaire Raj*, pp. 164–88.

son, Akhilesh Yadav, won the elections in 2014. Meanwhile, UP continues to lag behind other Indian states in terms of economic development, gender equality, job creation, healthcare, education, and other key indicators. However, it is a bit unfair to single out his failure to improve UP. Amethi and Rae Bareli are the strongholds of the Gandhi family but they have also made little difference for the region's development.

Apart from the fact that many ministers are utterly corrupt as well as incompetent, their arrogance is particularly mind-boggling. Recently, the chief minister of Jharkhand, Raghubar Das, had his feet washed in milk by two women on camera.[23] Last year, Madhya Pradesh chief minister Shivraj Singh Chouhan was carried around by two policemen through flood-hit regions in the state, which he was supposed to be inspecting, his feet shod in a pair of white sneakers.[24] There are so many incidents about politicians treating police and other top government officials with little or no respect, and transferring them at will.

But nothing much happens to such corrupt politicians—certainly not in relation to their grave crimes. They are neither held accountable nor sanctioned for bad behaviour. In the more than seventy years since Independence, hardly any politician has served serious jail time for corruption and other crimes. For instance, A. Raja, the former telecom minister, was acquitted in December 2017 after spending fifteen months in jail. That was the longest jail time for those accused in the 2G scam. His colleague and MP, Kanimozhi, the daughter of the Dravida Munnetra Kazhagam (DMK) chief M. Karunanidhi, spent just six months in jail while the others involved were all out on bail.[25] Bangaru Laxman, the politician from Andhra Pradesh, was convicted by a special CBI (Central

---

[23]   B. Sridhar and Jaideep Deogharia, 'Video of women washing Jharkhand CM Raghubar Das's feet sparks row', *The Times of India*, 10 July 2017, https://bit.ly/2Z5SI0h
[24]   'Kissa kursi ka: Cops carry Madhya Pradesh CM Shivraj Chouhan through flooded area', *India Today*, 22 August 2016, https://bit.ly/2z4Bh5O
[25]   PTI, '2G case: Raja spent longest period among accused in jail during trial', *The Economic Times*, 21 December 2017, https://bit.ly/2YQxyb7

Bureau of Investigation) court on 27 April 2012 for taking bribe and was sentenced to four years in jail on 28 April 2012. But he was granted bail due to health concerns and died on March 1 2014.

We have a broken system. Even if the corrupt are sentenced to prison for a few years like Jayalalithaa was, they are out faster than Houdini could get out of a box. Former chief minister of Bihar, Lalu Prasad Yadav, who was sent to jail for 14 years on various corruption charges related to the fodder scam, had petitioned the Supreme Court seeking bail on health grounds and his intention to run for the 2019 Lok Sabha polls.[26] As if we need another corrupt politician at the helm.

I wonder on what grounds he could petition. He and Rasheed Masood, a former minister, were already debarred from contesting elections for six years after their jail terms are completed.[27] Sentences need to be much more stringent in order to deter crime in politics. Moreover, bail should not be granted to the convicted barring exceptional circumstances. The media needs to hound corrupt politicians, the lawyers must go for the jugular, and the courts need to grow some real teeth. A criminal conviction should permanently bar politicians from running for any elections. Instead, what we have is a system where criminal politicians seem to do quite well.

Because politicians do not face any consequence for their criminal behaviour, they keep on doing them. That is because the electorate keeps on voting for them. Most people think that if the nation's leaders can play it so dirty, what is preventing them from raking in the loot too?

Development economist Paul Collier has said, 'Electorates get what they deserve.'[28] I happen to think they also get the governance

---

[26] Ashish Tripathi, 'Lalu Prasad Yadav moves SC for bail', *Deccan Herald*, 21 February 2019, https://bit.ly/2N95OHy

[27] Navin B. Chawla, 'Criminality in the Indian political system', *The Hindu*, 21 November 2013, https://bit.ly/2KCAK1f.

[28] Paul Collier, *The Bottom Billion: Why the Poorest Countries Are Failing and What Can Be Done about It* (New York: Oxford University Press, 2007), p. 176.

they deserve. If there are no widespread calls for governance reform, why should the government care?

The Role of Black Money in Campaign Financing

Democracy in India is very much a flawed enterprise, although the participation in the electoral process is impressive. Every so often, voters by the hundreds of thousands line up to cast votes in huge states such as Bihar, Madhya Pradesh and Uttar Pradesh. The cost of campaigning in a thousand villages, which make up a constituency, is enormous. There are many constituencies in such huge states which are larger and more populous than some countries. It takes massive amounts of money to finance elections in India. So how do parties finance state and local elections let alone the general elections to select a government at the Centre?

Just consider the enormous expenses involved in buying votes. While buying votes makes up a significant part of election expenses, paying party workers and meeting the costs of rallies and feasts quickly rack up the costs of campaign financing.[29] The *Times of India* reported that in the 2018 Karnataka state elections, voters were openly offered cash (as low as Rs 500 and as high as Rs 1000) to get them to vote for a party. Parties also distributed cases of liquor and Rs 15,000 for a community of 300 houses.[30] Given the size of the electorate, buying votes can get very expensive, very fast. All parties play this 'vote-for-sale' game regularly even as they tout the need for electoral reform. The hypocrisy is breathtaking. They resort to the same corrupt practices that they routinely decry from the pulpit. Once in office, the elected members of the party also use black money to deliver goods and services to their constituency.

---

[29]   Simon Chauchard, 'Why are elections getting more expensive in India?' *Hindustan Times*, 25 July 2018, https://bit.ly/2I3eKgd

[30]   Sandeep Moudgal, 'As Karnataka votes, cash is king for many voters', *The Times of India*, 12 May 2018, https://bit.ly/2Z9RSnd

Severe restrictions on how political parties can raise money have driven campaign finance underground and fostered a culture of corruption and kickbacks. There are two main factors responsible for the critical role of black money in financing elections. First, corporate contributions to finance elections was banned in 1967 by the then prime minister Indira Gandhi. The ban was introduced as part of her election strategy to limit the financing of opposition parties that relied more on corporate financing. But the effect of this ban reached far beyond the 1967 elections.

As Prem Shankar Jha wrote in the magazine *Tehelka*, 'The ban on company donations closed the only honest, open and transparent avenue of raising funds to fight elections.' The roots of corruption then started spreading their tentacles further into all aspects of public and private sector transactions in India. Jha correctly noted that the harm done by this ban is beyond measure. Actually, the financing gap left by the 1967 ban has been increasing year after year due to inflation, the fragmentation of parties, vote-bank politics, and an expanding electorate, leading to a vice-like grip of black money in the financing of Indian elections.

Second, as Jagdeep Chhokar notes, political candidates and political parties have recently complained that the limit on expenditure set for election campaign 'is too low and needs to be increased'. He further states that the limit has been raised from time to time (from Rs 25,000 in 1951 to Rs 1 lakh in 1979, to Rs 4.5 lakh in 1994, to Rs 15 lakh in 1997, Rs 25 lakh in 2003, and Rs 40 lakh in 2011). However, the fact remains that adjustments to the expenditure ceiling have failed to close the gap between the new limits and actual expenditures.

Politicians use their power to grant licences and permits as a leverage to raise funds through 'donations' which are really bribes. If donors do not pay these bribes, and their chosen party does not win, the next government will blacklist them and shut them out from getting any contracts.

Hence, enormous amounts of black money are involved not only to fund elections but to sustain those in power. The latter then turn around to award lucrative contracts to the donors who brought them to power. Black money is also used to play vote-bank politics to ensure victory in future elections. Minimizing the role of black money and barring criminals from running for elections are probably two of the most important electoral reforms that need to be made urgently.

One way the use of black money in financing elections can be gradually reduced is by having the Election Commission of India increase the limit on expenditures in inflation-adjusted terms. If, for example, inflation is increasing by 10 per cent per annum, the Election Commission could raise the limit by say 20 per cent in one year. The reverse has happened in the past when the ceiling was increased by less than the rate of inflation. Between 2003 and 2011, the limit on expenditures was increased by 60 per cent while prices increased by 78.5 per cent during that eight-year period. Adjustments to the ceiling needs to be significantly higher than the rate of inflation because election expenses have also been driven by an expanding electorate and the fragmentation of parties leading to an increase in candidates.

While every candidate to the Lok Sabha is required to submit a statement of expenditure incurred to the Election Commission of India, only a paltry few ever exceed the limit on expenditures. For instance, of the 6,753 candidates that contested the elections in 2009, only four candidates declared that they exceeded the limit. Small wonder that the Supreme Court in 1994, termed the ceiling on election expenditures as 'mere eyewash' making a mockery of election laws. Apart from the judiciary, several commissions have also pointed out the adverse impact of dirty money in politics. Yet, nothing ever gets done about the problem. The reason is an utter lack of political will as politicians are loath to go against a system that brought them to power and continue to serve them well.

The outsize role of black money in financing elections can and should be seen as a national security issue. This is because nobody shells out hundreds, even thousands, of crores of rupees without a motive. There is always a quid pro quo when it comes to money. Issues of national security arise if we ask the simple question: what motivates these financiers of elections? How do the holders of black money who finance elections plan to make good on their 'investment'? It will be naive to believe that their hidden agenda is to do good for the country! Rather, it is much more realistic to assume that the agenda of black money financiers of elections is to simply line their pockets when the government, the party or the politicians they have supported come to power.

A few ways black money financiers make a good return on their investment is by winning lucrative tenders for government contracts and obtaining exclusive licences to mine minerals and precious stones. Contractors win such contracts by paying bribes or they win them because they have already earned their keep by financing the government to power.

Of the parliamentarians implicated in criminal wrongdoing, some 12 per cent faced serious criminal charges including rape, murder, armed robbery, kidnapping, blackmailing and extortion. Moreover, the representation by politicians with criminal backgrounds is increasing rather than declining.

Milan Vaishnav, a senior fellow at the Carnegie Endowment for International Peace, notes that the share of MPs facing criminal cases increased from 24 per cent in 2004 to 30 per cent in 2009 and further to 34 per cent in 2014. Of these shares, those facing charges for serious crimes increased from 12 per cent to 15 per cent and further to 21 per cent during those years.[31] In March 2018, the Centre informed the Supreme Court that 36 per cent of MPs were facing criminal charges in 3045 cases.[32]

The ability to self-finance expensive campaigns is one of the key reasons why Indian politics attracts criminals to run for

---

[31]   Vaishnav, *When Crime Pays*, p. 9. His data are based on those compiled by the Association for Democratic Reforms (ADR).

[32]   Amit Anand Choudhary, '36 per cent of MPs facing trial in 3045 criminal cases', *The Times of India*, 12 March 2018.

office. They are the ones who know how to generate black money and where to stash the funds until they are needed for maximum political gain. Because parties are typically strapped for cash, they welcome such candidates.

Looking at a large data set of candidates in state elections, Vaishnav concludes that wealth significantly enhances the criminal candidates' electoral prospects. In fact, those convicted of serious misdeeds are three times as likely to win parliamentary elections as those with a clean slate.[33] One of the reasons why the electorate seem to favour them is that they have muscle power and know how to use black money to deliver services, even jobs, to the poor. I feel that criminals also fill the space left empty by an inefficient and ineffective state and local government apparatus.

Illiteracy among the electorate also plays into the hands of criminals. The illiterates are impressed by superficial things such as charisma and muscle power. They are unable to analyse the facts about the candidates and to ask themselves whether the politicians of their choice are good for their state or community, let alone for the country. Sometimes people believe that charges against their favourite candidate have been trumped up by the opposition. They get woolly thinking that their candidate is a 'social worker' who will represent their interests against a distant Central government oblivious to their plight.

The more illiterate the electorate, the more gullible they are. A largely illiterate population is much easier to manipulate (such as through vote-bank politics) than an educated one. Corrupt politicians would like to keep it that way. By 'illiterate' I mean those without basic knowledge about candidates, their stand on policies, means of delivery, etc., rather than a mere ability to sign their name on a piece of paper. They do not realize that the financing of Indian

---

[33]   'Why many Indian politicians have a criminal record: A penchant for criminality is an electoral asset in India, the world's biggest democracy', *The Economist*, 4 February 2017.

elections by black money clearly presents a national security issue which is compounded by the utter lack of transparency regarding campaign financing.

Yet, police continue to seize hundreds of crores of rupees hidden in trucks and rooftops of buses during state elections as has happened in the Karnataka and Tamil Nadu (2018) elections. Regional parties as well as mainstream ones get busy wooing alienated voters along caste, region and religious lines. These voters in turn pick candidates they best think will represent their interests. Often, mainstream parties lose out to narrow regional or caste interests as the voters feel that mainstream parties with a national footprint are not best placed to represent their own, often narrow, interests.

There is also a strong link between the real estate sector and black money, which is used to invest in property and other tangible assets such as precious stones, gold and silver. The speculative investment of black money in such assets rather than the financing of productive ventures is well known. Often, there is a cosy relationship between developers who benefit from political doles and the politicians who invest their illicit assets in real estate. At election time, these investments finance the political campaigns of politicians leading to a downturn in the construction sector and a significant reduction in cement consumption.

Milan Vaishnav and Devesh Kapur, professor of South Asian Studies at Johns Hopkins University, found evidence of this nexus between real estate developers and politicians in India.[34] They found that consumption of cement typically went down in the run-up to elections when developers had to divert cash to support their favourite candidates. But their short-term pain is more than compensated by long-term gain following their candidates' electoral win when the builders get lucrative contracts and other deals helping their business (such as cheap utilities or relaxation of regulations).

---

[34]   Vaishnav, *When Crime Pays*, p. 62.

Dirty politics is not confined to India alone. It is a familiar story across most developing countries in Asia, Africa, the Middle East and South America. Recently, there was an article on the state of democracy in Mongolia.[35] It was reported that every post in Mongolia's government bureaucracy comes at a price—around USD 400,000 to become a cabinet minister, USD 120,000 to be the director of a government agency, USD 4000 for a senior specialist's role within the bureaucracy. The Mongolian People's Party openly offered more than 8000 government jobs if it won parliamentary elections, in return for the money the party needed to run its campaign. Parties also routinely raise money from business elites to meet election expenses. One of the biggest political scandals to hit Mongolia in recent times was a case that exposed the fundamental weakness at the heart of that democracy.

Mongolians are convinced that the source of corruption is the way elections are financed. They feel that those who finance political parties control the country and the government. Voters feel that their interests are not represented and they are disillusioned with this so-called democracy. This disillusionment is gradually sweeping across many countries, giving rise to populist 'outsiders' and demagogues.

Voter turnouts have been declining in Mongolia. In 1993, turnout in the country's first free presidential election was nearly 93 per cent. In 2017, turnout fell to around 68 per cent. Some 19,000 people out of 1.4 million voters cast a blank ballot signalling that they were not impressed with any of the candidates. Khaltmaa Battulga, a business tycoon and former wrestler who cast himself as a populist, anti-establishment figure, won the last elections.

Meanwhile, a law requiring political parties to report on their finances is simply ignored. In Mongolia too, as elsewhere, when businesses fund politicians, they expect something in return. So,

---

[35] Simon Denyer, 'Familiar ill in Mongolia's democracy: Money; Campaign finance breeds corruption, people feel alienated, and populism is rising', *The Washington Post*, 27 June 2018.

when politicians win elections, they pay back their funders. The proceeds from Mongolia's vast reserves of coal, copper and gold flow disproportionately to the elite, while nearly 30 per cent of the country lives below the poverty line.

In the US, the system is more transparent, but Americans are also wary of the role of big money in the financing of elections. They are convinced that business elites have vastly more influence over policy than average citizens.

4

India's VIP Culture

A recent report in the *Times of India* states that in India, at least three police personnel are assigned to each politician while there is only one for every 663 people.[36] According to the Bureau of Police Research and Development, which is under the Ministry of Home Affairs, out of a police force of 19.26 lakh, 56,944 are assigned to ensure the safety of 20,828 VIPs across twenty-nine states and six Union territories as existing then.

Bihar, with the poorest police to population ratio, has the maximum number of VIPs at 3200, guarded by 6248 officers. This is closely followed by West Bengal, Uttar Pradesh and Punjab. In Jammu and Kashmir, one of India's most militarized states (recently changed from a state to two Union territories), about 2075 VIPs are being protected by 4499 officers. In the state of Uttar Pradesh, where Chief Minister Adityanath has made noises about cracking down on the toxic 'VIP culture', 1901 such privileged members of society are being taken care of by 4681 cops. Last but not the least, in New Delhi, where the prime minister and the president reside, 489 VIPs have 7420 officers allotted to them.

Prime Minister Modi announced that Indians should embrace the fact that every person is important (EPI). He wants India to transition from special treatments for very important persons (VIPs)

---

[36]   Neeraj Chauhan, '3 cops to protect each VIP but just 1 for every 663 common man', *The Times of India*, 18 September 2017, https://bit.ly/2Z8IxrL.

to an EPI culture. Well said, but the fact of the matter is that little has been done to actually make that transition. At least the BJP government got rid of the twirling red lights from every VIP car, which had become an eyesore across India. The move remains largely symbolic, however, as long as the culture remains intact and is perpetuated in so many ways every day. I was told some of the VIPs are now using sirens to announce their presence.

One can think of a hundred things the government could have done which would have probably improved governance by a small measure rather than the recent demonetization which had a marginal impact on corruption in the short run and a significant negative impact on the economy. But I do not see demonetization curtailing corruption in the long run. If, instead of demonetization, the government would have made a serious push to dismantle the VIP culture and the lavish benefits showered on government ministers and high officials, that move itself would have made a far more meaningful (although a largely symbolic) contribution to improving governance in India. Instead, demonetization failed to reduce corruption on a sustainable basis and imposed painful costs on the middle class and the poor.

The VIP privileges are often abused. The late chief minister of West Bengal, Jyoti Basu, had an extensive security detail. Even after retirement, he used to go around in a helicopter.[37] He once tried to land in an army cantonment eliciting a strong protest from the army who argued that landing in a cantonment cannot be extended to civilians due to security issues. Another VIP recently slapped an airline worker over a scuffle for seats. Apart from these regular tamashas, we have these VIPs showing up at the airport (sometimes with their entourage) and demanding to board the aircraft without having to go through any security clearance.[38]

---

[37]   Labonita Ghosh, 'With Jyoti Basu unwilling to go, West Bengal has two chief ministers', *India Today*, 1 January 2001, https://bit.ly/309dzkD
[38]   Binoy Prabhakar, 'Dangers of India's VIP culture: Exemption from airport security checks may compromise safety of others', *The Economic Times*, 15 June 2014, https://bit.ly/2OVIyiS

This culture has become a pure nuisance. Apart from holding up traffic and even ambulances, the assignment of high-level (or Z category) security to politicians is a waste of money in a poor country such as India. There is an urgent need to work towards the goal of reducing to zero the attractiveness of holding a political office.

The ideal situation would be reached when nobody really wants to become a minister. 'Seats' and 'tickets' would go a-begging as potential candidates would say, 'The pay is poor, headaches are plenty, and there are zero perks and zero security to boot. Moreover, the risk of going to jail for making black money is close to 100 per cent. We don't want to become ministers.' India would then attract only genuine leaders who want to serve their country at considerable cost to themselves. That will be in keeping with the true spirit of public service.

Instead, now we have diehard politicians as well as criminals all falling over themselves to become ministers. It would be deeply satisfying if Prime Minister Modi could work with this privileged ruling class to make their jobs totally unattractive. People would remember him for this lasting contribution. That is the only way a subservient class of government servants as well as the public will stop placing politicians on a pedestal and garlanding them at every turn.

No 'VIP' Scourge in Advanced Countries

First of all, there is no VIP culture in the US, or other developed countries in the world. The late senator Kennedy, a face that was known to the whole world, had to line up for security check before boarding a flight just like the rest of us. In fact, all senators have to do that. No exceptions.

But Kennedy had trouble boarding flights in 2004 because he was mistakenly placed on the government's secret no-fly list.[39] Those on that list must undergo additional security screening before being

---

[39]   Rachel L. Swarns, 'Senator? Terrorist? A Watch List Stops Kennedy at Airport', *The New York Times*, 20 August 2004, https://nyti.ms/2N6TkjS

permitted to board. Mistake or not, Senator Kennedy could not cite any VVIP or even VIP privileges to get around the Transportation Security Administration (TSA) screw-up. He was stopped five times from boarding a plane that year!

Now, along comes Shah Rukh Khan. He was pulled aside for extra security checks while entering the US in August 2009. I was amused to read that Bollywood had erupted in anger.[40] The most hilarious one was by Priyanka Chopra on her Twitter: 'Shocking, disturbing . . . downright disgraceful. It's such behaviour that fuels hatred and racism. SRK's a world figure for God's sake. Get real.' Shah Rukh Khan? World figure? Someone needs to update Ms Chopra on what it takes to be a world figure!

Never mind, but why only blame Bollywood for such over-the-top reactions? One cabinet minister went so far as to suggest a tit-for-tat policy towards Americans travelling to India. This outpouring of grief and outrage in India at VIPs unable to avoid being frisked at airports is understandable because politicians, sports celebrities and film stars often flaunt their status to avoid security checks. I am told that the entire entourage accompanying VIPs and VVIPs also claims the privileges whenever or wherever possible.

What's the status of politicians in developed countries? Joe Biden, the erstwhile vice president of the US, a man second in line to take over the presidency if the president was killed or incapacitated, regularly commuted to Washington DC on public trains. The prime ministers of the United Kingdom, Norway, Denmark and other Scandinavian countries, as well as in other developed countries with more than thirty times the per capita income of Indians, also get no special privileges or benefits. I saw on television David Cameron, then the prime minister of Britain, travelling on the subway train just like ordinary members of the public. There were other prominent

---

[40]   Associated Press, New Delhi, 'Bollywood anger over actor Shah Rukh Khan's "detention" by US immigration', *The Guardian*, 16 August 2009, https://bit.ly/2YTVAlL

politicians like Boris Johnson, the then ex-mayor of London, who also did the same.

In fact, the privileges and benefits extended to ministers and MPs in India are unheard of in these countries. Citizens of advanced countries would stare at you in amazement if you informed them about the perks that ministers and MPs in India get.

In Sweden, representatives to the parliament live in state-owned housing (and you can be sure, these are not lavish, bungalow-style houses!). Japanese parliamentarians stay in accommodations next to the legislature, while Indian politicians live in Lutyens-designed bungalows in New Delhi.[41] It was reported that some US congressmen and congresswomen sleep overnight in their offices which saves them up to 10 per cent of their salary which they would otherwise have to spend on Washington's pricey housing.

Most senators, representatives, and delegates earn USD 174,000 per annum on which they have to pay federal and state taxes. Only the Speaker of the House of Representatives makes an annual salary of USD 223,500 while the president pro tempore of the Senate and the majority and minority leaders in the House and Senate each earn a salary of USD 193,400. These levels have remained unchanged since 2009 and are extremely modest compared to salaries in the US private sector. No senator, representative, Supreme Court judge, or secretaries of federal agencies (a rank equivalent to ministers in the Government of India) receive a housing allowance let alone a big fat bungalow to live in. They all have to meet their housing cost from their salaries. Moreover, none of them get chauffeured around in fancy cars. All of them drive their own cars.

How do the salaries of US Congress members stack up against those paid to Indian MPs? The salaries of the former are lower than mid-level executives of the US private sector and about 2.9 times the 2017 US GDP per capita (USD 174,000 divided by US per capita

---

41   Kate Allen, 'Where do politicians live? How MPs across the world find city digs', *Financial Times*, 13 April 2016, https://on.ft.com/2OY4Dxp

GDP of 59,895). In contrast, the average salary of Indian MPs is around Rs 1 lakh a month plus at least Rs 90,000 in allowances (not including any housing allowances) which translates to about USD 32,570 per annum or about 16.2 times India's 2017 GDP per capita of USD 2014.[42]

We need to make two adjustments to this estimate. First, India's GDP should be estimated on what is known as purchasing power parity (PPP) basis. The PPP takes account of the fact that a dollar goes much further in India and that Indian consumers have a different basket of goods and services than American consumers. A straightforward comparison based on GDP per capita would overstate the extent to which an MP's salary exceeds the nation's per capita income. Using PPP-based GDP of about USD 7287 in 2017 (based on World Bank estimates), an Indian MP's salary plus allowances are 4.5 times the PPP-adjusted per capita income.

Now, we should remember that this compensation package does not include generous housing, travel and other allowances which are not extended to their US counterparts. Once these allowances are factored in, we can expect a typical Indian MP's total compensation package to be many more times the country's PPP-adjusted per capita income. India is a poor country based on per capita income. A compensation package for MPs that is likely to be more than ten times the country's per capita income is quite excessive. And we keep hearing that some of these MPs do not even attend Parliament when it is in session.

So this is a clear case. What works for the US could work in India, with some appropriate modifications. If the US, a much richer country than India, can offer its politicians a modest salary with little or no perks, I find it difficult to understand why India cannot adhere to the same basic principle.

At a minimum, ministers, MPs, judges and celebrities should be stripped of their VIP and VVIP perks and privileges. And the sooner,

---

[42]   Refer World Economic Outlook Database, July 2019, IMF. Available at: https://bit.ly/2YlTp5p

the better. They are public servants and should be treated as such. This sick VIP culture needs to be wiped off from India and the clean-up needs to start with the politicians. Only the prime minister and the president should be provided with *reasonable* perks and privileges (comparable to developed countries, and no more) in keeping with the status accorded to the highest offices in the land.

5

Institutional Deficits

Strong versus Weak Institutions

It is no surprise that strongly governed countries tend to have strong institutions. After all, no matter how many sensible laws are on the books, it is the relevant institution, staffed with qualified professionals of personal integrity that need to implement them. In India, we have the reverse problem. There are too many laws (some of them outdated) and too few strong institutions to implement them effectively.

Hence, the public has been beset by all kinds of scams. There have been banking scams, tax scams, customs scams, housing scams, government contracting scams, ration card scams . . . 'etcetera, etcetera, etcetera,' as Yul Brynner declared in *The King and I*. That should cover other types of scams I may have missed.

Highly professional institutions are an essential feature of effective government. Such institutions are typically led by well-qualified staff of good personal integrity. Furthermore, the laws establishing these institutions and their rules and regulations grant significant autonomy and operational independence. Moreover, the professionalism and technical expertise of their staff lend them strong credibility in the eyes of the public and the Central and state governments, particularly in times of crisis. On critical issues within their areas of competence, the top management of strong, independent institutions are not likely to cave in to political expediencies floated by politicians for political gain. If push comes to shove, they would rather resign than allow their reputations to be sullied.

Moreover, leaders of independent institutions are forthright in their views breaking sharply from the views of senior government officials, ministers or even the heads of governments. They are ready to defend their opinions of the state of the economy, security or any other aspect of governance that falls directly under their mandate.

Heads of independent institutions do not suffer from a herd mentality, toe the line or make statements to please their political bosses, if in their considered opinion, they are wrong. The advantage of having such independent institutions is that the public as well as politicians get to hear and weigh carefully considered professional opinions of experts rather than hear from a bunch of yes-men. Heads of institutions who merely chose the path of least political resistance can never serve as custodians of effective policy or provide early warning of an impending crisis. The nation ends up facing serious risks from multiple quarters because politicians prefer to surround themselves with subservient staff. Sycophants would rather not say what they really feel and hide the truth to please the powers that be.

A recent testimony before the US Senate Intelligence Committee illustrates the point that the heads of independent agencies can disagree with their commander-in-chief (the president) regarding important issues of national security or foreign policy. During this testimony, the nation's top intelligence officials differed sharply from President Trump on several critical fronts.[43]

Daniel Coats, the director of national intelligence, pointed out that North Korea is unlikely to give up its nuclear weapons, throwing cold water on Trump's claims about reaching a détente with that regime. Coats also noted that while the Islamic State has suffered leadership and territorial losses, it is still capable of attacking the

---

[43]   Shane Harris, 'Spy chiefs, Trump differ on threats: Hill Testimony Exposes Divergent Views', *The Washington Post*, 30 January 2019.

United States. His views contradict Trump's claim that the Islamic State has been defeated, as a result of which US troops can be withdrawn from Syria.

Furthermore, Coats, along with director of the The Central Intelligence Agency (CIA), Gina Haspel, and The Federal Bureau of Investigation (FBI) director, Christopher A. Wray, held the view that Iran was not trying to build a nuclear weapon. Again, their testimony directly contradicted the Trump administration's claims that the country has been violating the terms of an international agreement reached during the Obama administration. It looks like the Trump administration's imposition of sanctions and unilateral abrogation of the nuclear deal may actually push Iran to develop nuclear weapons in the long run.[44] Coats also testified that he sees a continuing threat of Russian cyber-attacks and political meddling in the 2020 US presidential elections.

The rule of law enforced by strong, independent institutions are perhaps two of the most important characteristics that determine the state of overall governance of a country. In strongly governed countries, the rule of law not only reigns supreme (on the fundamental premise that nobody is above the law), strong institutions also ensure that the laws are implemented in a timely and fair manner.

Weak and servile institutions can be politically manipulated or affected by corruption either from within or without. Strong institutions, on the other hand, do a much better job of withstanding these insidious forces. That said, even relatively strong institutions are not invincible if a country's political leaders are bent on undermining them. We will refer to recent developments in the US in order to highlight how historically independent institutions can be undermined.

In strongly governed countries, the government in power prefers to adopt a hands-off policy in dealing with independent

---

[44]   James Griffiths, Joshua Berlinger and Sheena McKenzie, 'Iranian leader announces partial withdrawal from nuclear deal', CNN, 8 May 2019, https://cnn.it/2H7lWF6

institutions in keeping with the spirit of laws governing those institutions and the country's traditions. By tradition I also mean an implicit recognition among politicians that they will have to answer to voters and pay a heavy price for undermining the authority of the nation's institutions.

According to the worldwide governance indicators (WGI), voice and accountability scores are much higher in advanced countries than in developing ones. This implies that voters in developed countries are far keener about governance-related issues and demand more accountability from their politicians than do voters in developing countries.

For instance, the recent mid-term election victory of the Democrats in taking control of the House of Representatives away from the Republicans is widely seen as a rebuke of Trump's policies.[45] In fact, when the new Congress was sworn in in January 2019, more than 100 women became new Representatives in the people's House. This is the first time in US history when so many women have a hand in running the government.

We can judge an institution to be largely independent from the fact that it can conduct its operations free of political pressures. That is, the leaders of the institution can adopt policies which they feel are in the best interests of the country and not the political party in power. In such cases, the institutions act in a strictly apolitical manner based on the facts of the matter and their best judgement regarding an appropriate course of action. There is no attempt by any political party or politician to influence government institutions into taking a specific action or policy.

Furthermore, the statutes and acts governing independent institutions are written in such a way as to make it very difficult for the government to fire senior management. The rules governing the termination of their services are deliberately set on a high bar such as

---

[45]   Joe Scarborough, 'That was a wave, and Trump lost', *The Washington Post*, 9 November 2018.

conviction on a criminal offence, gross dereliction of duty, conclusive evidence of corruption and other serious offences or incapacities.

Such rules of employment provide a reasonably strong protection from termination without cause or on some flimsy grounds. They allow management to function with a far greater latitude compared to managers who could be fired by the government without cause.

Moreover, the charter of independent institutions typically does not allow the government to have a great say in their day-to-day operations. For example, government representatives either do not have a seat in the institution's governing board or are merely invited as observers. Government representatives also tend not to have a voting power. Moreover, the government does not have a big financial stake in the institutions. They tend to make their own money and are owners of their own capital. In short, government influence or participation in their operations is minimal or even non-existent.

And, as I mentioned before, politicians ought to be well aware of the heavy political price they will pay for playing politics with the nation's top institutions. In most advanced countries, the message to politicians is loud and clear—play politics with these institutions and you will be flirting with political hara-kiri.

In contrast, politicians in India often get off lightly for corruption or other maleficence. Is this observation an exaggeration? After all, did the UPA-2 government not pay a price for corruption? Did A. Raja not go to jail after he was implicated in the 2G scam?

Yes, but we should weigh the penalties in relation to the scale of the crimes and the damage inflicted. By that measure, I think the penalties were not severe enough to act as a deterrent. The Congress came back in December 2018 to defeat the BJP in three crucial state elections—Chhattisgarh, Madhya Pradesh and Rajasthan. Raja got out of jail after serving just fifteen months. These penalties and punishments were hardly punitive enough to instill a fear of the law. That is why scams happened with sickening regularity under the Congress-led government. While the number and extent of scams have declined under the Modi-led government, India still has a long way to go before it can claim a clean government. The electorate can and should send a message to politicians that they expect harsher punishment for the corrupt. At the end of the day, Collier says electorates get the government they deserve.[46]

So what is the state of some key institutions in India today?

A Servile Law and Order System

At a minimum, the government needs to ensure the independence of the police force. Instead, political parties in India are guilty of playing footsie with regulatory, judicial and investigative agencies that are supposed to be independent of political considerations and motivations. Today, the state police forces, which are completely beholden to the chief minister and the party in power, have become a political tool for the harassment of opponents and the mollycoddling of goondas on the state payroll. A police force used by state politicians on the premise that 'our goondas are better than your goondas' can never be a credible law enforcement agency. When institutions that should serve the people are abused for political expediency, corruption comes full circle and institutions are rendered totally powerless. Such institutions make a mockery of democracy, not uphold its principles.

Matters are probably much worse with the Central Bureau of Investigation (CBI) these days. While corruption and partisanship had infiltrated the CBI since its inception, they came to a head recently after the director of the agency, Alok Verma, charged his second in command, Special Director Rakesh Asthana, of corruption.[47] Verma is supported by the Congress party while Asthana is supported by the BJP. According to Verma's lawyer, Prashant Bhushan, Asthana is a 'blue-eyed boy of the Prime Minister'. Apparently, Asthana worked under Modi when he was the chief minister of Gujarat and gave

---

46   Collier, *The Bottom Billion*, p. 176.
47   Zeenat Saberin, 'India's CBI chief removed, critics call it a "misuse of power"', Al Jazeera, 24 October 2018, https://bit.ly/2MmLdAd

Modi a clean chit on the Gujarat riots which happened under his watch. So Modi seems interested in promoting Asthana as director of the CBI.

How can you improve law and order if the highest investigative agency as well as the police forces around the country are subject to political meddling? The penchant for political parties in power to use the CBI for their own purposes has a long history. My father-in-law, Sachindra Kumar Chatterjee, who was among the first batch of IPS officers in independent India, was the front runner for the post of director of CBI in 1978. This was based on the fact that he topped the list of candidates for the post based on performance. But the then prime minister Morarji Desai lost majority in the House when the Janata Party splintered. He resigned and was replaced by Charan Singh who brought in his own man for the post.

I remember my father-in-law quite happy with the abrupt change in prospects. He told me, 'I am glad I am not going. It is a thankless job.' Shortly thereafter, he took over as the inspector general of police (IGP) of undivided Bihar (there were no director general of police (DGP) in the 1970s).

The point is that the CBI should serve the country and not the fancies of political parties. In fact, the CBI should not be answerable to political parties at all but to the Parliament. It should be an independent agency in its own right. Political meddling in the running of the CBI and its operations has compromised its integrity, and ruined its reputation, credibility and legitimacy.

Fast forward to what is happening in the US. There was a time when the US was a beacon of universal values and global order. No longer. Today what is happening in the US is a reminder to the rest of the world of what to do as well as what not to do. Therein lies one of the benefits of comparing the governance systems of the world's two largest democracies—India and the US.

Recently, Trump fired Attorney General Jeff Sessions because he did not stop the investigations of his presidential campaign for possible links or coordination with the Russian government. These investigations, under Special Counsel Robert Mueller, a former director of the FBI, have led to the convictions of several Trump campaign officials who were sent to jail. Paul Manafort, Trump's former campaign chairman, was convicted of eight charges related to bank and tax fraud. Michael Cohen, Trump's former lawyer and 'fixer', pleaded guilty to making excessive campaign contributions and paying off two women who said they had affairs with Trump. Michael Flynn pleaded guilty to lying to the FBI, while Scott Pruitt was forced to resign due to ethical lapses. There were other high officials who were found guilty of similar illegal acts. However, the Mueller report essentially cleared Trump himself from any wrongdoing in connection with the Russia investigations.

Independence of the RBI versus the FRB

The Reserve Bank of India (RBI) is perhaps India's best professionally managed institution. But, of late, the RBI has also come under renewed political pressures. The independence of a central bank is typically determined by a number of clauses in the Act establishing the institution.

Two sections of the Reserve Bank of India Act amply illustrate the power of the government over the RBI: Section 11 (1) and Section 30 of the Reserve Bank of India Act, 1934, (as amended):

11. Removal from and vacation of office.

(1) The Central Government may remove from office the Governor, or a Deputy Governor or any other Director or any member of a Local Board.

According to Section 30 of the Act, the Government of India can hire and fire senior executives of the Reserve Bank at will. This is because the government retains the power to 'supersede' (meaning, take over) the entire governing board of the Reserve Bank in the event it fails to follow through on government orders.

(30) Powers of Central Government to supersede Central
Board

If in the opinion of the Central Government the Bank fails
to carry out any of the obligations imposed on it by or under
this Act, the Central Government may, by notification in the
Gazette of India, declare the Central Board to be superseded,
and thereafter the general superintendence and direction of
the affairs of the Bank shall be entrusted to such agency as the
Central Government may determine, and such agency may
exercise the powers and do all acts and things which may be
exercised or done by the Central Board under this Act.

When action is taken under this section the Central government
shall cause a full report of the circumstances leading to such action
and of the action taken to be laid before Parliament at the earliest
possible opportunity and in any case within three months from the
issue of the notification superseding the board.

The Act does not specify any reason, let alone set a high bar,
for the government to fire the governor, the deputy governor or
other senior managers. The terms of reference of the Reserve Bank's
management should be reasonably independent of the government.
For instance, while the governor and the deputy governor would
continue to be appointed by the government, their dismissal should
be made much more difficult than the procedures currently in place.

India should model the terms of reference of the governor, the
deputy governor and the board of directors along the lines of the
Federal Reserve Bank (FRB) of the US and central banks in other
developed countries. The independence of the Reserve Bank of India
needs to be strengthened if we are to avoid periodic banking scams
and the piling up of loans as non-performing assets.

Larry Summers, one-time Harvard University president and
treasury secretary, in an excellent review of *Unelected Power*, a book
by Paul Tucker, research fellow at Harvard Kennedy School, notes

that 'it is often said that the chair of the Federal Reserve is the second most important person in Washington'.[48] This second most important person in Washington is neither elected by the people nor directly held accountable to, or subject to dismissal by, elected officials. In fact, the president of the United States cannot fire members of the board of governors of the Federal Reserve Bank.

No such language exists in the Federal Reserve Act of 1913, as amended. So, the independence of the central bank is built into the legal provisions governing the terms of reference of its senior executives and the manner in which it operates with respect to the government. In short, the Federal Reserve Act provides a legal framework designed to insulate it from political pressures.[49]

Furthermore, a central bank that is relatively more independent has a built-in clause in its Act that places a formal limit on the amount of government debt it can hold. Such formal limits help to insulate the central bank's conduct of the monetary policy from the government's fiscal policy. Let me explain.

In many developing countries, governments spend more on various programmes (such as on defence, infrastructure, health and education, wages, etc.) than they collect through revenues. The deficit, that is the gap between the much higher expenditure and revenue, is financed in three ways. They are printing money and taking loans from the central bank, borrowing funds from abroad, and selling government bonds to the public. All three are problematic. The first leads to inflation, the second to rising external indebtedness, and the last to rising interest rates which may 'crowd out' the private sector as the pool of domestic savings shrinks.

---

[48]   Lawrence H. Summers, 'Bringing accountability to powerful, unelected officials', review of *Unelected Power: The Quest for Legitimacy in Central Banking and the Regulatory State*, by Paul Tucker, *The Washington Post*, 16 September 2018.
[49]   Paul Tucker, *Unelected Power: The Quest for Legitimacy in Central Banking and the Regulatory State* (Princeton: Princeton University Press, 2018).

When the government sells its bonds to the central bank in exchange for cash, the extension of credit creates money and fuels inflation. Such a 'captive' central bank obligated to finance the government's deficits invariably loses its independence. For example, situations may arise when the central bank feels that it should tighten credit and the money supply in order to fight inflation. But it may be obligated to finance the government against its better judgement, particularly in an election year thereby fuelling inflation.

In contrast, the government in advanced countries cannot compel the central bank to finance its fiscal deficits by simply asking it to hold government bonds. Either there are no provisions for the central bank to hold government bonds or there are strict limits stipulated in the Act beyond which the government cannot sell the bonds to the central bank. These limits allow the central bank to pursue monetary policy that is much more independent from the government's fiscal policy compared to the situation which generally prevails in developing countries.

The Reserve Bank of India Act could be amended to place formal restrictions on the amount of government bonds and securities that can be held by the Bank. Such limits would circumscribe the RBI's 'banker to the government' function in the interest of prudential monetary policy and discipline in the financing of the government's fiscal deficits. These restrictions would place limits on inflationary financing of the deficits, ensure the independence of the RBI from political tinkering, and insulate monetary policy from the election cycle.

The RBI and Banking Scams

The late finance minister Arun Jaitley blamed the RBI's weak oversight and audit functions for the Rs 11,400-crore fraud at Punjab National Bank, the second-largest state-owned bank. Jaitley said that not a single red flag was raised by the RBI when the fraud took place. He also blamed its top management for indifference and lack of awareness of the financial shenanigans that were going on.

Specifically, Jaitley noted that 'multiple layers of auditing system which chose to either look the other way or do a casual job' meant that the RBI had 'inadequate supervision'. He lamented, '[U]nfortunately in the Indian system, we politicians are accountable, the regulators are not.'[50]

But these criticisms of the RBI are unfair because they stand on very shaky grounds. As Governor Urjit Patel has noted, the RBI has 'very limited authority' over state-run banks and he called on the government to give the RBI more powers to regulate and oversee public sector banks.[51] Appearing before the Parliament's Standing Committee on Finance on 12 June 2018, Patel specified areas where the RBI cannot control the public sector banks (PSBs) and pointed out that the Banking Regulation Act would need to be amended in order for the RBI to exercise full control over them.

It is helpful to remind ourselves of the history of the PSBs. The birth of PSBs started with the nationalization of the Imperial Bank of India by the Congress in 1955. That bank later became the State Bank of India. Seven other state banks became the subsidiaries of the new bank with the passage of the State Bank of India (Subsidiary Banks) Act, 1959, under the Nehru government. This was followed by the nationalization of fourteen major banks on 19 July 1969 by the Indira Gandhi government, bringing 84 per cent of bank branches under government control.

Given the overwhelming control of PSBs by the Central government, their oversight by the RBI was almost non-existent. PSBs cannot serve two masters at the same time—the government and its diktats as well as an independent RBI. Rather, the government has always used the PSBs to further its political and economic development objectives. These include targeted lending to agriculture and other

---

50   PTI, 'Jaitley slams regulators' failure to detect PNB fraud', *The Hindu BusinessLine*, 24 February 2018, https://bit.ly/2MjowN6
51   Devidutta Tripathy and Abhirup Roy, 'RBI Governor Urjit Patel calls for more powers over state lenders in wake of PNB fraud', Reuters, 15 March 2018, https://reut.rs/2uyPKaG

sectors (called selective credit policies) and spreading rural banking that private banks would not undertake on grounds of cost-effectiveness.

Why is the expansion of banking in rural areas not profitable for banks? The main reason is that the majority of rural inhabitants are small depositors because of income limitations. Moreover, many are still not comfortable operating bank accounts. They mostly rely on cash transactions for their daily needs and are also paid in cash. The small deposit base and the limited capacity of rural customers to take on and repay loans would limit a bank's profit margins. In short, private banks would not consider the expansion of rural banking to be a viable business proposition. The Indira Gandhi government created public sector banks to expand banking into rural areas, a move that private banks would not undertake from a purely business perspective.

It is hard to see how the lending policies of public sector undertakings (PSUs) directed by the government would pass muster with the prudential regulations enforced by any truly independent central bank. After all, private banks would not extend such high-risk, loss-making credits. So, for Jaitley to turn around and blame the RBI for lack of oversight was nothing but political fodder. The whole problem with the Indian system is that the politicians are never held accountable. Things got so difficult for Patel that he resigned rather than be totally subservient to the government.

Banking scams could be curtailed by gradually diluting the government's holdings and control of PSBs. The nationalization of private banks served its purpose and now it is time to let them manage their own affairs based on sound banking principles overseen by a strong and independent RBI.

There have been calls from Arvind Subramanian and others that the government use the reserves accumulated in the contingency fund of the RBI to help capitalize the banks. In other words, the government should pay down the non-performing loans and improve the lending capacity of state-owned banks.

This is not a good idea due to risks associated with 'moral hazard'. The moral hazard arises from the use of funds earned by a relatively well-managed RBI to essentially bail out poorly governed and corrupt public sector banks. After all, the PSBs went on a lending spree, untethered by prudential banking norms. The government will be sending these banks the message that it stands ready to bail them out again should they run into trouble due to their reckless lending in the future.

The moral hazard of using the RBI's contingency funds can be minimized by the government gradually privatizing PSBs. This means the government must reduce its role in the ownership, management and control of PSBs. The government would be sending them a clear message—you have been bailed out but henceforth, you are on your own. These moves would preclude politicians from pressurizing banks into making massive unsecured loans to their business friends (known as 'connected lending') as was the case with Vijay Mallya.

The government could also request technical assistance from the IMF on strengthening the independence of the Reserve Bank of India in accordance with international best practices. These practices could be modified in light of India's particular stage of development.

Institutions are invariably much more independent from the executive (i.e., the political powers that be) in strongly governed countries than they are in weakly governed ones. The best way to do that is to ensure that the statutes governing these public institutions are written in such a way that they can protect themselves from political interference.

Next, the heads and deputies of these institutions must be people of strong integrity and professional excellence. In popular discourse, they should be expected to exercise independence as provided under the law. They will not bend to political pressure. So, while laws granting independence are necessary, that alone is not sufficient. These institutions must exercise independence in their dealings with the government. Otherwise, in spite of laws, government regulatory agencies would become toothless tigers.

Independence of the Federal Reserve Bank

Americans are understandably worried that the chairman of the Federal Reserve, Jerome H. Powell, may be next in Trump's cross hairs, given the latter's track record of undermining the independence of federal institutions.[52] Trump's efforts to undermine federal agencies for political purposes are driven by his need to gain an edge over opponents. He could do that by shutting down the government, derailing ongoing investigations, or by delivering on the promises he made to his base in the run-up to the presidential elections.

The independence of a central bank can be assessed with regard to goals and instruments. Goal independence goes hand-in-hand with instrument independence. Price stability, full employment and stimulating economic growth are three important goals or objectives. At any given time, an independent central bank such as the Federal Reserve has to decide which of these three goals is the most important for the sake of economic stability.

For example, if the Federal Reserve senses that inflationary forces are taking root, it would act quickly to deploy all 'instruments' or policy measures to defuse such forces. Instruments include manipulating interest rates on deposits and loans, changing banks' reserve requirements (thereby increasing or reducing their lending capacity), and buying or selling government bonds in the open market to influence market interest rates.

If the Federal Reserve senses a risk of inflation, it can raise its benchmark federal funds rate in several steps. The federal funds rate is the rate at which depository institutions (such as commercial banks) lend funds to one another overnight without any collateral. In fact, in pursuit of its anti-inflation strategy, the Federal Reserve has been raising this benchmark rate in successive meetings of the Federal Open Market Committee in 2018. The rise in federal funds rate has also led to the rise of automobile, housing, home equity,

---

[52] Matt O'Brien, 'Sessions's ouster suggests Trump's Fed fight over rates is about to get uglier', *The Washington Post*, 10 November 2018.

credit card, and other interest rates. These policy actions have raised the Trump administration's anxiety that monetary tightening is going to choke off the economic expansion currently underway and hurt the prospects of the Republican Party in the 2020 elections. Subsequently, in light of the fact that the signs of inflation have abated, the Federal Reserve has refrained from further increasing the federal funds rate.

So, instrument independence means that the Federal Reserve is free to deploy any and all instruments which it deems are best suited to meet its primary goal, which in this case is price stability. As the FRB restricts credit growth by hiking up the interest rates that banks charge on their loans, the economy starts to slow down. Wage increases may be postponed and companies may shed workers as the credit squeeze raises the cost of doing business.

The restrictive monetary policy is likely to be quite risky for politicians in an election year. Goal independence and instrument independence means that a central bank such as the FRB is free to pursue them in the nation's interests *regardless of the political risks and costs involved*. The Federal Reserve Act grants the bank both goal and instrument independence in pursuing its objectives at any time independent of any political considerations. In other words, politicians do not get to influence, let alone decide, either the goal of the FRB or the instruments at its disposal.

Recently, signs have emerged of economic weakness, even a recession, probably starting sometime next year. Accordingly, the Federal Reserve has cut its benchmark interest rate by a quarter point, a move that is seen by the Trump administration as too feeble and insufficient to ward off a potential recession.

Trump is concerned that any economic downturn in the run-up to the presidential elections in 2020 can harm his re-election prospects. But the Federal Reserve is convinced that it needs to adopt a policy stance that is consistent with market conditions at any given point in time rather than take account of political compulsions dictated by the White House.

There are many examples where the Federal Reserve's strong regulatory oversight has worked for the people. One of them is the instance of Riggs Bank, which was one of the largest and most important commercial banks headquartered in Washington DC. The two main regulators of Riggs Bank were the Federal Reserve Bank and the Office of the Comptroller of the Currency (OCC), a part of the US treasury. When these regulators asked Riggs in 2000 for a list of its accounts controlled by political figures, the information turned in by the bank did not include any deposit accounts held in the name of the Chilean dictator General Augusto Pinochet.

Then, in April 2002, following the 11 September 2001 terrorist attacks on the US, the OCC began vetting the international banking operations of US banks more thoroughly. They found that the bank had changed the name on the accounts of the general and his wife from 'Augusto Pinochet Ugarte & Lucia Hiriart de Pinochet' to 'L. Hiriart &/or A. Ugarte', ensuring that searches for Riggs accounts named 'Pinochet' would draw a blank.[53]

The Senate's Permanent Subcommittee on Investigations found that sometime in the spring or summer of 2002, Riggs tried to withhold information about the Pinochet accounts from both the regulators. According to the customary laws, the bank should have frozen the accounts, closed them and returned the money to General Pinochet.

The Senate Subcommittee found that Riggs executives and bank regulators, even after the events of 11 September 2001, failed to monitor suspicious financial transactions involving hundreds of millions of dollars. Senate investigators said that while the bank never made any sincere effort to do so, as required by law, the regulators never considered fining Riggs in 2002 or referring the Pinochet accounts to law enforcement officials. In fact, the OCC's lead Riggs examiner at the time, R. Ashley Lee, took an executive position at Riggs later that year.

---

[53]   Timothy L. O'Brien, 'At Riggs Bank, A Tangled Path Led to Scandal', *The New York Times*, 19 July 2004.

Digging further into the operations of Riggs Bank, the Senate Subcommittee found that the Federal Bureau of Investigation (FBI) was examining Saudi Arabian Embassy accounts at the bank in connection with the 11 September attacks. Once again, the Subcommittee found that Riggs executives were indifferent to suspicious transactions that were being carried out right under their nose. Although the FBI found no evidence that the money from Prince Bandar's wife went to the hijackers involved in the 11 September attacks, regulators dug up outsized movements of cash that ought to have raised red flags but regarding which Riggs executives displayed gross negligence.

The Senate Subcommittee's report on Riggs Bank's operations gave a detailed picture of events that eventually snowballed into a financial scandal and permanently damaged the bank's reputation. On 13 May 2005, Riggs Bank was acquired by PNC Financial Services of Pittsburgh for USD 779 million.

All the regulators acted independently. Neither the Federal Reserve Bank nor the OCC called the White House seeking permission to launch an investigation into the transactions and operations of Riggs Bank. The Senate Permanent Subcommittee also acted independently from any political considerations arising out of the Chilean and Saudi funds. The investigations culminated in the closure of this large and reputed commercial bank after regulators found enough evidence of wrongdoing and financial transgressions. At no time did the Office of the President get involved in the ongoing investigations.

Now, let us recount what happened after the former RBI governor Raghuram Rajan 'dropped a bombshell' (the way one of Kolkata's leading newspapers put it) on the Modi government pointing out a list of high-profile bad loans extended by public sector banks in India.[54] As it turned out, the 'bombshell' was a dud.[55] Rajan may

---

[54]   Jayanta Roy Chowdhury and R. Suryamurthy, 'Rajan reveals alert to PMO on dud loans', *The Telegraph*, 12 September 2018, https://bit.ly/2Z9ShCa

[55]   Simrin Sirur and Rajgopal Singh, 'Economic Times Thinks Raghuram Rajan's note on bad loans is not a page 1 story', *Print*, 12 September 2018, https://bit.ly/2YUPrWa.

have dropped a bombshell on the government but the newspapers did not think that was a bombshell worth the name—few picked up the story. While the lack of media attention on the daylight robbery of banks was surprising, the fact that Rajan could not launch any investigation into the scams without the blessings of the prime minister was only to be expected given the outsized statutory role of the government in RBI operations.

Rajan noted that 'unscrupulous promoters who inflated the cost of capital equipment through over-invoicing were rarely checked'. The *Telegraph* article lacked depth of analysis. It failed to note that apart from the RBI, customs should also have been involved in carrying out an investigation of the fraud perpetrated on public sector banks. The customs and the RBI should then have alerted the CBI, which should then have tipped off the Bureau of Immigration and other agencies to prevent the likes of Vijay Mallya, Nirav Modi and Mehul Choksi, from absconding abroad.

But, as subsequent events have shown, all these regulatory and investigative agencies failed to carry out their mandate in protecting the public from financial fraud. I had written an article in the *Telegraph* in 2009 arguing the prevalence of export under-invoicing and import over-invoicing as a means of transferring black money abroad.[56]

But, as the subsequent banking and trading scams related to Nirav Modi show, neither the Customs nor the RBI has yet to implement sufficient checks and balances to curtail fraudulent trade mis-invoicing. First, imports of diamonds were over-invoiced. These over-invoiced imports were used to apply for massive loans from banks. On the one hand, the repeated over-invoicings should have alerted customs to strengthen its valuation methods. Appropriate checks and balances would have ensured that the imports are properly valued against the world market price for the goods in question.

---

[56] Dev Kar, 'Filters, Wrong Signs, Backdoors and Black Money', *The Telegraph*, 5 May 2009.

On the other hand, multiple requests for massive loans should have alerted bank management and government regulators responsible for sanctioning them. It is no use trying to close the barn door after the horse has already bolted.

In short, two main factors combined to provide the perfect environment for India's serial financial scams and non-performing assets. First, public sector banks, which have been established, and largely owned and managed by the government, did not follow the guidelines for prudential lending. Second, the regulatory and investigative institutions such as the RBI, the CBI, and the customs, have always been weak and politicized, thereby reducing their independence and effectiveness.

6

The Vortex of Corruption

The question may be asked—what is corruption?

Corruption, as defined by the IMF, is 'the abuse of public office for private gain'.[57] So when a government official receives a bribe to grant an individual or a company a licence, mining contract, tax exemption, or any other favour in exchange, that is a typical example of an abuse of public office for private gain. As the IMF mainly deals with governments and seeks to influence policy, this definition is appropriate for the work of the organization. But the definition is incomplete.

The actions resulting from corruption are typically illegal and therefore hidden. There are many other forms of corruption such as insider trading. These often involve company officials' use of privileged information (e.g., pending business merger) to make a profit in the stock market. In short, there are many faces of corruption. The hidden and diverse nature of corruption makes it difficult to measure it.

Daniel Kaufmann, an expert on corruption who helped develop the World Bank's worldwide governance indicators (WGI), points out that corruption is not only 'a challenge for public officials in developing countries' but is also behind the 2008 global financial crisis

---

[57] *The Role of the Fund in Governance Issues—Guidance Note* (Washington DC: IMF, 1997), footnote 3.

which originated in the US.[58] For example, large businesses could influence regulators and lawmakers through intense lobbying efforts or influence peddling, although no bribes are paid to specific individuals. These kinds of 'non-pecuniary' corruption would still fall within the definition of 'abuse of public office for private gain' as lawmakers who favour businesses obtain political campaign contributions for their party or, say, future employment at a lobbying firm.

Apart from defining the nature of a bribe, the more fundamental point is that private companies can also break laws to make huge profits, without the knowledge of the government. While there are several examples of this, I will focus on mis-invoicing of exports and imports and abusive transfer pricing by multinational companies.

Exporters and importers can make huge profits illegally by fraudulently mis-invoicing their customs declarations. We will explore these practices in more detail in Chapter 10. The question of government officials seeking a bribe (or imposing a penalty) will only arise if they are able to interdict the fraudulent transaction. But if the transaction escapes detection, the question of a bribe or penalty does not arise. This is a perfect example of the abuse of private office for private gain. The vast majority of fraudulent trade transactions are never caught—in fact, the portion interdicted represents the proverbial tip of the iceberg.

Now, consider a second example of the abuse of private office for private gain. It is well known that multinational companies carry out a multitude of financial and other transactions among their subsidiaries. Such transactions among different branches of a multinational company spread across the world is known as 'related transactions'. Transactions carried out by other companies are considered unrelated.

Now, transactions between related parties need to follow certain guidelines which are set by the Organization for Economic

---

58   Daniel Kaufmann, 'Corruption and the Global Financial Crisis', The Brookings Institution, 27 January 2009, https://brook.gs/33FsPbd

Cooperation and Development (OECD). The most important guideline is that related transactions must be priced within a permissible band. If they are outside this permissible band, the specific transaction is deemed to be an 'abusive transfer pricing' or ATP. Multinationals are permitted to shift some profits where the underlying price is within the band set by the OECD. However, sometimes a multinational engages in ATP in order to shift profits from a high-tax jurisdiction to a low-tax one.

While the majority of multinational transactions are not ATP, poor developing countries may not be able to interdict all ATPs. The main reason is that most developing countries do not have the highly trained manpower necessary to monitor transfer pricing and take multinationals to court on suspected ATPs. ATPs which are not caught are another example of the abuse of private office for private gain.

A comprehensive definition of corruption is important because government officials, researchers and activists cannot, and should not, ignore corruption. This may not be confined to government officials but can involve the private sector acting alone. Therefore, in order to go after fraud that is hiding in plain sight, we need to revise the IMF definition as follows:

Corruption not only involves the abuse of public office for private gain but also the abuse of private office for private gain.

How Corruption Is Assessed

The extent of corruption in a country is based on surveys of the perceptions of corruption among its citizens. It is therefore a qualitative, opinion-based measure. Two of the world's leading corruption perceptions indicators are compiled by the World Bank[59]

---

[59] Control of corruption sub-indicator of the worldwide governance indicators (WGI), which was discussed in Chapter 2 and in the Appendix.

and Transparency International (TI). To be sure, corruption affects countries in varying degrees.

According to Transparency International's corruption perceptions index (CPI) for 2017, the world's five least corrupt countries were Denmark, New Zealand and Sweden (all three tied) followed by Singapore and Finland. The five most corrupt countries in the world that year listed in increasing order were Afghanistan, Haiti, Iraq, Myanmar and Somalia. In fact, as far as perceptions of corruption are concerned, the bottom 15 per cent of advanced countries fare worse than the top 15 per cent of developing countries.[60] For example, the five developing countries Barbados, Bhutan, Chile, the United Arab Emirates and Uruguay were ranked significantly less corrupt than the advanced countries of Israel, Italy, Malta, South Korea and Spain.

More than two-thirds of the countries scored below 50 which TI considers to be highly corrupt. India, with a score of 40, is also considered highly corrupt, ranking eighty-first out of 180 countries in 2017. Among developing countries and territories in Asia, corruption is more rampant in India than in Hong Kong (77), Bhutan (67), Taiwan (63), Malaysia (47) and China (41).

The Nature of Corruption in India

Dozens of books and hundreds of articles have been written about the endemic and entrenched nature of corruption in India.[61] They talk about how corruption has become such an issue and how it undermines democracy, impacts the economy, and corrodes society. I will first present a summary of these views before focusing on measures to curtail corruption with reference to those that have worked in other countries.

---

[60]   Staff Team from the Fiscal Affairs Department and the Legal Department, *IMF Staff Discussion Note—Corruption: Costs and Mitigating Strategies* (Washington DC: IMF, May 2016), p. 2, footnote 4.
[61]   *When Crime Pays: Money and Muscle in Indian Politics*, Milan Vaishnav (Yale: Yale University Press, 2017).

In reviewing the literature on corruption, I have come to the conclusion that corruption in India has become intractable due to the benign neglect, indeed outright abetment, of corrupt practices by successive governments. There has been no political will to deal with corruption head-on.

There is no dearth of fine political speeches or *bhashan*s against corruption in India as around the world. However, apart from lip service, which goes up predictably around election time, few countries have managed a significant reduction in corruption, let alone win that fight. India has not even launched a serious fight against corruption with the full support of the political leadership behind wide-ranging measures. Meanwhile, the Supreme Court, which is often seen as the saviour of Indian democracy, has done precious little to 'truly ruffle political feathers and challenge the state'.[62]

It has been pointed out in Chapter 3 that corruption in high places—that is, corruption in the way the nation's leaders are elected and maintained in power—serves as an example for the rest of society. It is not realistic to think that corruption can only be confined among elected officials and their financiers while the rest of the country is scrupulously honest! If the nation's leaders and political parties feel that it is perfectly acceptable to use vast sums of black money to finance elections, field criminal candidates and help them win, play vote-bank politics to pit this group against that, why do they think that the rest of the society will accept that honesty is the best policy? On the contrary, the example set by the political machinery is that crime pays and it pays big.

The time has come for leaders to stop giving bhashans about reigning in corruption and resorting to gimmicks like demonetization. They need to walk the talk by leading their lives as if honesty *is* the best policy. For starters, they should stop pampering themselves with

---

[62]   Devesh Kapur, Pratap Bhanu Mehta and Milan Vaishnav (eds), *Rethinking Public Institutions in India* (New Delhi: Oxford University Press, 2017), pp. 109–10.

all manner of outrageous perks and VIP/VVIP privileges that make a mockery of democracy and create a huge gulf between the lifestyle of 'leaders' and the electorate.

Instead, today, corruption has spread to every aspect of society, including the judiciary, the enforcement and regulatory agencies, the Central, state, and local governments, as well as the corporate sector. There is both large-scale corruption involving mega deals between business, government, and public sector banks, and small-scale or grass-roots corruption involving petty bribes for routine government services such as building permits and utility connections.

The rot is so extensive that most Indians have become quite used to corruption. Those who lose fighting it, simply decide to leave the country. Often, their very survival requires them to do so. The forces of corruption are so entrenched that few are willing to risk their lives opposing them. Those who do, sometimes have to pay the ultimate price.

For instance, Satyendra Dubey was an Indian Engineering Service officer who was the project director in the National Highways Authority of India (NHAI) at Koderma in Jharkhand. He was assassinated in Gaya on 27 November 2003 for exposing the corruption in the NHAI related to the Golden Quadrilateral highway project.[63] About two years later in November 2005, Shanmugam Manjunath, a sales officer at the Indian Oil Corporation, was murdered for closing down a corrupt petrol station in Lakhimpur Kheri, Uttar Pradesh. Eight murder suspects were caught. The primary convict was sentenced to death. On 12 December 2009, the Allahabad High Court commuted the sentence to life in prison and acquitted two of the accused. The rest are serving life in prison.

In addition, there have been cases where honest police officers and those in the Indian Administrative Service have been killed for trying to bring the sand and coal mafias to book. I often said to Raymond Baker, president of GFI, 'The cash cow is the only true holy cow. No one wants to kill it.'

---

[63]   Refer 'Satyendra Dubey', Wikipedia, https://bit.ly/2Io7n2F

No wonder then that the bulk of GFI's funding comes from advanced (mostly Nordic) countries. Only a fraction of GFI's funding comes directly from developing countries even though they are the beneficiaries of GFI's anti-corruption work. Who wants to kill the goose that lays the golden egg?

Today, it is difficult for most ultra-rich Indians to imagine life without black money which affords them the opportunity to buy luxury goods and accumulate a huge stash of illicit assets at home and abroad, totally out of proportion to their declared income. Addiction to black money is very strong because the entire stash is tax-free, with little risk of getting caught.

The Pernicious Impact of Corruption

There is no question that corruption has benefited a lot of people in India from all walks of life, from the ordinary policemen monitoring traffic violations to the petty government clerks pushing papers for various permits like driver's licences, passports, phone and water connections, land registration, etc.

To the extent that the provision of some of these services have been automated, opportunities for corruption have come down. However, many rural areas and transactions have not yet benefited from automated services. Corruption continues to benefit many, as vested interests to maintain the status quo have remained strong. But there is no free lunch. As the IMF notes, the cost of corruption is quite significant.

Kaufmann estimated that in 2015, the annual cost of bribes paid in both advanced and developing countries amounted to around USD 1.5–2 trillion (or about 2 per cent of world GDP).[64] This is only the direct cost of bribes—the overall economic and social costs are likely to be much larger.

---

[64] *IMF Staff Discussion Note—Corruption: Costs and Mitigating Strategies*, p. 5.

For every gainer from corruption there is also a loser forced to pay for goods and services beyond their market price. This added margin raises the cost of transactions, including those related to doing business, whether we are talking about private individuals or companies. Foreigners also shy away from investing in the country because corruption raises their cost and lowers their profit potential.

Paolo Mauro at the IMF found two important effects of corruption—first, it significantly reduces economic growth and second, when it is widespread, people no longer have any incentive to fight it even though 'everybody would be better off without it'.[65]

In fact, corruption can not only threaten sustainable growth over the long run but also seriously hinder inclusive growth.[66] When corruption is rampant, the elites gain a far bigger share of the economic pie and political voice than do average citizens. The elites have strong ties to political parties because they often financially help their elections using black money. So it is the vested interests of the corrupt elites in cahoots with politicians that are far more likely to prevail (such as investments in prestigious mega projects) than propensities to uplift the poor through inclusive growth (such as greater investments in primary schooling or healthcare for the poor).

Research at the IMF and the World Bank also show that poor governance can adversely impact investment and efficiency. The IMF observes that highly corrupt countries, as a result of weak governance, invest less in health and education than less corrupt countries. In fact, the IMF found that the share of the budget dedicated to education and health is a third lower in more corrupt countries.[67]

Corruption makes tax collection very difficult. Advanced countries, which are less corrupt than developing countries, collect

65   Paolo Mauro, *IMF Working Paper—The Persistence of Corruption and Slow Economic Growth* (Washington DC: IMF, November 2002).
66   *IMF Staff Discussion Note—Corruption: Costs and Mitigating Strategies.*
67   Vitor Gaspar, Paolo Mauro and Paulo Medas, 'Tackling Corruption in Government', IMF Blog, 4 April 2019, https://blogs.imf.org/2019/04/04/tackling-corruption-in-government/

much more taxes (by about 4.5 per cent of GDP) than developing countries. When corruption allows the rich not to pay their fair share of taxes, the government is unable to deliver adequate services to the poor and the disadvantaged. Moreover, corruption reduces the efficiency of government services through leakages in subsidies. By that we mean subsidies do not reach those who deserve them but are siphoned off by corrupt middlemen to enrich themselves (for example, diversion of goods at subsidized prices for sale in black markets where prices are much higher).

Corruption and Property Rights

One of the pernicious effects of corruption is to dilute property rights. If property rights are weak and cannot be enforced in a clear and timely manner, the incentive for investment and innovation (which is linked to property rights) would be limited as firms will invest less in productive activities.[68] Likewise, farmers will be less likely to make long-term investment in their land when they are unsure of their tenure.

Most Indians can attest to the fact that property rights are indeed very weak in India. We all know either a family member or a friend who has been a victim of a land grab, an illegal encroachment on his private property by a neighbour or pavement dweller, or a tenant who refuses to leave after you have served him notice. There are many cases in India where a tenant has been paying a largely fixed rent for the last thirty years. At today's prices, that measly rent cannot pay for one day's groceries.

Anyone can be a victim, including the Central or state government! Every time pavement dwellers or footpath vendors encroach on public lands or pavements meant for pedestrians, they have effectively usurped government property without any legal basis, claim or procedure.

---

[68]   *World Development Report 2017—Governance and the Law* (Washington DC: World Bank, 2017).

Years ago, in 1976, I helped my father, a mid-level government servant, purchase a flat in south Calcutta. The flat, on the second floor of a ten-storey building, was in an excellent location and in high demand even at that time. My parents planned to live in Calcutta when my father retired from government service. So, after he paid the final instalment for the flat in 1978, he got final possession and a key to the flat. But, wonder of all wonders, when he opened the door to the flat, he was flabbergasted to find that there was a person already occupying that flat.

He said, 'Who are you? I am the owner of this flat.' My father said, 'Who are you? Here are my papers giving me full possession of the flat and I have the key to it too.' To cut a long story short, he could not move into his own home and there was nothing I could do being away in the US. In his old age, he had to do several rounds of the inept, inefficient and corrupt court system of West Bengal. It turned out that the illegal occupant was a retired judge of the Calcutta High Court!

One day, after about two years of doing the rounds of the courts, he was invited to a friend's home where he recounted his terrible experience. He said, 'I was in the Indian National Army (INA) with Subhas Chandra Bose in Rangoon and have fought for India's independence. I was jailed by the British. But today, I cannot enter my own home and have to go around knocking on the courts for justice. But there is no justice. The builder's lawyer finds some excuse or other as to why his client could not show up and the court simply goes through the motion and grants him an extension. Is this how someone who has fought for the country should be treated? Is this what an honest government officer should have to go through after retirement in the evening of their lives?'

There happened to be a gentleman in that gathering who held a high position in the Forward Bloc party, which was then a coalition partner in the Government of West Bengal, led by the Communist Party of India (Marxist) (CPI[M]). He said 'Mr Kar, I am so sorry to hear this and am frankly embarrassed by what you are having to go through in your retired life. These things simply should not happen. Let me see what I can do.'

I don't know what happened but that high court judge was ousted from my father's flat within a month—something the courts could not do in two years. Going by the horror stories we hear from friends and relatives, I am sure the courts would have taken at least thirty years to render justice, if that. My father simply got lucky. You can imagine how difficult it is to oust a retired judge of the Calcutta High Court in a country where you cannot oust an ordinary person illegally occupying your home.

Later, we heard that the builder had accepted money from sixty buyers knowing fully well that he is only building forty flats. He was fully confident that the courts would take at least thirty years to refund the money (without interest) to those left holding the bag! Meanwhile, our builder and model citizen would use the excess funds for business purposes at zero interest. What a brilliant idea.

What happened to him? Nothing at all. He was still a prominent builder of Calcutta the last time I checked. In the US, such a fellow would be behind bars faster than you can say 'pronto' and his licence to build forever revoked.

Recent Legal Provision to Improve Transparency and Accountability

The Rajya Sabha passed the Real Estate (Regulation and Development) Act on 10 March 2016 which is aimed at protecting homebuyers and helping boost legitimate investments in real estate by curtailing the use of black money. The bill, which was originally introduced by the UPA government in 2013, establishes the Real Estate Regulatory Authority (RERA) which will be responsible for overseeing the implementation of the legal provisions in each state.

It seems that as of November 2018, many of the states have not implemented the law in its true letter and spirit. They have failed to notify a Permanent Regulator, Appellate Authority, or make a website. Implementation of the RERA is still a work in progress. Moreover, how the RERA would actually work in practice, when the courts are clogged with past cases, remains to be seen. Nevertheless, stiff penalties under the law such as withdrawal of licence to build and prison sentences for builders found violating the RERA can potentially discourage cases of fraud and corruption in the sector.

But the RERA offers little solace to the millions of property owners across India who are unable to dislodge renters paying a pittance for those properties. I talked to several friends in Kolkata who complained bitterly about the injustice. The result is that owners tend not to maintain their properties which look like they are falling apart. The irony of it all is that the owners are not multimillionaires who can afford to lose meaningful rent.

Another friend in Tamil Nadu confides that the law favours renters and other possessors. He opines that while such laws may not exist in the statutes, they are nevertheless followed in practice. For instance, if someone somehow gets to possess real estate, it is difficult to restore the property to its rightful owner. The longer the possession, the greater the difficulty dislodging these so-called renters. While owners have moved the courts, their cases have languished there for years if not decades.

If you feel that the practice is meant to favour poor renters you would be mistaken. I asked a relative how this unwritten law favouring possessors actually operated in Mumbai given the city's reputation for exorbitant real estate prices and a shortage of affordable housing. He said owners typically rent their flats on short-term leases of two to three years which may at most be renewed once. The result is that the renter had to move five times in fifteen years. I guess it is great for the moving business.

Needless to say, RERA and other laws notwithstanding, corruption abounds in India. It infects the entire system including the Central as well as state governments, lawyers, courts, police, corporations, banks, and everyone in between. There is hardly any risk of getting caught. Even if by some bad luck someone does get caught, just bribe the guy catching you. Anyone can be bought for a price. If, by some misfortune, some utterly corrupt fellow lands up in jail, chances are that he will get bailed out in a short time. Meanwhile, the jail simply serves as a change of scenery, as comfort and privileges are extended to VIPs there for their short stay. I am sure that the sheer speed and compassion with which bail bonds are granted would have perplexed Mother Teresa!

Neither the IMF studies nor those by the World Bank focus on how corruption generates illicit financial flows (or the cross-border transfer of black money). Empirical studies at GFI show that corruption creates black money, which in turn drives the black markets and the underground economy. The link between black money and the underground economy was found to be significant in case studies on Brazil, India, Mexico, Myanmar, the Philippines and Russia carried out at GFI.

The implication is that corruption tends to drive the underground economy directly, which may or may not benefit the official economy. For instance, corruption will drive speculative investments in real estate (part of the underground economy) far more than it will increase legitimate incomes such as the collection of registration fees, real estate brokerage commissions, state taxes, etc. The link between the overground and underground economies is complex and varies between countries and over time.

7

Corruption after Economic Reform

Corruption has always figured prominently in India since Independence. A number of writers have looked at how corruption has evolved in India and the factors that have driven it.[69] Normally, when the government loosens its control over the economy, corruption should decline. So, when import licences are removed, allowing foreign goods to come in, there is no longer an incentive to smuggle them into the country. Similarly, when controlled prices are freed, they rise as dictated by market forces. Any black markets for those goods can no longer survive and smugglers lose the opportunity to make money illegally.

Research at GFI showed that corruption and the generation and transfer of black money abroad seemed to have increased rather than declined after the economic reforms of 1991. There are three reasons for this growing corruption.

First, the stranglehold of the Congress party started to loosen. The decline in Congress's dominance was replaced by greater fragmentation of parties. The new parties catered to voters along caste, class, ethnic and religious lines. Vote-bank politics became a major feature of Indian politics as parties sought to maintain the loyalty of supporters. But vote-bank politics is an expensive game to play and requires lots of black money.

---

[69] For instance, see Vaishnav, *When Crime Pays*, pp. 31–33.

Second, changes in campaign finance laws initiated by Indira Gandhi placed severe restrictions on private sector financing. As white money for elections dried up, increasingly expensive elections came to be financed by black money. The quid pro quo between black money financiers and the politicians meant that the latter ensure that their financiers make a good return on their 'investment'. This is how opportunities to make even more black money are built into the system.

Third, as controls over the private sector were relaxed, the economy took off. The rich who were connected with the global economy became much richer. Globalization and economic growth benefited the elite far more than the average Indian. The result was abject poverty amidst untold wealth. Tax evasion by the rich increased because they felt they were already paying too much. The transfer of black money abroad is mainly carried out by the ultra-rich and not by the *aam aadmi* or common man.

Thus, the tectonic shifts in India's political, economic and societal landscapes provided more fodder to corruption rather than less. The licence raj gave way to goonda raj because the rise of regional parties also meant the chance to play vote-bank politics, which required more muscle power to extract and deliver political rents. Thus, economic liberalization in the face of weak governance has provided a greater impetus to corruption.

Scams in Modern India

There have been many scams in India in the post-reform period. I will only highlight two of them—the 2G and the mining scams. The main objective will be to illustrate how they could have been prevented.

The 2G Scam (Background)

The demand for cellphones started to increase in the early years of the new millennium as incomes rose and the middle class expanded. In order to meet the growing demand, the Department of Telecommunications, headed by A. Raja, started to issue licences in 2008. Raja became the face of the scam for a number of reasons.

First, the licences were issued to telecom operators on a first come, first served basis, which was clearly not recommended as subsequently ruled by the Supreme Court. Second, the licences were issued at 2001 and not 2008 prices. This was confirmed on 16 November 2010 by the Comptroller and Auditor General of India (CAG) Vinod Rai. The throwaway prices led to a loss of Rs 1.76 lakh crore to the Government of India (about USD 26 billion). Third, the licences were issued to applicants who violated all the rules. They deliberately suppressed facts, provided incomplete and misleading information, and submitted fictitious documents. In other words, the applicants committed fraud in obtaining the licences and their access to spectrum.[70]

In fact, the CAG said that within a short time, the owners of the licences simply turned around and sold significant stakes to other Indian and foreign companies at huge markups. Raja and his co-conspirators rigged the licensing process in another important way. They advanced the cut-off date of the auction and changed the rules several times in order to throw the bidders off-balance. In fact, officials at the telecoms department physically shut the counters to prevent telecom companies from bidding. Had the process of granting 2G licences been free and fair, these profits would have accrued to the Government of India.

The CBI took up the case and filed an 80,000-page charge sheet before the trial court. The charge was that Raja got Swan's Shahid Balwa to invest Rs 200 crore in Kalaignar TV Pvt. Ltd, a company controlled by some members of the DMK's first family. Raja was a minister in the UPA government from the DMK. The CBI also

---

[70] '2G spectrum allocation scam: A timeline of how the case progressed', *Hindustan Times*, 21 December 2017; James Crabtree, *The Billionaire Raj: A Journey through India's New Gilded Age*, Chapter 5: 'The Season of Scams' (New York: Tim Duggan Book, 2018).

charged DMK Supremo M. Karunanidhi's daughter Kanimozhi of being a key stakeholder of Kalaignar TV channels and therefore directly involved in the scam.

Further investigations revealed that A. Raja had received more than Rs 3000 crore as bribe in the allotment of the 2G licences. There were many other private and public officials who benefited directly from the scam at the expense of the people of India. The CAG in its 2010 report ruled that the 2G scam was the biggest in the history of independent India. Estimates of the total loss to the Government of India has been pegged at USD 40 billion, a staggering amount by any measure let alone for a poor developing country.

Subsequently, on 2 February 2012, the Supreme Court of India ruled that the allotment of spectrum was 'unconstitutional and arbitrary'. It cancelled the 122 licences issued in 2008 under A. Raja who wanted to 'favour some companies at the cost of the public exchequer' and 'virtually gifted away the important national asset.'[71]

How the Scam Could Have Been Prevented

The method of checks and balances required to prevent such scams are there for all to see. For example, the Organization for Economic Cooperation and Development (OECD) has played a pioneering role in promoting transparency and good governance in government contracts.[72] It is not rocket science. The government is well aware of these anti-corruption methods. What is stopping it is a lack of political will to make a start and the refusal to clean up dirty politics. How would have such checks and balances prevented the 2G scam?

First, the 2G licensing process would have violated the OECD's first principle—that of transparency. The totally opaque and confusing manner in which the Department of

[71] PTI, '2G verdict: A Raja "virtually gifted away important national asset", says Supreme Court', *The Times of India*, 2 February 2012.
[72] Refer *OECD Principles for Integrity in Public Procurement* (Paris: OECD, 2009), https://bit.ly/2m8nV5c

Telecommunications set about asking for bids on a first come, first served basis and making frequent changes to the rules made a mockery of transparency. Moreover, the OECD guidelines say that, 'Conditions for participation, such as selection and award criteria as well as the deadline for submission should be established in advance. In addition, they should be published so as to provide sufficient time for potential suppliers for the preparation of tenders and recorded in writing to ensure a level playing field.' Clearly, these guidelines were violated.

Second, OECD guidelines note that in order to 'ensure sound competitive processes, governments should provide clear and realistic rules on the choice of the optimum method'. The optimum method of allocating licences should have been deliberated with different stakeholders—not just the Department of Telecommunications. It seems that Raja chose the first come, first served basis in order to favour a few companies and receive kickbacks for doing so.[73] As it turned out, the Supreme Court pointed out that the allocation of licences should have been done on a basis of competitive bidding and not on a first come, first served basis.

Third, the guidelines recommend that for large projects such as the 2G spectrum licensing, the government should have linked public procurement with public financial management systems to foster transparency and accountability and improve value for money. In other words, the CAG, as the supreme audit institution together with appropriate parliamentary committees should have been involved from the very beginning on this spectrum allocation project. It should not have been up to Raja and his team to decide such matters by themselves. There is a dire need to monitor the management of public funds in order to ensure and verify that funds are used as intended. This basic principle was also violated.

---

[73] 'Supreme Court directs CBI and ED to wrap up investigations in 2G spectrum scam within six months', Scroll.in, 12 March 2018, https://bit.ly/2OT3KFQ

Fourth, the involvement of Raja roping in another DMK member, the party chief's daughter Kanimozhi, and involving the DMK-run television channel should have set off alarm bells in regulatory institutions such as the CAG. Instead, it was caught napping at the wheels. That is another clear violation of the guidelines against conflict of interest.

To cut a long story short, there were many violations of the basic principles which should govern public procurement and contracting of mega projects. Has the government learnt anything from such mega scams? I don't think so and would not be surprised to see more such scams in the future. What is clear is that the government can put a stop to such shenanigans if it chooses to do so. The guidelines have been painstakingly developed by reputed international organizations such as the OECD and the IMF based on decades of experience working in various countries around the world. But, it seems that the political will to set matters right and improve governance is not there.

Mining Scams

While the 2G scam was the largest single scam in the history of independent India, the total loss to the public resulting from the many mining scams is even larger. There have been widespread mining scams in various mineral-rich states of India such as the Belekeri Port scandal in Karnataka (from where illegally mined iron ore was being exported); illegal mining in the Aravalli range; bauxite, iron ore, chromite and coal mining in Odisha, and illegal sand and iron ore mining in Madhya Pradesh and Goa.[74]

Illegal mining, besides plundering state resources, can also be extremely dangerous for workers because the owners have little regard

---

[74] Paranjoy Guha Thakurta, 'Why mining in India is a source of corruption?', BBC News, 12 August 2011, https://bbc.in/2KOGLXM; Deepak Patel, 'Illegal mining of minor minerals in Karnataka: "Inadequate workforce led to difficulty in monitoring"', *The Indian Express*, 20 May 2018, https://bit.ly/2MiGDmB

for worker safety. On 13 December 2018, fifteen workers were trapped in an illegal mine in Meghalaya, after the frigid waters of the Lytein River flooded it. All miners perished following the state's belated and botched attempt to rescue them. This also exposed an utter lack of infrastructure and trained manpower to launch such operations.

Extensive mining of Meghalaya's 24,000 mines, in spite of the state's mining ban, has polluted its rivers rendering the waters highly acidic. The state government blames a lack of manpower for its inability to enforce the ban. However, the fact of the matter is that elections are funded with black money generated by these illegal coal mines. When many of the mine owners also happen to be elected officials, it's all a family affair.[75]

Meanwhile, Rahul Gandhi sees a political opportunity to take the BJP to task over the mining accident. Politicians are interested in securing political advantage over the pain, suffering and death of poor workers in order to further their own ambitions. But Rahul Gandhi does not talk about the following case when the Congress was in power.

In the run-up to the 2008 Olympics hosted by China, demand for Indian steel shot up. As steel prices increased fifteen-fold, Bellary in Karnataka boomed as a result of illegal iron ore mining to feed the steel mills. Gali Janardhana Reddy, a modern-day robber baron, made oodles of black money and built a sixty-room mansion for himself.

The Supreme Court finally cracked down on Reddy in 2011 and sent him to jail.[76] But, having made billions of dollars in black money, I am sure that the four years he spent in jail flew by real fast. Truly, it wasn't a bad deal for Reddy. Now, Lalu Prasad Yadav, mastermind of the fodder scam, is also awaiting a compassionate

---

[75]   Joanna Slater and Sannio Siangshai, 'Hopes fade for 15 workers trapped in illegal Indian mine', *The Washington Post*, 13 January 2019.
[76]   Rama Lakshmi, 'In Indian mining district, the barons are back', *The Washington Post*, 2 May 2013.

consideration by the courts. It is doubtful that the government will ever recover the amount plundered by illegal mining ventures.

An ombudsman report on mining in Karnataka found that the promoters of private mining companies in the Bellary region bribed politicians and joined politics. Some of them rose up the ranks in the state government. A couple of years later, business tycoon Birla's reputation was dragged into the muck when his company, Hindalco, benefited from an arbitrary allocation of coal deposits.

India's mainstream media taunted the then prime minister Manmohan Singh to throw more light on this shady deal given that he was also the coal minister. He argued that no laws were broken when Hindalco got the mining lease. But when the CBI raided Hindalco's offices in Delhi, it found 25 crore rupees in black money. If Hindalco had played by the rules all along, how could it explain the 25 crore rupees in black money in its coffers? Although Indian newspapers reported the incident, they did not dwell on it for too long.[77]

What could be done about mining scams?

One would think that with so many scandals, the government would be receptive to joining the Extractive Industries Transparency Initiative (EITI) to improve transparency and accountability of its operations in the extractive industries. But neither the government nor Indian companies show any inclination of joining the EITI.

The EITI is a coalition of governments, companies, investors, civil society organizations and partner organizations which promotes greater transparency and accountability in the management of oil, gas and mineral resources. Thus far, the fifty-one countries that have signed on to the EITI are required to disclose information about their extractive industries.

The information relates to each stage of the process, from identification of resources, extraction, production and exports, to

---

[77]   Manu Joseph, 'Indian Billionaires Get a Pass', *The New York Times*, 23 October 2013, https://nyti.ms/2KNTYjn

how much revenues accrue to the government and how they are utilized. Accordingly, the EITI framework ensures better governance in the management of natural resources by promoting transparency and accountability of government contracts and involvement in the mineral, oil and gas sectors.

A spokesman of the Ministry of Petroleum and Natural Gas insisted that the idea of EITI was driven by the West and that India's own New Exploration Licensing Policy (NELP) is 'robust' enough. In other words, don't tell us. We know it all! Meanwhile, states continue to be plundered of their mineral resources, governments receive paltry royalties, workers face grave risks, and the locals suffer extensive environmental degradation.

Because more than half of foreign bribery cases occur in the process of winning government contracts, sound management of such contracts with maximum transparency and accountability is crucial. High-prestige, high-impact and high-cost, large-scale infrastructure projects are particularly vulnerable to political interference, corruption and mismanagement. India's history is replete with foreign procurement cases that led to massive scams and bribes such as the Bofors scandal and the more recent 2G scandal.[78] The OECD notes that commitment at the highest levels of government is necessary for speedy reform of public procurement systems.

In conclusion, corruption is a complex phenomenon that is more difficult to eradicate the longer the country remains in its grip. The results of anti-corruption strategies undertaken by various countries have been disappointing mainly because eradicating corruption requires a holistic approach whereas past attempts have been rather narrowly focused and piecemeal.

Given the nature of these attempts and the lack of political will to do any better, there is a strong tendency for these efforts to peter out before long. Hope for progress against petty or 'grass-roots'

---

[78] 'India's 2G Telecom Scandal Spans the Spectrum of Abuse', *Knowledge@Wharton*, 2 December 2010, https://whr.tn/2KCCqI5

corruption largely centres on the use of technology in streamlining the delivery of services and reducing direct interaction between citizens and government officials delivering the services they need. But there are limits to the extent to which technology can reduce corruption. It cannot enforce laws, make up for weak institutions, or solve the problem of clogged courts and dirty politics.

8

Law and Disorder

The rule of law is not only necessary for good governance but also for stable and equitable development. In fact, what sets apart weakly governed developing countries from strongly governed advanced countries is the primacy of the rule of law. But what is meant by the rule of law?

In countries where the 'rule of law' prevails, government officials and citizens are bound by, and act in accordance with, the law.[79] So, it is not enough for the laws to merely exist on paper. In fact, as the World Bank has noted, in many countries laws are either not implemented or selectively implemented. Sometimes these laws are impossible to implement for various reasons. What good are laws that remain largely on paper? As people clamouring for justice know too well, they are not worth the paper they are written on!

There is a reason why laws are sometimes difficult to implement. For instance, Pratap Bhanu Mehta, former president of the Centre for Policy Research (CPR) in New Delhi, notes that while the Supreme Court has been occupying a front-row seat in Indian politics, it must carefully weigh whether its decisions can be implemented by dysfunctional public institutions. Ignoring the ground reality would

---

[79]   *World Development Report 2017, Governance and the Law* (Washington DC: The World Bank), pp. 83–101.

lead to decisions that cannot be implemented and hence largely irrelevant.[80]

In the US, when celebrities and prominent politicians go to jail, ordinary citizens are reminded that the rule of law applies to all. Americans have a deep respect for the rule of law. That does not mean there are no crimes in the US. But the healthy respect for the rule of law ensures that everyone follows rules and procedures in accordance with the law. The penalties for transgressions are sure, swift and severe. As far as compliance with the law is concerned, Americans are not better than Indians. They are just more afraid of transgressions and their consequences.

In contrast, the rule of law prevailing in India leaves much to be desired. As we have seen, the country scores a 'D'—barely a passing grade in some scoring systems or a failing grade under somewhat more stringent standards. In fact, the rule of law has declined perceptibly from the sixty-first percentile rank in 1996 (meaning that 39 per cent of countries scored above India then) to the (nearly) fifty-third percentile rank in 2017, meaning that 47 per cent of countries scored above India when it comes to upholding the rule of law. The average percentile rank for the period 1996–2017 is 56.3 which is consistent with a 'D' grade. Note that the percentile ranks are based on the feedback received from Indian citizens. In 2017, India's percentile rank came in at 52.88. In comparison, many countries and jurisdictions in Asia did much better in maintaining law and order—Bhutan (74.04), Hong Kong, China (93.75), Singapore (96.63), South Korea (85.58), and Taiwan (84.62), while Sri Lanka (55.29), and Thailand (54.81) did somewhat better. Interestingly, mainland China (44.71) scored significantly worse than India.

In addition to criminals getting a free pass into running for high office (with their criminal background helping rather than hurting

---

[80]   Devesh Kapur, Pratap Bhanu Mehta and Milan Vaishnav (eds), Rethinking Public Institutions in India (New Delhi: Oxford University Press, 2017), p. 110.

their electability), the rule of law takes a severe beating when weak institutions are headed by servile officials grovelling before politicians rather than standing up to them in upholding the law. For instance, the newspapers are replete with news about netas flaunting their power over high-ranking police officials.

In a recent incident, some newspapers reported that the chief minister of West Bengal, Mamata Banerjee, had the director general of police of Karnataka transferred by the chief minister of that state just because the DGP had requested Banerjee to walk a few metres to the dais due to traffic congestion.[81] This was refuted by other accounts saying that the chief minister denied that the DGP was transferred.[82] Whether or not the DGP was transferred for the audacity of asking Mamata to walk a short distance is not the issue. The larger point is that Mamata is not alone. Ministers in India think nothing of expecting police officers to treat them like royalty and grovel before them.

One could easily write a book documenting such abuses. But the voters who have elected these politicians don't seem to care. There is no public outrage over the humiliation suffered by police officials at the hands of politicians. I am amazed at the lack of accountability of politicians. They seem to have a wide latitude in their norms of behaviour. Perhaps they are endowed with some type of divine power!

I don't mean to be tongue-in-cheek about these incidents but I don't understand why people are not fed up with such shenanigans. Where is the rule of law? The message to politicians should be loud and clear. Your divine power has been withdrawn. Stick to the narrow path and make sure your actions conform to the law and to the Constitution of India. Or we, the people, will hound you and throw you out of office.

Lack of respect for the rule of law by politicians (and, indirectly, by the people who elect them) leads to horrific consequences for

---

[81]   'Karnataka DGP, who earned Mamata's ire during Kumaraswamy oath ceremony, transferred', *DNA*, 24 May 2018, https://bit.ly/2Z90OFh
[82]   'Karnataka DGP, with whom Mamata was miffed, not transferred', *The Statesman*, 25 May 2018, https://bit.ly/2TEvtJA

human rights. For instance, the TV serial *Crime Patrol* routinely shows the police beating and torturing those they arrest (often without a warrant) on mere suspicion. The poor seem to bear the brunt of brutal police interrogation methods to extract key information or a confession to the crime. If the suspect comes from a rich or influential family, speaks good English, you can see the police behaving quite politely and with a lot of restraint. The difference in treatment of those the police arrest based on social strata, income, education, caste, etc., is shocking to say the least.

Yet nothing much has been done to improve police procedures and in improving their human rights record. After all, even suspects in criminal cases should be accorded basic human rights. If they are sent to prison after conviction, they still have certain inalienable rights under the Constitution. These rights are seldom respected in India and those arrested are hardly aware of them.

The 1980 Bhagalpur blinding case (which happened when my father-in-law was the IGP, Bihar) probably stands out as one of the darkest days for the Indian police. The case highlights the human rights consequences of a criminal justice system severely compromised by political interference.

In that case, prison inmates in Bhagalpur, Bihar, were blinded by prison officials while under police custody. These criminals had a long history of rape, murder, extortion and kidnapping, but they never seemed to remain behind bars for long. They were always released on bail with the blessings of some minister or the other. Police would repeatedly track them down, often at considerable risk to their lives, only having to release them a short while later due to political pressure. In frustration, the police, in cahoots with prison personnel, blinded the criminals to stop them from committing these crimes. The fact remains that *political interference in the criminal justice system not only led to a deterioration of law and order but also to a serious violation of human rights.*

Rather than resorting to a gimmick like demonetization, one could think of many areas where the Modi government could make a real difference. For instance, the hands of the Supreme Court of India could be strengthened to severely censure politicians big and small who penalize or humiliate public officials going about fulfilling their responsibilities under the Constitution. Censure must come with a painful bite and should include various penalties, including nullification of unlawful and vindictive actions (such as frequent 'transfers', obstruction of well-deserved promotions), barring from holding public office, and running for future elections. The message to politicians should be loud and clear—the rule of law reigns supreme in India and those who flaunt it will be held accountable. Severely censuring a few ministers will get the message out very quickly and put a stop to such misadventures. *A demonstration effect is sorely needed.*

There is a lesson behind the extraordinary events that tested the rule of law in two democracies a world apart—India and the US.

On 26 June 1975, Indira Gandhi, after convening a meeting of the Indian cabinet at 6 a.m., declared over All India Radio that 'the President has proclaimed Emergency' and that 'there is nothing to panic about'. This state of affairs, under which Indira Gandhi suspended the Constitution, abrogating the civil rights of citizens and restricting the freedom of the press, has since come to be known as India's darkest hour. The state of Emergency would continue for the next twenty-two months.

She declared that Emergency rule was a necessary response to the 'forces of disintegration' and 'communal passions' that were threatening the unity of India. Anyone deemed a threat to the Congress such as leaders and legislators from other parties, student activists, trade unionists and sundry others were jailed. Many were jailed without evidence and simply on mere suspicion. What were the events that led up to the declaration of Emergency?

Indira Gandhi had won the 1971 Lok Sabha election contesting from the Rae Bareli constituency in Uttar Pradesh defeating socialist leader Raj Narain who challenged her electoral victory in the Allahabad High Court. He alleged that Prime Minister Indira

Gandhi had resorted to election malpractices and violation of the Representation of the People Act, 1951.[83] The verdict of Justice Jagmohanlal Sinha found her guilty of electoral malpractices, disqualified her from Parliament, and imposed a six-year ban on her holding any elected office.

However, on an appeal filed by Indira Gandhi, Justice V.R. Krishna Iyer, a vacation judge of the Supreme Court, granted a conditional stay on Justice Sinha's verdict on 24 June 1975.[84] The very next day, she imposed the Emergency suspending all fundamental rights, jailing her opponents, and imposing strict censorship on the media. Her son Sanjay Gandhi also took on autocratic powers and initiated a programme to forcefully sterilize millions of Indians, mostly the poor. This programme can be considered to be one of the most heinous crimes against humanity in modern India. With the Emergency in effect, the Supreme Court later overturned her conviction on 7 November 1975.[85]

This was achieved by changing the electoral laws retroactively which automatically rendered Justice Sinha's guilty verdict null and void. However, Justice Sinha's guilty verdict is still hailed by democracy advocates as perhaps one of the greatest triumphs of an independent judiciary in India.

While the unanimous reversal by the Supreme Court of Prime Minister Indira Gandhi's conviction of two electoral offences removed the threat of her having to resign from office, it did not end the state of Emergency. Her opponent, Raj Narain, asked the court to strike down the amendment itself arguing that it was unfair to change the election laws retroactively on the grounds that the change tampered with the 'basic structure' of the Constitution. But the judges did not accept

---

[83]   Satya Prakash, 'The court verdict that prompted Indira Gandhi to declare Emergency', *Hindustan Times*, 26 June 2015, https://bit.ly/31Ip1E2
[84]   A vacation judge takes the place of regular sitting judges of courts that are in recess.
[85]   William Borders, 'Mrs. Gandhi wins court reversal of her conviction', *The New York Times*, 8 November 1975.

these arguments. Had Raj Narain prevailed and the prime minister's conviction upheld, she would have had to resign under the law. Finally, the court absolved Indira Gandhi of all charges declaring that the court had no power to adjudicate the election of the prime minister.

The use of the courts to legitimize Prime Minister Indira Gandhi's election was a 'corollary to the politics of dynasty . . . a deepening of the instinct to centralize power and have loyalists in key positions . . .'.[86] So we have a demonstration of what an independent judiciary looks like followed immediately by what capitulation to political leaders looks like.

Some are of the opinion that the Supreme Court, eager to re-establish judicial independence, created the concept of public interest litigation (PIL). This was a legal avenue through which citizens could improve the country's governance and administration. While the PIL system has been a positive development, the Supreme Court's caving in to political pressure was a dark chapter in the life of the nation.

Since then, the Supreme Court has demonstrated from time to time what judicial independence looks like in the finest of traditions. For instance, in a landmark ruling in September 2018, the Supreme Court abrogated Section 377, which criminalized homosexual acts. That section of the law was provisionally invalidated in 2009, only to be reversed in a regressive ruling in 2013 bowing to pressures from self-styled moralists and religious groups.

The late 2018 landmark judgement, opening with a quote from Goethe ('I am what I am, so take me as I am'), reflected the Supreme Court's endorsement of human rights for India's LGBTQ (lesbian, gay, bisexual, transvestite and queer) community at par with those applicable for all Indian citizens. In striking down the 2013 ruling, the justices opined that the arguments were 'fallacious' based on 'constitutionally impermissible' reasoning and '. . . meaningless; like zero on the left of any number'. The justices saw this ruling as a move from 'bigotry to tolerance' to serve 'as the herald of a new India'.

---

[86]   'The legacy of Indira Gandhi's Emergency', Livemint, 27 June 2018.

In stark contrast to the judges delivering the 2013 verdicts who declared that they will not be swayed by progressive international judgments on gay rights, the recent panel of justices quoted them extensively to support and extend those same rights to the LGBTQ community in India. This landmark judgment has huge implications in extending gay rights in many other countries in Africa and Asia and stands testimony to the judicial independence of India's Supreme Court. Bravo!

Halfway across the world, we are witnessing an almost daily assault on the independence of key government institutions of the US that Americans have come to accept as an essential feature of democracy. Separation of powers between the executive (i.e., the president), the legislature (i.e., Congress), and the judiciary (i.e., Department of Justice) is enshrined in the US Constitution and is a salient feature of America. But ever since President Trump won the election, he has escalated attacks on the Department of Justice, the FBI, and the Federal Reserve Bank and has corralled the Republican-dominated Congress to essentially support his policies.

For instance, Trump escalated his attacks on Attorney General Jeff Sessions suggesting that the Department of Justice had put the November 2018 mid-term elections in jeopardy by indicting two Republican congressmen—Rep. Duncan Hunter of California and Rep. Chris Collins of New York. Both were accused of separate charges—the former of charges that included the use of campaign funds for personal expenses while the latter for insider trading. On 7 November 2018, one day after the mid-term elections, when Democrats won the House, Trump fired Sessions.

Trump's suggestion that the Department of Justice make decisions based on political considerations amounts to a blatant disregard of the separation of powers between the executive and the judiciary. Investigators are supposed to be blind with regard to the political affiliations of the persons they are prosecuting. American judicial independence reached its lowest point that day.

Trump has also remarked on many occasions that he is extremely displeased with the FBI, which is carrying out an investigation on whether Trump and members of his campaign colluded with the Russian government in the run-up to the 2016 presidential elections. The FBI operates under the jurisdiction of the United States Department of Justice and reports to the Attorney General. The Department of Justice conducts its own investigations into possible breach of law. Given the separation of powers between the executive and the judiciary, past presidents have also avoided commenting on pending or ongoing cases being pursued by the FBI.

Apart from the judiciary, Trump has also commented publicly on his dislike of the Federal Reserve raising interest rates in the run-up to the November 2018 mid-term elections. On 23 December, some leading newspapers in the US reported that Trump asked his advisers about his power to fire the chairman of the Federal Reserve, Jerome Powell. News of Trump's inquiries invited sharp rebukes from lawmakers as well as lawyers, academics and Wall Street executives. Treasury Secretary Steven Mnuchin tweeted a statement from Trump the same evening saying, 'I totally disagree with Fed policy . . . but I never suggested firing Chairman Jay Powell, nor do I believe I have the right to do so.'

The Federal Reserve has traditionally been completely independent of the executive in the conduct of economic policies under its mandate and past presidents have avoided commenting on its policy in keeping with that independence. One of his advisers must have informed Trump that according to the Federal Reserve Act, a Fed governor could only be removed 'for cause', which courts have interpreted as criminal activity or malfeasance, as in other cases regarding independent agency leaders.[87]

As a result of statutory independence, and a long culture of respecting these statutes, key investigative and regulatory agencies

---

[87] 'Trump reportedly asked advisers about his power to fire Fed chair', *The Washington Post*, 23 December 2018.

have held firm in the conduct of their operations, in spite of an almost daily onslaught on their independence. Neither the FBI, the Department of Justice, nor for that matter the Federal Reserve, have caved in to political pressures coming from President Trump.

The Federal Reserve is widely expected to continue setting interest rates according to its own best judgement regarding the state of the economy. And, notwithstanding Trump's strong objections, the FBI continued with its investigations into whether there was any evidence of collusion between the Trump campaign and the Russian government in the run-up to the 2016 presidential elections. The bottom line is that in spite of Trump having appointed the heads of these key agencies expecting that they will cave in to his demands, every single agency has thus far acted independently in carrying out its duties as prescribed under the Constitution and its own mandate.

In strongly governed democracies, there are sufficient checks and balances which ensure that key regulatory and judicial institutions remain independent from political interference. The constitutional guarantees of independence allow the institutions to carry out their mandates in the interest of the nation.

9

Two Types of Regulatory Agencies

There are two types of regulatory agencies. They can be best described with reference to the canine world—attack dogs and poodles. Criminals fear attack dogs but love poodles. They are fearful because attack dogs lie in the dark waiting for their transgressions and attack without warning. And once they bite, they typically do not let go until the criminal is behind bars.

A strong system breeds good attack dogs that only recognize boundaries set by the law. Anyone who steps out of that boundary will be attacked. Attack dogs make no distinction between 'our' criminals and 'their' criminals—both will be attacked if they trespass legal boundaries.

Poodles are an entirely different breed. They snuggle up to their political masters and are often in their pocket, so to speak. Of course, they never bite but just want treats and cuddles. What is the point of putting up a sign that says 'Beware of poodles'? Criminals know that they have a free reign in a system overseen by poodles.

In the US, the Federal Reserve, Office of the Comptroller of the Currency (OCC), FBI, Department of Justice, Customs and Border Enforcement, the Securities and Exchange Commission (SEC), and the various law and regulatory agencies at the state level, are all widely recognized to be good attack dogs.

And so, Punjab-born New York attorney Preet Bharara himself became an attack dog working in an attack-dog institution. Bharara was instrumental in sending one-time Wall Street icon Rajat Gupta to jail for two years for insider trading.[88] Insider trading involves the sharing of privileged information to make personal profit through stock market trading. Gupta's co-conspirator Raj Rajaratnam was sentenced to eleven years in jail. The former was released in January 2016 after serving his full sentence while the latter is eligible for release in July 2021. Prior to those cases, Bharara sent the infamous super fraudster Bernie Madoff and crime bosses such as the Gambinos to serve lengthy jail sentences. There is no bail for any of them. Well, good for Bharara and for the US.

Criminals who take a chance transgressing the law face a much higher risk of getting mauled by these attack dogs in the US than do criminals breaking the law in India. It should be noted that all applicable laws are on the books in India—there are no shortages of them. But the regulatory agencies charged with upholding those laws behave like poodles. In fact, the Supreme Court out of frustration with the CBI, called it a 'caged parrot' and 'its master's voice'.[89]

That is why we have seen so many scams in India including the latest ones involving the defrauding of thousands of crores of rupees from public sector banks. I agree with former RBI governor Urjit Patel. The RBI Act does not provide any statutory powers to the central bank to oversee and exercise control over the transactions and operations of the public sector banks. In other words, the RBI is expected to act like a poodle when it comes to these banks. How can we then turn around and say that the RBI has failed on its watch? Is it realistic for us to expect a poodle to act like an attack dog?

---

[88]   Chidanand Rajghatta, 'Preet Bharara vs Rajat Gupta: An Indian-American Saga', *The Times of India*, 26 October 2012, https://bit.ly/2TDLaRp
[89]   Ross Colvin and Satarupa Bhattacharjya, 'A "caged parrot" - Supreme Court describes CBI', Reuters, 10 May 2013, https://reut.rs/2z4Tos1

Justice Delayed Is Justice Denied

The long time taken by a lower-level court to reach a decision often seriously erodes a state's capacity to enforce private contracts or to preserve property rights. For example, most Indians are aware of the fact that it is often extremely difficult to remove those who illegally occupy or encroach upon property that we rightfully own. Court cases to enforce one's property rights can drag on for so long that many people just give up and compromise with the illegal occupiers, or worse, hire goons to enforce the contract. Some states have improved upon an owner's right to enforce the contract and remove occupiers who break the terms of the contract. But progress has been slow and the problem with enforcing property rights continues in most states. Let me provide an illustration of the problem.

An elderly couple in Kolkata had arranged for a caretaker to look after them in the absence of their daughter living in the US. The daughter, who is our family friend, recounted what happened when she went back to sell the ancestral property after her parents passed away. On reaching home, she found that the caretaker had moved his family into her home and claimed that he was now the rightful owner of that property as he had spent the last twenty years caring for her parents! Yet, during her annual visits to see her parents, the caretaker never revealed his intentions—he had carried out his duties as expected.

But the caretaker now claimed that his rights to the property accrued over the two decades he lived there taking care of her parents. Never mind the logic. Our friend called the police when she was unable to enter her own home. But when the police arrived, they sided with the caretaker upon hearing all sides of the story!

Left with no choice, she hired an eminent lawyer at considerable cost and filed a court case. After four years and tens of thousands of dollars in airfare, hotel, lawyer fees, and other costs, she was finally able to have the court evict the caretaker from her ancestral home.

Such cases are unheard of in developed countries where the sanctity of private contracts is respected and enforced in a timely and fair manner. If renters fall behind in their rental payments for more than thirty days, the owner can have the relevant court evict the renter forthwith. And the court does not take thirty years to render a verdict to evict. The owner typically does not have to hire a lawyer in such open-and-shut cases. Furthermore, the owner can raise rents as allowed under the terms of the contract. Renters are allowed a reasonable time (normally thirty days) to decide whether they accept the higher rent or move elsewhere. The contracts are neat, clear and enforced with impunity.

Goons and encroachers take advantage of the fact that the courts at all levels are clogged in India. Recently, Dipak Misra, the then Chief Justice of India (CJI), declared that there were a rising number of pending cases before the courts.[90] An unbelievable 2.84 crore cases were clogging the subordinate (or lower) courts, while the high courts and the Supreme Court (SC) had a backlog of forty-three lakh and nearly 60,000 cases respectively. Five states with the highest number of pending cases were Uttar Pradesh (61.58 lakh), Maharashtra (33.22 lakh), West Bengal (17.59 lakh), Bihar (16.58 lakh) and Gujarat (16.45 lakh).

Misra also worried that the large number of undertrials, who were languishing in jails across the country and who do not get bail, may end up being incarcerated longer than their original sentences. Of all pending cases, 60 per cent are more than two years old while 40 per cent are more than five years old.

The CJI asked all high court judges to take stock of pending cases before them as well as the subordinate courts with a view to disposing of the five- to ten-year-old cases in a time-bound manner. In addition, the CJI called for a new mechanism, in addition to the arrears committees, to reduce the backlog of cases at the high court and district court levels.

---

[90] '3.3 crore cases pending in Indian courts, pendency figure at its highest: CJI Dipak Misra', *Business Today*, 28 June 2018, https://bit.ly/2TkfLCP

The pattern of backlogs in lawsuits show that it is the lower courts where most cases get stuck.[91] The notion that backlogs are caused by a shortage of judges is not universally accepted because some courts tend to perform better in clearing cases than others even though they also deal with an equally heavy caseload. So, the efficiency with which court cases are filed and disposed of, has an impact on the volume of backlog.

The Law Commission of India recommended a series of measures to reduce the backlog in court cases, including (i) strict guidelines for the adjournments of cases, (ii) reducing vacation time for judges in the higher judiciary, (iii) curtailing time devoted to oral arguments unless strictly necessary, (iv) framing clear and decisive judgments to avoid further litigation. Furthermore, the Law Commission also suggested the incorporation of technology, where possible, to reduce the pendency of cases such as digitization of court records and the incorporation of artificial intelligence to carry out routine and repetitive legal procedures currently carried out by lawyers.

However, there are also other problems with the Indian judicial system. First and foremost, there is a need to determine for each court, how many cases it can hear each day while rendering full justice to each one. If, as is often the case, a judge has to hear 100 cases a day, one can be sure that justice may not be fully served in all of them. It is not humanly possible to do so when you are handling such a heavy caseload. Hence, the first order of business is to determine, in a methodological way, the number of cases a judge can reasonably handle in a day. Complex as well as reasonably open-and-shut cases need to be evenly distributed so that a judge is not burdened with hearing too many complex cases on a single day. Otherwise, not only the quality of adjudication will suffer but it is also probable that a number of cases may not even be heard, adding to the backlog.

---

[91]   'How to make Indian courts more efficient', Livemint, 15 September 2017, https://bit.ly/2zeCIi9

Second, Indian courts often lack adequate infrastructure—from a dearth of support staff for judges (such as those carrying out research and secretarial work) to poor courtroom facilities. For instance, judges often complain that although they hear up to seventy cases a day, it takes two days or more for the stenographers to finish typing the orders. India has yet to harness the power of technology where the use of stenographers has been replaced, or greatly reduced, by real-time digitized transcription carried out at the speed of oral arguments, interventions and decisions. Courts must also apply modern management principles to optimize case progression and judicial time. While some courts in India have created dedicated court management posts to fulfil these functions and have hired MBA graduates to manage the workflow, there is scope to better utilize their full potential.

The tussle between the government and the judiciary in the appointment of judges is a long-standing one. One of the main reasons for the build-up of vacancies for judges has been this cold war running between the government and the judiciary in the procedures for filling those vacancies. The judiciary began excluding the government from playing any role in the appointment of judges after the Second Judges Case in 1993, thereafter making the CJI the primary player in higher judicial appointments. The government tried to win back some of its authority in the selection and appointment process but the SC derailed that move.

Corruption within the judiciary would argue against assigning it a primary role in the selection and appointment of judges. It is a well-known fact that the Indian judiciary system has many corrupt judges who are merely recirculated under a collegium system of judges appointing judges.

The current procedures for removal of errant or corrupt judges is simply too cumbersome to act as a deterrent. While the Parliament is the only body which can impeach bad judges, this has never come to pass. As of 2018, over a period of some seventy years since Independence, six higher court judges have faced impeachment proceedings. But, no high court judge has ever been actually removed through such proceedings. For instance, Justice Soumitra Sen, resigned before facing imminent impeachment.[92] Another judge, Justice Veeraswami Ramaswami, who was appointed to the Supreme Court on 6 October 1989, faced impeachment proceedings in the Lok Sabha for corruption related to ostentatious expenditures on his official residence during his tenure as chief justice of the Punjab and Haryana high court. However, the motion to impeach him failed to pass in the Lok Sabha on 10 May 1993 and he retired on 14 February 1994.[93] Meanwhile, the SC as well as the government has done little to help weed out corrupt judges in spite of having a free hand to do so.

Consequently, the PIL has become a key instrument for delivering justice. It has enabled ordinary NGOs to present their case directly to the courts to seek redress. However, the PILs have also contributed to the backlog of cases clogging the Indian courts. According to data provided as a result of a Right to Information case, the number of PILs before the SC shot up from two in 1994 to 1,598 in 2015. The number of PILs before the SC capture only part of the backlog in such cases.

Riots and the Rule of Law

A second example of the link between poor rule of law and human rights is the frequency of riots along religious, caste and ethnic lines in India. Violence in one state can spread to another if people believe that justice has not been served in a fair, timely and credible manner. The role of an independent police and transparency in the criminal

---

[92]   'Justice Soumitra Sen resigns after Rajya Sabha voted to impeach him', NDTV, 1 September 2011, https://bit.ly/307SU0r; 'Impeachment Motion: Sixth judge to face impeachment but none removed thus far', *Free Press Journal*, 21 April 2018, https://bit.ly/2P995cS

[93]   The Hindu Net Desk, 'List of judges who faced impeachment proceedings', *The Hindu*, 25 May 2017.

justice system driven by evidence-based dispensation of justice are critical factors in improving the credibility of the courts. There are also other cogs in the wheel of the judicial system that are extremely important and need to be strengthened.

First, India should devote significant resources in building up its police force in terms of manpower, techniques, state-of-the-art forensic labs, police equipment for defensive and offensive use, better riot control, surveillance, etc. The police departments are lagging behind in technology and there is a lack of coordination between them across states.

Second, the police need to be made much more independent of politicians and there should be a mechanism to challenge decisions to transfer senior personnel by politicians. Undue political interference into police matters is a leading cause of the deterioration of law and order, low morale among police personnel, and sinking confidence in the rule of law.

Third, police personnel should be required to undergo periodic training in the latest methods of investigations, crowd control, collection of forensic evidence, respecting human rights, improving interactions between police and the society at large, and increasing awareness of gender issues. The minimum requirements to enter into the police force at the lowest levels need to be considerably tightened.

Finally, India's forensic labs need to be improved in terms of facilities, testing equipment, DNA analysis, advanced blood work, fingerprint identification techniques, etc. Sometimes, in complicated cases, the evidence collected at the crime scene are sent abroad due to lack of advanced forensic lab facilities in India. This need not be the case if adequate investments are made to bring existing crime labs to match the advanced labs in developed countries.

The Rule of Law Fails Indian Women

It seems after the 16 December 2012 gang rape and murder of Nirbhaya in a private bus on New Delhi streets, nothing much has changed as far as women's safety goes. Women are raped and even killed with a sickening regularity throughout India. The number of incidents of rape and violence against women in general has been rising fast in the country over the past few decades.

More than two rapes occur every hour on average in India (a statistic that is under-reported because women are often reluctant to file charges) but women still face many barriers to obtaining justice in India's courts. Poorly trained doctors, callous and corrupt police, lack of good crime labs with latest testing facilities, shoddy forensic work by investigators, and a clogged court system leading to inordinate delays in court decisions are the main barriers to justice. While India has responded by increasing the punishment for rape and creating fast-track courts to hear rape cases, these courts have also become clogged given the large number of rapes occurring in the country. Moreover, the court records show strikingly low rates of conviction for rape given the barriers.

If the complainant is a poor, low-caste, illiterate woman, her chances of getting a rape charge registered against powerful men is almost zero. Even if by some stroke of luck, she manages to file a first information report (FIR), the chances of winning a court case against her rich, high-caste assailants are also close to zero.

Part of the problem is that the police force at the lower levels of constables and sub-inspectors are typically male and either illiterate or semi-illiterate. They are trained poorly in police procedures and lack education on the role of the police in society, and the rights of citizens, particularly women, under the Constitution. The system favours those in the upper echelons of society with loads of money to hire the best lawyers.

Today, there seems to be a heightened awareness about the rights of women in India. Moreover, young women have begun to assert their rights vociferously wherever they are found wanting.[94]

---

[94]   Sameera Khan, 'Five years after Nirbhaya what has changed for women in public places', *The Hindu*, 19 December 2017, https://bit.ly/2z2v9uu

Thousands of women clamour all over the country asking for justice in a male-dominated society that claims to venerate the Divine Mother but fails to extend respect and equality of treatment to women in their daily lives.

10

Getting Rich without a Trace

The Basics of Black Money

When someone does something in secret, he obviously has something to hide. But unlike secrets that break no laws, secrecies involving money are typically illegal. Thus, a bribe to a government official is paid in secret and is illegal anywhere in the world.

The sharp distinction between white and black money is that the former is legal and recorded while the latter is illegal and unrecorded. In short, barring errors in recording, there is no reason why legitimate funds and related transactions should go unrecorded. So, when we say someone is trying to get rich secretly, we mean he or she is accumulating wealth in a clandestine manner—without the knowledge of the government. Typically, the individual is keeping the whereabouts of the funds secret either because he earned it illegally (such as a bribe or a kickback) or because he does not want to pay taxes on them.

Black money is internationally known as illicit funds and its cross-border transfer is known as illicit financial flows. The main characteristic of black money or illicit funds is that they must have broken laws somewhere along the line when they were earned, transferred or utilized. Accordingly, even if the funds were earned legally, such as from the profits of a legitimate business, they become illegal the moment they are transferred abroad, in violation of the tax, foreign exchange or other regulations of a country.

The other important point to note is that all black money is held by the private sector and never by the government. Even if the individual is a government servant or a minister, *he acts on his own behalf and is the sole owner of the illegal funds.* The government neither has any compulsion to steal from the private sector nor can it steal from itself.

For example, if it overcharges on taxes or makes some other mistake which penalizes the private sector, the government will ultimately have to rectify the situation under the law. Even in the case of the Russian Central Bank's misuse of the IMF's loan in 1999, certain individuals were involved in that elaborate money laundering operation to help elect Boris Yeltsin. The Russian government itself was not involved. So, illicit funds or black money deposits abroad are always associated with either private individuals or companies, never the government.

Today, black money constitutes a significant part of the Indian economy. How can we say that? The significance of black money shows up in various indicators that have been estimated by economists. One such indicator is the size of India's underground economy. The size of the underground economy is derived using indirect methods. While estimates vary according to the method used, most economists agree that it is very large (50–60 per cent of official GDP) and still growing.[95]

Research at GFI found that weak governance is the single-most important driver of illicit funds abroad. In fact, economists have typically found a significant positive relationship between corruption (as captured by the size of the underground economy) and outflows of black money from most developing countries.

Often, a weak government presiding over its weak judicial, administrative and executive branches provides an inadequate level of public services, most of which are of poor quality. These

---

[95]   Arun Kumar, *The Black Economy in India* (New Delhi: Penguin Books, 1999).

factors, along with 'grass-roots corruption' in the private sector (involving individuals, private households and enterprises) drive the extensive corruption permeating the entire civil society. Grass-roots corruption fuels growth of the underground economy. In India's case, we found that over the period since Independence, the growth of the underground economy, reflecting deteriorating governance, had been the major driver of black money transfers abroad.

Sources of Black Money

Black money, which is always unrecorded, is generated through three types of activities—criminal, corrupt and commercial. Some of the criminal sources of black money involve smuggling, drug, sex and human trafficking, kidnapping, extortion and blackmail, illegal fishing, illegal arms trade, and the theft of copyright material or intellectual property (such as pirated videos and the manufacture and distribution of goods that carry fake brand names).

Smuggling can happen without the knowledge of customs and tends to be rampant when there are significant differences in cross-border prices of certain goods, particularly between countries that share a long and porous border.

Gold smuggling often tends to be rampant in India due to the high domestic demand for gold and a price differential in favour of smuggled gold (due to high duty rates on declared gold imports). The profits from smuggling generate massive amounts of black money which the smugglers hide from government officials. In poorly governed countries, smugglers make lots of black money in collusion with or by bribing corrupt customs and other government officials.

Corruption, as I shared earlier, involves not only the abuse of public office for private gain but also the abuse of private office for private gain. The sources of corruption include bribery and kickbacks. For example, the bribing of government officials and ministers in order to win government contracts is a typical example of how corruption generates black money. The Bofors scandal and more recently, the 2G and the Commonwealth Games scandals are typical examples of the abuse of public office for private gain. However, when the private sector makes illegal profit and does not get caught (and there are many such instances), those transgressions amount to an abuse of private office for private gain.

The greater the bureaucratic red tape involved in the granting of licences and permits, the greater the scope for government servants to accept bribes for services that should be routinely provided. Not only that, the admission of children in highly selective schools and colleges in exchange for a payment is a form of bribe arising out of corruption in India's educational system. Calling these payments 'donations' does not change their basic nature. If the required payment is not noted on the admissions form as a requirement or is not declared to the government, the so-called 'donation' is nothing but a bribe.

While crime and corruption ruin many lives, by far the most important source of black money is commercial in nature. However, only a small portion of commercial black money can be directly estimated. It was only through extensive surveys that Raymond Baker was able to obtain a rough idea of the criminal, corrupt and commercial components of black money. He concluded that on average the commercial source of dirty money is the largest (accounting for about 64 per cent of the global total), followed by the criminal (around 33 per cent) and the corrupt (about 3 per cent).[96] The survey respondents included regulatory officials, such as tax, central banking, and customs officials, industry executives, and other people who are knowledgeable about the generation and transfer of black money.

No Data on Total Black Money

No government in the world has any clue about the totality of black money coming out of a country. Economists know that only a small

---

[96]   Raymond W. Baker, *Capitalism's Achilles Heel: Dirty Money and How to Renew the Free-Market System* (Hoboken: Wiley, 2005), p. 172.

portion of these flows is measurable. The main reason is that there
are no data on black money generated through the illegal sources
discussed above. Such transactions are always unrecorded. If total
black money flows represent an iceberg, what is measurable merely
accounts for its tip. The hidden portion of this iceberg is larger for
countries affected by drug trafficking, trade in contraband, human
trafficking and other illegal activities such as cross-border smuggling
and black market transactions.

A 2010 study carried out at GFI found that over the period
1948–2008, India lost a total of USD 213 billion through black
money transfers abroad.[97] This is only the measurable portion of
black money lost through transfer. The total value of this transfer
in today's dollars would be worth at least USD 500 billion. For the
reasons discussed in this and the next chapter, even this amount is
likely to be significantly understated.

How Fraudulent Trade Shifts Black Money

A preferred method of sending black money abroad is by manipulating
invoices of exports and imports. There are four types of fraudulent
invoicing in trade—export under-invoicing, export over-invoicing,
import under-invoicing, and import over-invoicing. Export under-
invoicing (EU) and import over-invoicing (IO) shift black money
abroad while export over-invoicing (EO) and import under-invoicing
(IU) shift black money into India.

Traders choose a particular type of mis-invoicing depending on
whether and how they stand to gain from doing so. *And the government
always makes a loss, regardless of the type of mis-invoicing.* The
private gain through mis-invoicing is exactly offset by a public loss.

---

[97]   Dev Kar, *The Drivers and Dynamics of Illicit Financial Flows from
India: 1948–2008* (Washington DC: Global Financial Integrity, November
2010).

The following example illustrates how export under-invoicing shifts black money out of the country.

Let us say an Indian exporter under-invoices a consignment of goods to Nigeria at USD 15 million to Indian customs when its actual value is USD 20 million. Because there are no duties to be collected on exports, the Indian customs do not really care much about the valuation. But the Nigerian importer still owes the Indian exporter the true market price of the exports (USD 20 million).

The Indian exporter simply asks the Nigerian importer to remit USD 15 million to his account in India and pay the USD 5 million into his account held in a tax haven such as the Cayman Islands or Hong Kong. The importer does not care how or where the total payment is to be made—all he cares is that the payment should not exceed the agreed price of USD 20 million. There is no way that Indian authorities can trace the USD 5 million that was deposited into the account of a shell company owned by the director of the company.

The Nirav Modi Trading Scam in Diamonds

Now consider how Nirav Modi shifted funds through import over-invoicing of diamonds. His basic strategy was to create sham import transactions of expensive diamonds to apply for massive letters of undertaking (LoUs) from Punjab National Bank (PNB). The LoU is basically a bank guarantee which allows the holder (in this case, Nirav Modi) to take loans from another Indian bank's foreign branch. These loans are given on a short-term basis (less than a year).

A total of 153 LoUs were issued by PNB but these were never recorded on the bank's books, thanks to Modi's contacts there. In fact, even the interbank instructions between PNB and the other banks issuing credit to Modi were never recorded in SWIFT, the interbank messaging network widely used by banks all over the world.

The amount of fraud perpetuated by PNB officials to help Nirav Modi launder black money is mind-boggling. Over a period of some seven years, these LoUs saddled PNB with massive 'non-performing' loans totalling USD 1.8 billion. A non-performing loan is one on which payments are past due for over ninety days. Actually, Nirav Modi never intended to repay any of these loans. In the meantime, he fled India and is currently fighting extradition from the United Kingdom.[98] How did he pull off one of the biggest daylight robberies of an Indian public sector bank?

First, Nirav Modi set up three shell companies in order to help him launder the black money—Firestar Diamond Inc., A Jaffe Inc., and Fantasy Inc. These were global sham entities set up with the sole purpose of throwing bank regulators off-track through a complicated global web of financial transactions and helping Modi launder the money he obtained from PNB.[99]

Customs officials were also duped into allowing fraudulent transactions right under their noses. This is because diamonds are extremely difficult to value correctly without knowledge of the industry and special instruments to evaluate the diamond's cut, colour and clarity. So when Modi overvalued a certain consignment of diamonds backed up by an LoU from PNB, customs went along with the valuation. The difference between the inflated value and the much lower actual value was probably shifted into one of the shell companies under Nirav Modi's direction. I say probably because any of the world's many tax havens would have been happy to accept the deposit.

Import over-invoicing is also used by companies to reduce their corporate taxes. As import costs eat into sales profits, companies can declare reduced profits on which they pay lower corporate taxes. In countries where the corporate tax rates are higher than import duties, companies could save money even after paying higher import costs as a result of the overvaluation. So Nirav Modi, to the extent that he

---

[98]   Cleve R. Wootson Jr, 'One of Hollywood's favorite diamond dealers has vanished amid an epic Indian fraud case', *The Washington Post*, 24 February 2018.

[99]   Radhika Merwin, 'US Bankruptcy Court orders probe into Nirav Modi's ties with Firestar Diamond', *The Hindu BusinessLine*, 29 April 2018, https://bit.ly/30f1pqA

declared business profits in India, could also fraudulently lower his corporate taxes while shifting the inflated value abroad.

Actually, as the examiner in the United States Bankruptcy Court found out, the three US entities (Firestar, A Jaffe, and Fantasy) were directly involved in the Nirav Modi scam. The examiner found evidence of a number of fraudulent transactions where the diamonds were repeatedly round-tripped between Firestar global entities, Modi firms and other shadow entities. The examiner found one transaction where the overvalued diamond was round-tripped between two Modi entities simply to obtain LoU financing. In some cases, the diamond purportedly being traded (a 1.04-carat Fancy Intense Pink Emerald Cut S12) did not even exist!

In fact, examiners in the US courts investigating the Nirav Modi case served to highlight the complex manner in which Indian companies move cash in and out of India and other countries. Often, such movements of funds fall under a practice known as Trade-Based Money Laundering (TBML). This is a preferred technique to move funds into and out of countries where customs and other regulatory institutions are weak or corrupt and the rule of law is tenuous.

Hawala Transactions

Hawala is a method of transferring money through word of mouth. It is quite common in the Indian subcontinent and in parts of the Middle East. A hawala transaction is simply based on trust between the person transferring the funds and the one who operates the hawala known as a hawaladar. The huge diaspora of Indian workers in Dubai and other parts of the Middle East often rely on hawala transactions to send money to India safely and securely. Because hawala transactions are not recorded at either end, it is difficult to put a figure to the amount of money being shifted in and out of India using this technique.

In February 2009, a report by the US assistant secretary of state for International Narcotics and Law Enforcement Affairs, David Johnson, quoted RBI estimates that while remittances to India sent through formal channels (such as commercial banks) amounted to USD 42.6 billion, funds transferred through hawala were estimated to be between 30–40 per cent of the formal market. The hawala market for India could therefore amount to USD 13–17 billion per annum in 2009. The report noted that large illegal funds (black money) were often laundered through hawala and that the system could be linked to terrorist financing.[100]

Take the case of someone in India with a large holding of black money in Indian rupees. Now, let us suppose that he needs to send his son to college in the US and the annual expenses are in excess of those allowed by the RBI or his declared income. He would simply arrange with a hawaladar to deposit the needed amount in dollars into his son's account in a US bank against the deposit of Indian rupees in the hawaladar's local account in an Indian bank.

The convenience, transaction cost, and the exchange rate offered by the hawaladar could provide additional incentives to use his services rather than official channels, even if the transfer amount was within the legal limit. Such 'currency swaps', or hawala transactions, are almost impossible to trace. In any case, in most countries, hawala transactions are not illegal.

Global Use of Black Money

Getting rich secretly involves more than just transferring black money abroad. The black money could also be used to purchase expensive real estate, fancy cars, precious stones and other tangible goods.

Besides stashing USD 8 billion in Swiss banks, Indian stud farm owner Hasan Ali Khan owned several luxury cars, a number of flats in posh neighbourhoods, and other real estate abroad.[101] If tracing

---

[100] 'Hawala money in India linked to terrorist financing: US', *The Indian Express*, 28 February 2009, https://bit.ly/2N9jp1y

[101] 'India stud farm owner arrested for "illegal money"', BBC News, 8 March 2011, citing Dev Kar, *The Drivers and Dynamics of Illicit Financial Flows from India: 1948-2008* (Washington DC: Global Financial Integrity, 2010).

black money into numbered bank accounts in tax havens such as Switzerland becomes almost impossible over time, finding evidence of such investments in real estate and other tangible assets is even more difficult.

London, Miami, Paris and New York present tantalizing real estate investment opportunities for well-heeled black money holders around the world. Such investments have turned these cities into the illegal savings accounts of the glitzy corrupt. As regulators have failed to stem such investments, prices of real estate in these cities have skyrocketed, shutting out local buyers and helping corrupt foreigners launder their black money.

To combat the problem, some governments are gradually fighting back. Instead of proving that a particular real estate investment by the owner utilized illicit funds or black money, governments in advanced countries are now asking the investor, 'How did you pay for that?'[102] So, instead of the state having to prove that the investment was made with black money, the onus is now on these investors to show that they purchased the real estate using legitimate funds.

This is obviously a huge change in legal tactic and one with which some lawyers are not comfortable. Moreover, this change in strategy by the British government is just starting. There is no guarantee that the legal strategy will succeed in stemming the flow of black money into these cities.

The latest case involves Zamira Hajiyeva who was living a lavish lifestyle in Britain with a USD 15 million townhouse in the posh Knightsbridge neighbourhood of London, a golf club in the English countryside, and gold-plated shopping privileges at Harrods. While Ms Hajiyeva has not been charged with a crime in Britain, she is under an 'unexplained wealth order' to clarify how she is able to maintain this lifestyle. In other words, what were her sources of income and what are they now?

---

[102]   Jeanne Whalen, 'To combat dirty money, Britain asks: How did you pay for that mansion?', *The Washington Post*, 14 December 2018.

The 'unexplained wealth order' is issued when law enforcement agencies have 'reasonable grounds to suspect' that the person in question lacks sufficient legitimate funds to purchase an expensive real estate and maintain such a lavish lifestyle. If the person cannot show that they have used and are using legitimate income, then the court may allow the government to seize the property. The entire case turns on the moral ground that Britain cannot allow people to acquire and retain property and other assets in the country using dirty or black money obtained from crime and corruption.

Australia has also started to adopt this approach. However, the approach has had mixed results in other advanced countries. For example, while the US has a strong anti-money-laundering mechanism in place, its regulations of lawyers, accountants and real estate agents who help such shady investments are weak, offering many opportunities to do so.

11

Why India Cannot Get the Money Back

A few years after retiring from the IMF, I applied for the position of lead economist at GFI, then a fledging think tank based in Washington DC, headed by Raymond Baker. He had just written the widely acclaimed book which I referred to earlier. For the first time, here was a book that put a figure on all the 'dirty money' sloshing around in the world.[103] GFI was instrumental in introducing the term 'illicit financial flows' to represent flows of dirty money around the world.

I was called for an interview during which Raymond said, 'We have received some funding from the Ford Foundation to carry out a study. The objective of the study would be to estimate the total volume of illicit funds coming out from developing countries. The second part of the project would be to determine where the money goes. What are your views on these projects, can you do them?'

The Ford Foundation felt that people would be interested to know whether Raymond's survey-based estimates could be corroborated through economic methods. I said, 'I am confident about estimating the volume of illegal capital flight from developing countries, but I am not sure whether the second part of the project could be done.' I knew that the illicit funds went into 'black holes', about which economists knew precious little.

---

[103]   Baker, *Capitalism's Achilles Heel.*

It was probably the first time someone got a job by doubting they could actually do it! I would not suggest anyone giving it a try at a job interview. Far from being whimsical, I knew that there were enormous difficulties in carrying out the second part of the Ford project.

As it turned out, within one year, with the help of some bright economic interns, I was able to complete the first part of the project, namely estimating the total volume of illicit funds coming out from developing countries. The second part—where black money goes after it leaves a country—was completed the following year using a number of heroic assumptions about the way the world's shadow financial system behaves. These were some of the most exciting projects I ever worked on during my long career as an economist.

On Tax Havens and Other Black Holes

To make a reasonable start, I assumed that the black money coming out from developing countries could either be deposited in the banks of advanced countries or in tax havens. Both can be likened to black holes—destinations that cannot be traced, monitored or contacted by any investigating or regulatory agency regarding the funds.

Even if you manage to get in touch with these black holes, the answers to your questions would be evasive. Their skimpy 'publications' tend to raise more questions than they answer. Literally, these black holes emit no light. By that I mean the light of information and of transparency. In fact, the word 'transparency' is alien to the people running that world.

No wonder that tax havens and most advanced countries are called 'secrecy jurisdictions'. Advanced countries such as Singapore, Switzerland, the United Kingdom and the US are closely connected to tax havens because of their strong financial linkages. After all, most of the banks operating in tax havens have their headquarters in the advanced countries.

Business Is Great!

Business has been so good for tax havens that their assets and liabilities have grown exponentially. Assets are what tax havens invest abroad while their liabilities consist of deposits by foreigners. Even the world's best investigative agencies such as the CIA, the FBI, the Interpol and Scotland Yard have few clues about who holds what and how much in these tax havens.

You would expect that the advanced countries, if not the tax havens themselves, would be a little more sympathetic to your queries. But the banks of advanced countries are equally secretive about such information. For instance, you cannot get any bank in any of the advanced countries to provide you with a detailed breakdown of public and private sector deposits of developing countries by type of financial instruments. They gave me all sorts of excuses as to why they could not provide me that data. That is why I call them black holes. The name is most appropriate.

Some of them such as the Cayman Islands grew so much in the dark that they went bust. The United Kingdom had to bail them out. Now, not all tax havens are under the jurisdiction of an advanced country and when these go bankrupt (such as Cyprus), you are out of luck.

The Panama Papers

One day in 2014, a person named 'John Doe' (meaning he did not wish to reveal his identity) called Bastian Obermayer, a reporter working for *Süddeutsche Zeitung*, a German newspaper. He said he wanted to talk about data but that his life was in danger. There is no way he is going to give Obermayer a personal interview. Doe suggested that they chat using encrypted files. Is Obermayer interested in what he has to say? Naturally, this made the reporter prick up his ears. Still, he asked Doe why he wanted to spill the beans.

Doe said he wanted to 'make these crimes public'. He was seriously concerned about the growing income disparity between the rich and the poor and the widespread corruption in many countries. He was angry about the injustice meted out by firms such as Mossack Fonseca, which helped the rich hide their money in tax havens and evade taxes. Shortly thereafter, he began to digitally transfer nearly 11.5 million documents from the law firm Mossack Fonseca based in Panama.[104]

Süddeutsche Zeitung verified that the documents were authentic and shared them with the International Consortium of Investigative Journalists (ICIJ) as well as the *Guardian* and the BBC. Finally released to the public, the documents became known as the Panama Papers. What were the main findings and consequences of these documents?

The Panama Papers revealed that the rich and famous tend to take advantage of tax havens or offshore financial centres to avoid paying their fair share of taxes. The documents show the extent to which law firms such as Mossack Fonseca, accountants and investment advisers help the rich to hide their wealth from tax authorities for an annual fee. Such companies are run on a worldwide basis. They have specialized knowledge of tax havens and the rates of interest offered on the various types of investments. Generally, these tax havens charge little or no taxes on these investments, which are maintained safely and securely in total secrecy.

Moreover, high public officials use companies and trusts to hide the fact that they are the true owners of the funds held there. Even the managers of these brass-plate companies and trusts based in tax havens such as the British Virgin Islands and the Cayman Islands have no idea whom they are working for. In other words, there is zero information on the actual persons who own these companies which only exist on a brass plate in some building in a tax haven.

---

[104] 'The story behind the massive Panama Papers leak', *USA Today*, 4 April 2016. See also, Frederick Obermaier, Bastian Obermayer, Vanessa Wormer and Wolgang Jaschensky and *Süddeutsche Zeitung*, 'About the Panama Papers', website of the International Consortium of Investigative Journalists, https://bit.ly/2DWWBKl

I remember listening to Barack Obama in the run-up to the 2008 presidential elections saying that he knew of a building in the Cayman Islands that was home to some 12,000 brass-plate companies. He said, 'That's either the biggest building or the biggest tax scam on record.'[105]

This does not mean that all the funds deposited in tax havens consist of black money. Offshore financial centres such as the Cayman Islands, Hong Kong, Singapore and Switzerland also hold a lot of legitimate funds. For instance, they also take deposits from central banks, other government agencies and commercial banks. Such deposits are legal and are made for convenience and high rates of return.

However, the Panama Papers revealed that 143 politicians (including twelve national leaders and their friends and relatives) as well as thousands of the rich and famous around the world have deposited their funds in tax havens. While it is true that having a deposit in a tax haven is not necessarily illegal, the public revelation of these depositors does not reflect well on their honesty and integrity. Caught up in the dragnet were politicians such as Vladimir Putin and his best friend Sergei Roldugin; Nawaz Sharif, the former prime minister of Pakistan; Petro Poroshenko, the former president of Ukraine; Alaa Mubarak, the son of Egypt's former president, and the former prime minister of Iceland, Sigmundur Gunnlaugsson.[106] Sharif was convicted of corruption and sent to prison while Gunnlaugsson had to resign in embarrassment.

A second set of 1.2 million documents related to the Panama Papers revealed the names of at least 12,000 Indians, including the CEOs of several companies, some lower-level politicians, iconic Bollywood celebrities like Amitabh Bachchan and a few individuals connected to the underworld. These documents revealed that the

---

[105] 'Obama targets Cayman "tax scam"', Politifact, 9 January 2008, https://bit.ly/2z30ihy

[106] Luke Harding, 'What are the Panama Papers? A guide to history's biggest data leak', *Guardian*, 5 April 2016, https://bit.ly/29RFjU7

Indian clients of Mossack Fonseca reacted differently to the initial revelation—some renewed their relationship with the company, some actually increased their deposits there, while others rushed to liquidate the firms that Fonseca managed.

India's Central Board of Direct Taxes (CBDT) said that it could only investigate 147 of these 12,000 individuals. The Enforcement Directorate (ED) said that the violations of five out of the forty-five cases it was investigating were serious in the sense that the individuals did not disclose their relationship with the tax havens. The violations of the rest were of a technical nature and probably not punishable. Amitabh Bachchan, who is under investigation, has denied any link to the offshore companies and accounts.[107]

How Much Do Indians Actually Hold Abroad?

Mossack Fonseca is only one among hundreds if not thousands of such law firms operating globally helping to hide the assets of the rich from the tax authorities. In fact, Panama is a relatively small player of dirty money compared to others like the Cayman Islands, Hong Kong, Singapore and Switzerland when ranked by the volume of offshore deposits. More to the point, there are much bigger law firms than Mossack Fonseca with a larger global footprint and assets under management.

Given the lack of transparency, we can only provide rough estimates of the amount of black money held by Indians—roughly USD 500 billion accumulated since Independence. But nobody has a hard number—certainly not the CBI or other agencies of the Government of India. To make matters worse, Indian media reports on black money add to the fog rather than clarify matters.

For example, a recent article in an Indian newspaper claimed that Modi's 2019 campaign would get a big boost because Swiss

---

[107] 'Panama Papers 2.0: New leak reveals fresh 1,200 documents linked to Indians', *Business Today*, 21 June 2018, https://bit.ly/2N8j4wh

bank deposits showed that India was winning the fight against black money.[108] Unfortunately, the arguments extended to support this tall claim are fallacious for the following reasons.

First, the data published by international organizations such as the Bank for International Settlements (BIS) located in Basel, Switzerland, cannot be used to track deposits by the Indian private sector accurately. I can say this because I worked extensively with the BIS data over the period 2008–14 when I was at GFI.

It would be more accurate to say that the BIS data can provide an *indication* of the amount of deposits received by Swiss banks from both the Indian public and private sectors. A clear disaggregation is not possible. Because government funds are not illegal, the total volume of deposits cannot be attributed only to the black money holdings of individuals.

Second, there is no way to break down the total deposits into the black and white money portions. As the Panama Papers show, not all the so-called private sector deposits are black. It was one thing for those papers to reveal the names of certain individuals. *It is quite another to actually prove them guilty of a crime in a court of law.* For example, India has progressively allowed more foreign exchange to be transferred out of the country. As a result, people have been allowed to hold more white money abroad than ever before. Hence, as a result of financial liberalization, we can expect a greater portion of those deposits in Swiss banks to be entirely legal.

Third, Switzerland is only one among more than a hundred tax havens and secrecy jurisdictions spread around the world. Therefore, the decrease in total deposits in Swiss banks cannot be indicative of the total black money flows from India. It may well be that Indian black money holders, wary of the government's focus on Swiss banks,

---

[108] 'Modi's 2019 campaign gets a big boost! Swiss banks show India winning Black money battle', *Financial Express*, 24 July 2018, https://bit.ly/2OZsqgs

have decided to park their loot in other secrecy jurisdictions! When it comes to black money, there are more than a hundred ways to skin the cat. The point is we cannot assert that India is 'winning the black money battle' based on totally incomplete information on how deposits are behaving in one secrecy jurisdiction.

Can India Get Back the Black Money Orbiting in Black Holes?

Since 2011, I have been asked by the media whether India could ever get back the hundreds of billions of dollars in black money it has lost to these black holes since Independence.[109] I told them not to hold their breath.

In the run-up to the 2014 general elections, which ushered in the BJP with Prime Minister Narendra Modi at its helm, Baba Ramdev called me at home four times, each call lasting close to two hours. He had many questions on the repatriation of black money and tried to float some ideas which I had to shoot down.

One such idea was particularly bizarre. He waited until I had exhausted all the reasons (enumerated below) as to why India cannot get back the black money. Then he said, 'The Government of India can simply declare that all the black money of Indian citizens deposited in foreign accounts belongs to the Government of India.' He was talking of confiscating the illegal funds.

I said, 'Please go right ahead. Why only make one declaration? Make a hundred declarations that the black money in foreign accounts belongs to the Government of India. It will make no difference.' Then I had to explain *why* it will make no difference.

First of all, before declaring that all the black money held abroad belongs to the Government of India, the question is how would it know that the money in a particular account is black or white, that

---

[109]   See, for example, Sanjay Jog, 'Getting black money back is a myth: Dev Kar', *Business Standard*, 15 February 2011, https://bit.ly/31JSzRH

is, legal or illegal? After all, the Government of India does not have extrasensory perception (ESP)!

Next, who can be charged with making that determination? The courts in India, of course. The government cannot simply bypass the courts and declare someone's deposit as black money. As far as democracies are concerned, there is something called private property and laws have to respect private property.

There are huge legal hurdles to overcome to prove that the funds deposited abroad by an individual are in fact illegal. The hurdles exist in both India and the country holding the funds. The following hypothetical case illustrates the difficulties.

Let us assume that on 8 June 2018, the Government of India filed a case in the Delhi High Court (which happens to be the competent court to hear the case) that Mr X, the then secretary, Ministry of Mines, received a bribe of Rs 10 crore on or about 12 September 1978 from Mr Y, CEO of TT Mines and Minerals, which was then transferred out of India on 21 September 1978.

The government has to bring both Mr X and Mr Y to court and place all the evidence that Y gave X the bribe on or about 12 September 1978, nearly forty years ago. Then, it has to prove that Mr Y received a specific favour in exchange for that bribe (for example, X awarded the contract to Y).

There could be a complication that X or Y, or both, are deceased, but let us assume for the moment that they are still alive and well enough to come to court. Just imagine trying to present hard evidence before a judge that Mr X did receive the bribe from Mr Y nearly forty years back. Even if evidence may be presented, the judge may well ask the government lawyer what he was doing all this time. Suppose the lawyer says that they were trying to collect all the evidence, absurd as it may sound. But then Mr Y says, 'Where is the evidence that I paid him?'

In a country where the courts take thirty years to restore a property to its rightful owner, how long do you think it will take for the court to establish that Mr X took the bribe from Mr Y some forty years ago? Now, even if the Delhi High Court renders a judgment that Mr X did receive the bribe from Mr Y, *tracing the money is next to impossible*. It is like trying to convict a murderer without a murder weapon or a body! The simple question the defence lawyer can ask the prosecutor is: 'Show me the money! Where is the money? If the Government cannot provide any evidence on where that bribe money is, what are we talking about?'

In this electronic age of moving funds, it would take seconds to move the money from Switzerland (where the equivalent of Rs 10 crore was originally deposited) into, say, the Cayman Islands, a tax haven. Moreover, Mr X had already split and shifted the funds into a shell company with an account in a bank in the Cayman Islands as well as a portion of the proceeds into a massive hedge fund based in New York. Both of them are excellent black holes.

So the case falls flat because the government could not trace that bribe to a specific account held by Mr X in either the Cayman Islands or sloshing around in a mega hedge fund. *Mr X had done his homework and made sure from day one that any black money he held abroad could never be traced to him!*

Moreover, international agreements such as the Double Tax Avoidance Agreement (DTAA) has a 'no fishing expedition' clause. That clause says that a country cannot use the DTAA to go after 'black money' in a blanket fashion. The 'no fishing expedition' clause in turn arises from the 'innocent until proven guilty' clause and strong privacy laws in almost all advanced countries. Moreover, Switzerland could point out that the DTAA with India was signed much later than the date of the transfer, which in our case was 21 September 1978. So it is not a valid request for an exchange of information.

Now let us suppose that the transfer of funds took place after the DTAA was signed. In that case, Switzerland would start to look for the funds belonging to Mr X. But Mr X had already made sure that the black money he holds can never be traced back to him. He holds the funds in several trust funds or shell companies with a brass plate in, say, the Cayman Islands and New York.

In both places, his bribe is working overtime as a small part of a USD 500 million derivative held in the name of some obscure company. Both the shell company in the Cayman Islands and the company in New York managing the derivative have no information whatsoever that it is really Mr X who is the beneficial owner of the funds. *The utter lack of information on beneficial ownership is a primary feature of the world's financial system.*

There is no international regulation that says shell companies must know and declare who their ultimate beneficiaries are. In other words, shell or brass-plate companies are run by managers who have no clue about the beneficial owners of those companies. Good luck on trying to find Mr X's bribe in those black holes.

Now, that is just the case of Mr X's bribe which was paid on a certain date for a favour done on a certain project. There are thousands of such cases that make up the nearly USD 500 billion at present value of India's black money deposited abroad. And each of these cases presents its own daunting legal challenge to, first, prove guilt and, second, to trace the proceeds to the accused black money holder. How long will it take for the Government of India to get all the black money back? *Forever is one word. Eternity is another.*

No wonder that efforts to date by various countries and international organizations to bring back black money have been very disappointing. For instance, the World Bank's Stolen Asset Recovery (StAR) Initiative has been able to bring back only a minuscule fraction of the total volume of illicit assets that have been spirited away from poor developing countries over the past several decades. Despite the significant resources of the World Bank, in terms of funding, staff, country legal expertise, and the political backing of member governments, the StAR Initiative has thus far managed to retrieve only about USD 1 billion since its inception in 2007 out of the more than USD 1 trillion stolen from all countries.

Expropriation of black money is only possible in a limited number of cases where the transfer of funds was very recent or if investigative agencies were already hot on the trail of the culprit such as in the case of Vijay Mallya or Nirav Modi. Even then, it may take years before the government gets its hands on any stolen funds, and the portion finally retrieved is likely to be a fraction of what the culprit stole.

It would be far more productive to curtail the internal generation and external transfer of black money in the first place. This involves a two-prong strategy. India must strengthen governance in all its various dimensions in order to restrict the generation of black money. Simultaneously, it must push developed countries against taking in tainted funds. For example, developed countries and tax havens need to do a much better job of getting information on these depositors and sharing the information with developing countries like India. If these steps are not taken, an emphasis on getting the money back is meaningless. Even if the money were to return, it will leak out again. It's like pouring water into a bucket full of holes. That's not a strategy!

Greater efforts should be made to rein in tax evasion by improving the capacity of India's tax authority. In fact, most developing countries do not have enough tax officials to collect taxes. For example, whereas Kenya and Nigeria employ 3000 and 5000 tax and customs officials for populations of thirty-two and 140 million, respectively, the Netherlands employs 30,000 tax and customs officials for a population of ten million. Therefore, in order for a country to effectively collect taxes and follow up on suspected cases of tax evasion, it is imperative that it gradually shore up its staffing and training of tax officials. In addition, India needs to enter into various agreements to exchange information with developed countries regarding depositors based in India.

PART 3

THE FALLOUT

12

A Taxing Problem

There are many scholarly books and academic papers devoted entirely to tax problems and policies in developing countries such as India. Even the problem of tax evasion and policies to eliminate such practices is a huge subject with many complexities.

It is not possible to cover such vast subjects in this short chapter. Rather, the intent here is to provide readers with a brief overview of the main challenges facing the government in raising revenues, and India's poor record in doing so thus far. Obviously, boosting government revenues is crucial given the multiple demands on the government to meet India's development challenges such as improving healthcare and education.

Ever since Independence, India has had two main problems with taxation—a narrow tax base and significant tax evasion. A narrow tax base means only a small portion of India's population is paying income taxes. Out of a population of some 1.3 billion people, only about 4 per cent file (but not necessarily) pay income taxes, which make up the largest part of direct taxes. Other types of direct taxes include taxes on corporations, wealth, estate, inheritance and fringe benefits.

The label 'direct taxes' refer to the fact that the individual or corporation pays them directly to the government. They cannot shift the burden of paying these obligations to another party. Indirect taxes, on the other hand, are value-added taxes (VAT) like the goods and services tax (GST) and customs duties (typically on imports).

The burden of paying indirect taxes is typically shifted to others such as when importers recuperate import duties by charging the consumers a higher price.

Causes and Consequences of a Narrow Tax Base

Causes

Many developing countries such as India tend to have a narrow tax base due to a large informal sector which is the major source of employment for the vast majority of the country's workers. According to the International Labour Organization (ILO), while the share of workers in the unorganized sector fell recently, the share of informal workers in the organized sector (defined as workers without social security or other benefits) increased significantly. This increase was due to the greater use of contractual and other types of casual labour. Hence, the overall share of informal workers in total employment has remained relatively stable at around 92 per cent.[110]

Globally, the agriculture sector accounts for 93.6 per cent of all informal sector jobs. Among the five South Asian countries studied, India and Nepal have the highest share of labour in the informal sector, most of them employed in the agricultural sector. The youth constitute a major share of those informal labour markets.[111]

A major reason for the growth of the informal sector is that the formal job market is not creating enough jobs to absorb the millions looking for work. Moreover, most new entrants into the job market are poorly educated with little skills. They are therefore unable to find gainful employment in the formal sector anyway.

The ILO finds that while informality is a global phenomenon, the level of informality decreases the more a country's labour force is

---

[110] *India Labour Market Update* (New Delhi: ILO Country Office for India, July 2017).

[111] The demographic dividend is likely to peter out if the youth are stuck in low-skilled jobs in the informal labour markets.

educated or undergoes vocational training. In sum, poor investment in education and training has adverse implications not only for employment generation but also for attaining inclusive growth, developing a wider tax base, and increasing government revenues relative to the GDP. The ratio of government revenues to GDP is an indicator of revenue performance which will be used extensively in this chapter.

Consequences

A country trying to raise adequate tax revenues from a narrow base ends up running large fiscal deficits given increasing government expenditures to meet multiple development objectives. Fiscal deficits in turn hamper economic growth and lead to economic instability through rampant inflation, higher interest rates, or increasing foreign debt. It is the poor who suffer disproportionately.

A relatively small number of taxpayers means the government faces a serious problem of raising tax revenues because any increase in tax rates is likely to result in an increase in tax evasion. A narrow tax base is susceptible to tax fatigue, which occurs when a relatively smaller number of taxpayers feel that they are already paying too much in relation to the quantity and quality of government services they are receiving in return. Taxpayers feel that the system is unfair. They are being asked to finance an increasing share of the government budget while the vast majority of the population is getting a free ride. Tax fatigue leads to greater tax avoidance as well as tax evasion. There are important differences between the two.

Tax avoidance is legitimate in the sense that all taxpayers seek to minimize their taxes. This means taxpayers avoid paying more than what they owe after accounting for all permissible deductions and exemptions allowed under the law. Thus, the employment or advice of tax accountants and lawyers with a view to minimizing personal or corporate tax obligations to the government is carried out routinely around the world. No one likes paying more taxes than what they owe.

Questionable tax avoidance is a murky area where the taxpayer (whether individual or corporate) uses tax loopholes or inflate deductions and exemptions well beyond their reasonable value. But they manage to fly under the radar of the revenue department, which does not have the resources to check the veracity of the loopholes or the accuracy of every deduction and exemption within a complicated tax filing. Questionable tax avoidance tends to rise along with tax fatigue.

Tax evasion, unlike tax avoidance, is illegal. There is a popular misconception that high tax rates lead to tax evasion. One has to only look at the Nordic and other advanced countries where compliance by taxpayers is high in spite of tax rates of 40 per cent or even higher. Tax compliance and collections are high in spite of high tax rates because taxpayers feel that they are getting their money's worth in terms of the quantity and quality of government services.

A few years back, on a work-related visit to Bergen, Norway, I struck up a conversation with my taxi driver. I asked him about life in Norway in general noting that the cost of living is very high and so are taxes in comparison to other advanced countries such as the US.

He said, 'I am very happy. Sure, taxes are high but everything is taken care of by the government, from the cradle to the grave, so to speak. I don't have to worry about my children's education, my pension is secure and guaranteed by the government on top of which I will receive a nice social security if I ever become disabled. Also, my family and I can avail of the best healthcare free of charge. I don't have any reason to complain.'

Norway is totally transparent about the taxes the government collects from its citizens. In fact, Norway is the only country where the tax returns of Norwegian citizens are posted online and any citizen can have access to that database. This tradition of publicly sharing the income and tax information goes back a long time—to 1882 when the personal income tax was first introduced. To be precise, the information was available in hard copies from the Norwegian Tax Administration prior to 2001, while since then, with the advent of the digital age, the information has been made accessible online. Back in the 1880s and 1990s, citizens would go to the City Hall to see who was paying what in taxes and make sure everyone pulled their fair share of the tax burden.

Transparency about the taxes one pays discourage tax evasion. The theory goes that if you have nothing to hide, you should have no problem in letting others see how much you paid and contributed to the nation's upkeep and development. Norway has a progressive tax system meaning taxes rise along with the income brackets ensuring that the tax burden is distributed evenly according to the taxpayer's capacity to pay.

Country comparison of tax systems is more difficult than what is suggested at first glance. This is because we may have different exemptions and slabs that are applicable in the countries being compared. Still, in 2018, the top personal income tax rate in Norway was 46.6 per cent while in India it was 35.9 per cent.[112]

Tax compliance is high not only because of transparency. Along with the high quality of government services such as excellent retirement benefits and social security, world-class infrastructure including education and healthcare ensures a high degree of tax compliance. People voluntarily pay their fair share because they know that their taxes are being put to good use. Why should anyone resort to tax evasion and risk getting caught and punished if they are enjoying high-quality government services and can look forward to a secure pension and social security? In contrast, tax fatigue and evasion set in when the relatively few are asked to shell out even more taxes in the face of shoddy, intermittent, or even non-existent government services while the vast majority go tax-free.

In India, tax evasion has long been a national sport. Arun Kumar, a retired professor at Jawaharlal Nehru University (JNU) who has worked extensively on India's black economy, estimates that

---

[112] 'Country comparison Norway vs India', countryeconomy.com, https://bit.ly/2ZeBSAg

uncollected taxes come to around USD 314 billion per annum.[113] There is evasion not only on direct taxes such as personal income and company profits but also on indirect taxes such as those payable on the sale of real estate.

Typically, the seller simply pays taxes on the declared price of an apartment or building. He asks the buyer to pay him in cash the difference between the actual price and the declared price in order to evade taxes on the full market price of the property.

There have been recent attempts by the government to ensure that the declared sale price of the property is realistic. In case the government suspects that the declared price is too low, it makes an offer to buy the property from the seller at the declared price. Such tactics have reduced the evasion of taxes on the sale of property but have not eliminated the problem entirely.

Often, the problem is corruption among income tax officials themselves. The bribe paid to tax officials is simply added to the sale price as an additional 'transaction' cost. The real estate sector in India attracts a lot of black money held by investors, brokers, lawyers, sellers, buyers, as well as the taxmen. If bribes and 'commissions' are to be paid along the way, those transactions simply recirculate the black money. And the government loses out on a good portion of tax revenues it was meant to collect at every step of the transaction. Vito Tanzi, a reputed economist and a former director of the IMF's Fiscal Affairs Department, coined the term 'fiscal termites'. Like termites that eat into the very foundation of a home and make the structure weak, fiscal termites characterize the many ways the government loses tax revenue and sees its subsidies for the poor (e.g., on rice and kerosene) eaten away by corrupt middlemen.

India lags behind China and other developing countries in Asia when it comes to tax collection. A high tax collection is an indicator of

---

[113] Tushar Dhara and Cherian Thomas, 'In India, Tax Evasion Is a National Sport', *Bloomberg Businessweek*, 28 July 2011, https://bloom.bg/2HbKQEb

good governance and a capacity to spend for economic development. In 2018, for example, the major advanced countries (i.e., Canada, France, Germany, Italy, Japan, the United Kingdom and the US) collected an average of 36 per cent of GDP in taxes. In comparison, tax collections in China and India amounted to 28.7 per cent and 20.8 per cent of their GDPs, respectively (see Table 2).

What is very interesting is that India was actually doing better than China when it came to tax collections during the 1990s up until the first half of the first decade of the twenty-first century, i.e., 2005–2009. But beginning 2010, China started outpacing India in tax collections. By the end of 2018, China's tax collections exceeded India's by a whopping 8 per cent of GDP. In fact, over the period 1990 to 2018, India's tax revenue to GDP only increased by a paltry 2.8 per cent while China's more than doubled from 13.9 per cent to 28.7 per cent of GDP (see Table 2).

What Led Chinese Revenue Performance to Outstrip India's?

Several factors enabled China to power ahead of India in terms of revenue performance. First, China started economic liberalization in December 1978, some six years after President Nixon's first official visit to the country in 1972. While China's complicated path to economic liberalization was implemented in phases, the fact remains that it had a much earlier start to liberalization than India where economic reforms began in 1991.

China's economic liberalization was mainly outward-oriented, meaning it relied on export-led growth. Its trade performance (exports plus imports) has been clearly superior to India's.[114] In

---

[114]   Nicholas R. Lardy, 'Trade Liberalization and Its Role in Chinese Economic Growth' (prepared for an International Monetary Fund and National Council of Applied Economic Research Conference 'A Tale of Two Giants: India's and China's Experience with Reform and Growth', New Delhi, 14–16 November 2003).

2017, while India's share of global trade in goods was around 2 per cent, China's share was almost six times larger at about 12 per cent. China's trade expansion has been so strong that it became the world's second largest trading economy behind the US, a mere seventeen years after it joined the World Trade Organization in 2001.

Trade-led Growth Boosted Revenue Performance in a Number of Ways

For one, China's export-led growth was mainly led by the manufacturing sector. Growth of the manufacturing sector helped move labour from the informal to the formal sector, thereby increasing income taxes. The larger fraction of workers in the formal sector has helped to expand the collection of income taxes in China. Meanwhile, the lack of decent jobs in the formal sector in India led to low and falling female labour force participation rate, while forcing both male and female workers to look for employment in the informal sector. In fact, more than 90 per cent of the workforce in India works in the informal sector with women accounting for just 20 per cent of formal sector jobs.[115]

According to World Bank data, Chinese industry (including manufacturing) accounted for 40.5 per cent of the GDP in 2017, compared to just 26.2 per cent in India. China has excelled not only at large-scale assembly line production employing workers at the lower skill ranges but also increasingly sophisticated manufacturing goods that employ many highly skilled workers.

India, on the other hand, has specialized in the services sector (e.g., IT, back office processing work for large multinationals), which have limited job opportunities. Recognizing the limited capacity of the service sector to generate jobs on a scale required to absorb India's burgeoning labour force, the Modi government has embarked on

---

[115]   Purva Khera, 'Macroeconomic Impacts of Gender Inequality and Informality in India', IMF Working Paper (Washington DC: IMF, 2016).

the 'Make in India' campaign. However, the rather shallow pool of skilled workers and the shoddy state of India's education system has effectively hampered the drive to expand manufacturing and other industry in India, which rely on an educated and skilled workforce. Still, the 'Make in India' drive is a laudable one which needs to be backed up by high-quality vocational training as well as educational opportunities for Indian workers.

In the meantime, China's success in trade participation has transformed its economy from a largely agricultural economy to an increasingly industrial one, shrinking the size of the informal economy. Estimates vary given the differing definitions of what constitutes informality but researchers agree that the informal sector in China employs somewhere between 40–60 per cent of workers compared to more than 90 per cent of workers in India. The informal sector's smaller footprint in China played an important role in boosting its revenue performance.

The expansion of exports and imports also increased both direct and indirect taxes. As Chinese firms expanded their exports to the world, their export profits soared which increased corporate taxes, a form of direct tax revenues. Meanwhile, as imports also increased commensurately with a growing economy, import duties (which fall under indirect taxes) also increased in spite of a decline in duty rates. As a result of all these factors, the gap between China's and India's revenue performances began to widen starting in 2010. In retrospect, China's faster pace of infrastructure and other aspects of economic development can be partly explained by its better revenue performance compared to India's.

13

Boosting Tax Collection

As Amartya Sen has pointed out, the 2004 Kelkar Committee report noted that India needs to widen its tax base and do away with many exemptions.[116] The country also needs to reduce tax evasion through various measures. These steps are discussed below.

The first order of business of the Department of Revenue is to widen India's tax base. A narrow tax base typically coexists with a vast majority of 'free-riders'. Free-riders are those who are consuming or enjoying existing government services such as infrastructure, subsidies (e.g., on food, water, electricity, transportation, etc.), and other public goods (e.g., police protection), but are not paying for them.

But how to bring these free-riders into the tax net and widen the tax base? For one, India needs to move more people from the informal to the formal sector where their incomes would improve and they can be taxed. An informal sector that employs an overwhelming majority of India's workforce has adverse implications for tax policy.

However, as far as designing and implementing a good tax policy is concerned, the concept of 'informality' is not operationally helpful or meaningful. Within the informal sector, there is a need to differentiate between income groups and consequently, their

---

[116] Jean Drèze and Amartya Sen, *An Uncertain Glory: India and Its Contradictions* (Princeton: Princeton University Press, 2013), p. 347.

capacity to pay appropriate taxes. Taxability, or the ease with which the government could target and tax individuals and businesses, is a much more relevant and operationally useful concept for the tax department.

There is little point in trying to expand the tax net to include low-income traders, vendors, taxi drivers, rickshaw pullers, agricultural workers, etc. This is because the taxes collected from such low-income workers will not be worthwhile compared to the expenses the government will incur in the effort. It will be far more cost-effective to charge the informal traders and vendors a Goods and Services Tax (GST) which they could then pass on to their customers. At least, the government would gain some revenues from such informal workers than would be the case by including them in the direct tax net.

For these and other reasons, the India-wide GST is a step in the right direction. Inevitably, there are and there will be, some teething problems with the GST such as excessively complicated rate structure, exemptions, uneven enforcement, corruption and evasion, etc. However, the experience of other countries show that revenue collection through such value-added taxes (VATs) improve significantly as experience is gained and tax departments become better trained and efficient at enforcement and collection. We therefore expect the GST to help broaden the tax base and gradually improve tax performance over time.

Measures to Improve the GST

The GST works best when there is a minimum of slabs at which rates are imposed. India has four non-zero rates of 5 per cent, 12 per cent, 18 per cent and 28 per cent and special low rates of 3 per cent on gems and jewellery and 0.25 per cent on rough diamonds. Moreover, India's GST is complicated to administer due to a lot of exemptions, exclusions, deductions and frequency of changes. In comparison, of the 115 countries that have a similar system, forty-nine have a single rate while twenty-eight have two rates.

The cost of administering such a tax system increases significantly with the number of rate slabs and legislative complexity. There is broad consensus among economists that India should strive for fewer rates (two or at the most three rates) and greatly simplify the legislative complexity in administering them.

There are hopeful signs. For instance, as of last year, there has been almost a 50 per cent increase in the number of registered GST payers, which points to better tax compliance. Arvind Subramanian, the former chief economic adviser to the Government of India expects that the GST will bring in at least 1–1.5 per cent of GDP in extra revenues once taxpayers become familiar with the system and improvements are made in light of experience.[117]

Other Sources of Revenue

Now, there are many other small businesses that are typically thought of as belonging in the informal market as they tend to largely operate outside government restrictions and pay no taxes. However, these small businesses should not escape the tax net simply because they are considered part of the informal sector. Many small businesses make a decent income which is likely to be well above the minimum income threshold.

Also, while low-skilled workers make subsistence incomes below the tax threshold, the same cannot be said of professionals in the informal market. We are talking about doctors, lawyers, architects, restaurant owners and the like. In fact, the incomes of many such professionals are likely to exceed the incomes of government, or even, many private sector workers in the formal sectors. Yet, such professionals in the informal sector pay little or no taxes and can be considered as free-riders.

---

[117] 'In the Trenches: A Market Unified', *Finance and Development*, Vol. 55, No. 2, June 2018. See also, *India: Selected Issues, IMF Country Report No. 18/255* (Washington DC: International Monetary Fund, August 2018), p. 4; IMF Country Report No. 18/255

In short, the time has come for India to look closely at broad labels in order to design and develop a comprehensive and fair tax system. Millions of workers and businesses in the 'informal' sector, agricultural sector, service sector, etc., who are free-riders need to be roped into the tax net. India cannot afford them. The message should go out loud and clear followed by implementation and enforcement. Enforcement, backed up by stiff penalties including significant prison sentences, is the key to compliance. Corrupt tax officials should also be subject to these same penalties.

Furthermore, India needs to ramp up the hiring of thousands of tax officers and train and post them in tax offices around the country. The current strength of income tax officers is woefully inadequate to shore up tax performance and compliance.

India also needs to invest in better education and vocational training for its workers. Investments in health and education take a long time to make a decent return (i.e., long gestation periods). However, it is crucial to do so in order to generate high-quality jobs in sufficient numbers to absorb India's expanding labour force. Otherwise, new entrants to the job market would have no option but to take up employment in the informal sector further limiting India's capacity to raise revenues. So, government spending on education and training can be looked upon as long-term investments to expand the tax base. Such investments have the effect of pulling workers from the informal to the formal sector and to prevent more workers from entering the informal job markets.

Policies to Counter Tax Evasion

Tax evasion needs to be countered through much better enforcement, together with heavy penalties meted out to evaders in a timely manner. Of course, this is easier said than done. If the court system is clogged and judgments take years to be handed down, the government can expect tax evaders to take full advantage of such weaknesses in the system. Not only that, tax evasion also tends to be rampant if regulatory institutions are infected with corruption, lack trained manpower or adequate resources to ensure tax compliance, or if the system is full of exemptions which can be abused.

We have already seen how businesses can shift income and profits abroad through deliberate mis-invoicing of exports and imports. This deliberate mis-invoicing is mainly undertaken to either shift profits abroad or to evade taxes. Import duties and GST on imports are together projected to amount to 4.6 per cent of GDP in 2019, which is a significant source of revenues for the government.

Without going into too many technical details, we note that the customs department can take a number of measures to curtail such practices. However, it faces many challenges. For example, the incentive for corruption at customs is very high. This is a general observation applicable to most developing countries. As the IMF has noted, a customs officer can make a lot more money colluding with businesses to evade duties and GST than what he brings home as salary.[118] So the overall reform of customs administration must improve its governance. Other reform measures include better training of customs inspectors and improving their pay structures in order to attract high-quality applicants. The Ministry of Finance would also need to exercise strict vigilance of customs revenue performance following such reform.

---

[118]   Michael Keen (ed.), *Changing Customs: Challenges and Strategies for the Reform of Customs Administration* (Washington DC: International Monetary Fund, 2003), p. 12.

14

Poverty and Inequality

Most middle- and upper-class Indians have absolutely no idea about how the poor live. They cannot understand their hopes and ambitions, much less their everyday trials and tribulations. The haves and the have-nots live in their own lifestyle cocoons. When I grew up in India, I moved around in my own circle of friends and relatives, doing typical middle-class things, eating out at cafes that my meagre student allowance could afford. My middle-class friends did the same, as did the rich at a 'higher orbit'. They shelled out money as if there was no tomorrow. Meanwhile, the poor, many of them working in our homes as cooks, maids and cleaners and living in slums not too far away from our homes, remained conveniently 'invisible'. By that I mean they were far from our collective consciousness.

Every once in a while, there comes along a writer such as Pulitzer Prize–winner Katherine Boo, whose book *Behind the Beautiful Forevers: Life, Death, and Hope in a Mumbai Undercity* expands your awareness of how the poor live.[119] It is then that the lives of the invisible and their daily struggles become somewhat more visible. Nevertheless, the experience is blurry because a book can only leave an impression. Heaven forbid that we ever have to live that life!

---

[119] Katherine Boo, *Behind the Beautiful Forevers: Life, Death, and Hope in a Mumbai Undercity* (New York: Random House, 2012). See Author's Note, pp. 247–48.

In order to write the book, Boo spent years reporting from India's impoverished cities and slums. *Behind the Beautiful Forevers* is about the lives of the poor in Annawadi, a makeshift slum in the shadow of luxury hotels near the Mumbai airport. She follows the hopes, aspirations and frustrations of slum dwellers. She asks what opportunities are being opened up by markets? How is the government helping with its economic and social policies? 'Whose capabilities are squandered? By what means might that ribby child grow up to be less poor? . . . Why don't more of our unequal societies implode?'

Recently, the IMF likened India to an elephant that has started to run.[120] That this elephant should be running is, in fact, very much in the natural order of things. We should not be surprised. Take the case of a malnourished child whose family could not afford to feed him properly. We see this not only in India but in poor countries around the world. Now, suppose that this child is fortunate enough to be adopted by a rich family. He never goes hungry again. Of course, he will gain weight faster during the catch-up phase than if he had normal weight at adoption and ate the same food.

In our analogy, this calorie-restricted child was the economy India inherited. It was straddled with all kinds of restrictions from 1947 to 1990, hampering domestic and foreign investment. As trade was stifled behind high tariffs and import quotas, business decisions were subject to the whims of a licence raj. This 'artificial, calorie-restricted diet' continued for more than forty years! But in 1991, this restricted economy, this malnourished child in our analogy, started benefiting from better policies. The economy was allowed to pursue its potential for growth. And so the economy has been growing rapidly since then. What is so surprising about this turn of events?

We are not belittling the growth that India achieved in the post-reform period since 1991. That would be like downplaying the role of good food in helping the malnourished child. My point is we

---

[120] 'India's economy is an elephant that's starting to run, says IMF', *The Times of India*, 8 August 2018, https://bit.ly/2Z8x7UQ

should not be excessively fixated on achieving some stellar rates of growth. Now that the elephant has started running, we should be more concerned about the depth of the ditches lying across its path. Specifically, we should be concerned about the quality of growth as well as its sustainability. Growth must lift all boats.

It is not good enough that India has a burgeoning middle class and the rich are getting richer. What should occupy policymakers is whether the poor and the disenfranchised are really benefiting all that much from growth? I think there is a lot of 'irrational exuberance' regarding growth—particularly among those who have been able to take advantage of expanding opportunities. For the vast majority of India's poor, who are struggling in dead-end, low-paying jobs, tethering on the margin between destitution and poverty, growth hasn't made much difference in their lives.

This is precisely the point that Amartya Sen makes. The per capita incomes and expenditures of the poor have been increasing at a snail's pace.[121] While incomes have increased just enough so that they can no longer be called poor, their lives have not been transformed because of stellar rates of economic growth.

Two Key Concepts of an Economy

Poverty and inequality are two key features of an economy. They measure different things. We can talk of poverty in terms of income per person or per family. It is typically defined by some income threshold. For example, the World Bank defines two types of poverty—extreme and moderate. Those who are earning USD 1.90 or less per day are considered to be extremely poor while those making less than USD 3.10 per day are called moderately poor. These dollar amounts are adjusted in such a way that incomes are comparable across countries.

---

[121] Drèze and Sen, *An Uncertain Glory*, p. 29.

Inequality, on the other hand, measures how incomes are distributed within a country or across countries. Economists can assess the extent to which incomes vary among different groups of workers in a country. Thus, in a totally egalitarian country, because everyone has the same income, there is no disparity. In contrast, a country where one person owns everything would have the worst inequality.

In order to study inequality, economists have also looked at a breakdown of income groups within each country. For example, they considered the lowest to the highest 10 per cent income earners. To gain a further understanding of inequality, they also focus on income changes of the top 1 per cent of income earners.[122]

Yet another measure of income inequality is the share of national income accruing to each income group. By that measure, in 2014, the top 10 per cent of income earners in the US captured 47 per cent of total national income. In India, the top 10 per cent income earners capture 56 per cent of the nation's income. So, income inequality is worse in India than in the US, which itself has one of the most unequal incomes among advanced countries.

Poverty and inequality therefore capture different aspects of an economy. In fact, they could very well move in opposite directions over time. For instance, while economic growth can generally be expected to reduce poverty, growth need not reduce inequality at all. In fact, economic growth may well lead to an *increase* in inequality. This is one of India's most important development challenges. While successive years of growth have reduced poverty, higher growth rates have led to greater income inequality, not less.

How is this possible? This is because economic growth says nothing about *how* it is going to impact different groups. In severely unequal societies, the poor or the bottom 10 per cent have limited access to healthcare. They are malnourished, and have limited opportunities for acquiring education and job-related skills. In

---

[122]   Alvaredo, et al. (eds.), *World Inequality Report 2018*.

other words, the poor are unable to take advantage of the growing opportunities available to those who are better educated and healthier. Therefore, the benefits of growth such as increasing incomes accrue mainly to the upper income groups. The rich get richer while the poor either languish or do not benefit much. This worsens income inequality.

The effectiveness of government policies plays a significant role in reducing poverty and income inequality. If high rates of growth are pursued for their own sake, they may lead to rising inequality. This can become a serious drag on growth itself.

Regarding income inequality in India, Thomas Piketty, the well-known French economist and professor, found that:

(i) Income inequality has reached historically high levels; in 2014, the latest year for which data were available, the top 10 per cent captured 56 per cent of total national income. The top 1 per cent captured 22 per cent. He found that inequality has risen significantly since the 1980s whereby the top 1 per cent captured more than the bottom 50 per cent combined.

(ii) Income inequality also increased within the top 10 per cent income earners. The higher up the income strata we look, the faster are the shares of national income accruing. In other words, *India has only been shining for the top 10 per cent of the population*.

(iii) Income inequality is highly correlated with wealth inequality. Unequal income growth at the top drives wealth inequality across the population.

If the wages of rank-and-file workers are not growing enough, we have a demoralized workforce with low productivity. Low income growth also reduces consumption. There are many ways through which rising inequality can drag down growth in the long run. More importantly, increasing income inequality can feed group grievances posing a serious threat to peace, stability and security.

The fragility indicators, which are more current and forward-looking than governance indicators, are signalling an urgent need for policies to reduce income inequality and improve human development outcomes.

15

The Bhagwati and Sen Debate

Jagdish Bhagwati and Amartya Sen are eminent economists of Indian origin who live in the US. The former is a professor of economics at Columbia University who has made seminal contributions in the field of international trade. The latter is a professor at Harvard University and won the Nobel Prize in economics in 1998. The Bhagwati versus Sen debate on what should be India's policies for economic development has been extensively discussed elsewhere. I will not rehash them here except to present a brief synopsis for easy reference.

Roughly speaking, the debate is about whether we should pursue faster rates of growth in order to develop the country or should we pay greater attention to the *quality* of growth? Essentially, Bhagwati's strategy involves increasing the rate of growth through extensive liberalization. There is a need to reform key sectors of the Indian economy where excessive regulations have hamstrung growth and productivity. Besides the agricultural sector, the government also needs to liberalize the labour markets. As the tethers of regulation are dismantled, economic liberalization would thrust the economy into a higher growth trajectory. Increasing incomes will then generate additional tax revenues which can then be devoted to improving social indicators.

According to Bhagwati and Panagariya, economic growth is most important to reduce poverty. In a December 2010 speech before India's Parliament, Bhagwati argued that it was the reforms of 1991 that enabled even the lowest social classes in India to improve their lot. According to the Brookings Institution, the level of extreme poverty in India is expected to decline from fifty million people to forty million people by the end of 2019.[123]

In order for the Indian economy to grow faster, Bhagwati recommends that policy reform be rolled out in two stages. Track I reforms would involve liberalizing international trade, foreign direct investment, and the agricultural sector. For instance, Bhagwati and Arvind Panagariya note that India imposes an average duty rate of 12 per cent on industrial goods. This is still too high in the era of globalization. Hence, the liberalization of external trade would essentially involve bringing down tariff rates on trade in these goods.

Regarding foreign direct investment, Bhagwati and Panagariya prescribe further opening up the market. One way is to invite large foreign retailers such as Walmart and PepsiCo in order to develop domestic supply chains and help build export capacity.

There is also a need to introduce greater competition in the market for agricultural produce. As agriculture is a state subject, only the state could loosen the restrictive rules related to the sale of agricultural produce by farmers. Currently, farmers are compelled to sell their produce to state-owned mandis or marketing committees where middlemen squeeze the prices received by farmers. These marketing arrangements have proved to be very inefficient and detrimental to farmers' interests. Moreover, there are also significant restrictions in the interstate movements of grain. These restrictions have led to market fragmentation breeding inefficiency and raising costs. Track I reforms would dismantle such restrictions in order to raise agricultural productivity.

---

[123]   Homi Kharas, Kristofer Hamel and Martin Hofer, 'Rethinking global poverty reduction in 2019', The Brookings Institution, 13 December 2018, https://brook.gs/2PQ8ibM

Track II reforms would involve direct transfers to the poor or through employment in government infrastructure projects (such as the building of roads, bridges and schools) at above-market wages. After a discussion of various types of transfer schemes, Bhagwati and Panagariya recommend unconditional cash transfers. These measures are expected to help meet the basic needs of the poor related to food, clothing and shelter. Furthermore, vouchers for elementary education, and insurance for major illnesses with government payment of premiums will help improve their productivity.

The important point about the Bhagwati and Panagariya strategy is that Track I reforms would complement Track II reforms. Track I would cause enough growth to generate additional tax revenues. This will be used to finance Track II reforms. In other words, without the growth-enhancing benefits of Track I reforms, there would not be sufficient tax revenues for Track II reforms. Both are needed to ensure faster economic development of the country.

The Sen and Drèze Development Strategy

Amartya Sen and Jean Drèze point out that high rates of growth are not enough to ensure shared prosperity. While the standard of living of the middle class has improved significantly in the post-reform period, the living standards of the poor have barely budged. Sen and Drèze do not say that the lives of the poor have not improved at all but rather that their incomes have barely increased. Moreover, there is the 'density effect' whereby the millions who are just below the poverty line, get pulled up a little above the poverty line as a result of growth. Thus, while they are no longer statistically counted as poor, their quality of life has not improved much.

Studies by Sen and Drèze underscore the fact that significant social failures can coexist with high rates of growth. Unless growth is preceded, or at least accompanied, by huge government investments in health, education and other standards that lift human development, growth alone will not result in social gains. In that sense, there is nothing automatic about growth. Instead, the poor quality of growth as reflected in lagging human development indicators will, in the long run, lead to increasing income inequality. Ultimately, income inequality will drag down economic growth itself.

They also put forward other reasons why growth reduced poverty but failed to improve social indicators. For instance, they argue that 'Indian rulers have never been properly accountable to the needy majority'.[124] Defined by caste, gender, education and income strata, the country's ruling elite always had a callous neglect when it came to improving the lives of the poor. These are incisive observations. After all, how can we expect F-rated politics to deliver A-rated egalitarian outcomes?

High growth rates themselves will never be enough. With rampant inequality, the condition on the ground would still be dismal. This includes the utter lack of good-quality primary education or healthcare for the poor, awful sanitation and public hygiene, widespread malnourishment, extreme poverty, and appalling gender inequality and bias against women. This is the ground reality today.

So the Sen and Drèze strategy for economic development would involve a policy commitment for upfront and large government spending on improving human capabilities. They have little faith in Bhagwati and Panagariya's Track I reform to first boost economic growth followed by expenditure on human development.

I can see Sen and Drèze's point. Without an official commitment at the highest levels of government, there will be no implementation. The electorate should hold the politicians' feet to the fire on this matter. There has been enough foot-dragging and excuses made to justify the status quo.

Sen was quoted in the media as saying that while both growth and welfare programmes are needed, they should not be at the cost of each other. Wasteful subsidies such as those on electricity, cooking gas,

---

[124] 'Beyond bootstraps', *The Economist*, 29 June 2013, https://econ.st/2NcE0lI

and gasoline at the pump must go. Public investment must be focused on improving human capabilities. These include better healthcare and education because Sen knew of no example of 'unhealthy, uneducated labour producing memorable growth rates'.[125]

In contrast to the Bhagwati strategy, Sen does not think that the government first needs to increase tax revenues through liberalization and other high-growth policies. Economists call the capacity to spend, given existing levels of revenue, 'fiscal space'. Such spending does not push the country into a debt or solvency crisis. So, in Sen's view, rather than wait for growth to generate more tax revenues, the government should allocate more spending to improve health and education on a pay-as-you-go basis. Expenditures should be rebalanced and prioritized towards improving social indicators. As they improve, the growth that follows would not only be robust but inclusive as well. In other words, the prosperity arising out of growth would be more widely shared.

Why I Feel Sen Is Right

Sen is not saying growth does not matter. One does not need to win a Nobel Prize in economics to figure out that growth matters. Sen's focus is on the *quality and sustainability* of growth rather than growth itself.

There are at least two reasons why Sen's development strategy for India makes more sense than Bhagwati's. First, the link between economic growth and tax revenues has been weak. For example, according to the IMF World Economic Outlook database, over the period since 1991, growth has averaged slightly less than 7 per cent per annum while tax revenues averaged 18.7 per cent of the GDP. This is about half the average revenues collected (as a share of GDP) in advanced countries.

---

[125] Pramit Bhattacharya, 'Everything you wanted to know about the Sen-Bhagwati debate', Livemint, 25 July 2013, https://bit.ly/31Gmc6o

Second, the Indian economy grew by more than 7 per cent per annum during 1995–96, 1999, 2003–07, 2009–10 and 2016–17. In fact, during most of these years of relatively high rates of growth, the revenue to GDP ratio increased by less than 1 per cent. Such high rates of growth should have pushed up the tax to GDP ratio by at least a couple of percentage points.

What are the reasons for this middling revenue performance?

First, as late finance minister Arun Jaitley had acknowledged, tax collections in India are very low given the size of the economy. In other words, the tax to GDP ratio is small because of a narrow tax base. Of the 3.7 crore Indians who filed taxes in 2015–16, 99 lakh declared an income below the minimum of Rs 2.5 lakh per annum that is subject to tax; 1.95 crore declared incomes between Rs 2.5 and 5 lakh; 52 lakh declared incomes between Rs 5 and 10 lakh; and just 24 lakh people showed earning more than Rs 10 lakh. Thus, in that year, only 76 lakh out of 3.7 crore taxpayers Indian earned income of more than Rs 5 lakh.[126] This means just about 2.1 per cent of the population or 5.9 per cent of the working age group pay any taxes. And those are mostly concentrated in the lower income slabs.

Second, given India's severe income inequality, any increase in incomes tends to be disproportionate. This means the increase in income of those in the upper 10 per cent bracket is much more than those in lower income brackets. Yet, given the far larger number of lower-income taxpayers, economic growth does not yield as much revenues compared to countries where incomes are more evenly distributed.

Third, while economic growth increases the incomes of workers in both the formal and informal sectors, the burden of taxation falls mainly on those in the formal sector. The informal sector in India is notorious for not paying taxes. Rising incomes in the formal sector along with the ever-higher tax burden they shoulder lead to greater tax fatigue and evasion.

---

[126] 'Only 76 lakh Indians showed income of over Rs 5 lakh: Jaitley', *The Hindu BusinessLine*, 1 February 2017, https://bit.ly/2KENPHt

Researchers have found that when governments of countries with a large informal sector raise taxes, taxable income reported to the government actually drops significantly. Potential taxpayers start joining the informal sector to escape the tax net. In fact, the transformation of informal to formal economy is a very slow process because of the poorly educated and trained workforce and the lack of formal sector jobs.[127]

Fourth, endemic corruption and weak regulatory institutions facilitate tax evasion. This is also why the link between economic growth and revenue performance is weak. In fact, all the factors that weaken the growth–revenue link, such as large informal sector, narrow tax base, tax fatigue, corruption and weak institutions, can only be redressed gradually.

So, we cannot expect to see great results out of tax reform and growth over a few short years. Therefore, it will not be prudent to hold the development of India's human capital hostage to the expected glacial improvements in revenue performance. The caveat is that if the past is any guide, improvements to tax collections and the tax base is likely to be gradual.

Finally, economic reform leading to high growth rates in poorly governed countries typically leads to more tax evasion, not less. Of course, economic growth also increases reported incomes, which is white money. But why does growth create even more black money? First, while corruption is extensive and entrenched, the rule of law and regulatory institutions are weak. Hence, the opportunities to make tax-free black money without getting caught increases. Second, growth is lopsided in that it creates many more ultra-rich. India today has thousands of millionaires and more than a hundred billionaires in dollar terms. So, the ultra-rich make even more money due to growth as the benefits

---

[127]   Timothy Besley and Torsten Persson, 'Why Do Developing Countries Tax So Little?' *Journal of Economic Perspectives*, Vol. 28, No. 4, Fall 2014, pp. 99–120.

accrue to them disproportionately. Now, they owe even more taxes because their taxable income has gone up setting the stage for more tax evasion.

A 2010 study at Global Financial Integrity found that India's faster economic growth in the post-reform period (1991–2005, the last year for which Gini coefficients were available from UNU-WIDER World Income Inequality Database) seemed to go hand in hand with worsening inequality and larger, not lower, illicit flows (or black money transfers) from the country. This unmistakable trend towards worsening income inequality and larger black money transfers which accompanied the higher growth rates in the post-reform period was also corroborated by other researchers.[128]

Sen devotes one whole chapter of his book to the issue of corruption. He writes, 'Corruption has become such an endemic feature of Indian administration and commercial life that in some parts of the country nothing moves in the intended direction unless the palm of the deliverer is greased.'[129] He includes a fairly comprehensive discussion of how corruption can thwart the institutional change necessary for economic development in the long run.

There is an implicit recognition from the very beginning that no amount of growth is going to solve the problem of India's lagging social indicators. In raising questions about the poor accountability of public sector undertakings, Sen says that there is 'a fairly comprehensive neglect of accountability in operating this large sector'.

---

[128] See, for example, A. Sengupta, K.P. Kannan and G. Raveendran, 'India's Common People: Who Are They, How Many Are They and How Do They Live?', *Economic and Political Weekly*, Vol. 43, No. 11, 2008; see also, Sandip Sarkar and Balwant S. Mehta, 'Income Inequality in India: Pre- and Post-Reform Periods', *Economic and Political Weekly*, Vol. 45, No. 37, September 2010.

[129] Drèze and Sen, *An Uncertain Glory*, pp. 81–106.

Tax Revenues and Human Development

Greater investments in improving health and education for the poor has the effect of empowering them to take advantage of opportunities in a growing economy. Such investments help ensure that growth will be more inclusive rather than benefit only those in the upper income brackets. We have seen before how broad-based growth is likely to generate more revenues as poor workers become more productive and they find work in the formal sector due to better education and training. Thus, tax revenues increase more when growth happens. We examined the link between revenue performance and the Human Capital Index (HCI) as estimated by the World Bank. The HCI measures the productivity of future workers based on the investments in health and education for children starting at five years of age. The higher the HCI, the greater is the productivity of workers.

The goal of the HCI is to quantify the key stages in a child's development from birth to productive worker—through six indicators, such as the chance that the child will survive to age five, the quantity and quality of education he or she receives by age eighteen, the chance that the fifteen-year-old will survive until age sixty (which is a proxy for the quantity and quality of healthcare), scoring on standard tests, etc. Thus, the HCI captures, through six indicators, the trajectory from birth to productive adulthood of a child born today.

The greater the investment in health and education, the greater is human development—the child grows into a productive worker. After all, sick and poorly educated workers cannot be as productive as those who are healthy and better educated.[130]

The table below seeks to answer the simple question: Is stronger revenue performance absolutely necessary for achieving better human development scores or whether governments can improve development scores even with lower revenue performance?

---

[130]   Aart Kraay, *Methodology for a World Bank Human Capital Index* (Washington DC: World Bank Group, September 2018).

Table 2. Human Capital Index (HCI) in Relation to Government Revenue Performance, 1990–2018

| Country groups or countries | <======General Government Revenue as percent of GDP======> | | | | | | | | | | HCI |
	1990–1994	1995–1999	2000–2004	2005–2009	2010–2014	2015	2016	2017	2018	Average	1<HCI>0
Major advanced countries (G7)	...	...	34.1	35.3	35.3	36.2	35.9	35.9	36.0	35.5	...
Developing countries	...	...	23.6	27.4	28.1	26.4	26.0	26.3	26.8	26.4	...
Developing Asia	16.3	14.4	16.4	19.7	24.4	25.8	25.4	25.4	25.9	21.5	...
Bangladesh	11.2	9.6	9.1	9.5	10.8	9.8	10.1	10.2	10.9	10.1	0.48
China	13.9	11.1	15.1	19.6	27.0	28.5	28.2	28.4	28.7	22.3	0.67
India	18.0	17.0	17.8	19.9	19.3	19.9	20.3	20.5	20.8	19.3	0.44
Indonesia	14.9	13.3	16.4	17.9	16.6	14.9	14.3	14.0	14.6	15.2	0.53
Malaysia	29.7	24.6	22.8	23.5	23.8	22.5	20.7	19.6	19.6	23.0	0.62
Philippines	18.6	20.1	17.7	18.3	18.2	19.4	19.1	19.6	19.8	19.0	0.55
Sri Lanka	18.5	16.3	14.0	14.2	12.5	13.3	14.2	13.8	14.5	14.6	0.58
Thailand	...	19.2	19.3	20.3	21.3	22.3	22.0	21.1	20.9	20.8	0.60
Vietnam	...	19.9	22.9	25.9	24.2	23.8	23.7	23.6	23.3	23.4	0.67

General government revenue as percent of GDP; the human capital index varies between 0 and 1, with higher index values representing better human capital development outcomes. The HCI indicates productivity outcomes of future workers based on investments in health and education for children at five years of age. The revenue performance data for 2018 are estimated.

India's revenue performance increased from an average of 18.0 per cent of the GDP in the five-year period 1990–94 to an estimated 20.8 per cent of the GDP in 2018. But Bangladesh's revenue performance trailed India's significantly throughout this period coming in at just 10.9 per cent of the GDP in 2018. Yet, its HCI at 0.48 (meaning its children are expected to reach 48 per cent of their productive capacity as adult workers) is higher than India's at 0.44.

Similarly, the average revenue performances of Indonesia, the Philippines, and Sri Lanka have also lagged behind India's for the period as a whole. Yet, their HCI scores of 0.53, 0.55, and 0.58 respectively were significantly better than India's score of 0.44.

This goes to show that it is not necessary to generate revenues first in order to make greater investments in health and education. Quite a few countries in Asia have managed to deliver better human development outcomes with lower revenue performances than India.

Why then do politicians and policymakers fail to invest in human development? For one, these investments take a long time to yield results and are not as visible to voters as high-profile investments in infrastructure. That may be an important reason why those allocating resources are not sufficiently motivated to invest in human development. For another, in poorly governed countries, the vast majority of those who are poor are without a voice while the elite, who exercise a lot of influence over the government, are only interested in seeing prestigious infrastructure projects that expand their influence.

Concluding Observations

The Indian economy with its emphasis on liberalization and reform has reached a stage where there is little risk of it sliding back to one of controls and piddling rates of growth. Now, the best development strategy would be one that invests in human capital through larger investments in health and education for the poor. These investments need to be made on a pay-as-you-go basis rather than waiting for growth to generate greater revenues.

Perhaps as a result of the Bhagwati–Sen debate, the issue of 'inclusive growth', mainly extended by the IMF, World Bank, and other international organizations, has come to the fore in recent years. By inclusive growth is meant growth wherein the resulting benefits are shared more equitably in terms of increased prosperity, more better-paying jobs, improved access to better-quality healthcare and education, and increasing safeguards against environmental degradation. Only when growth is inclusive can we ensure that growth will be sustainable in the long run. If, on the other hand, the benefits of economic growth only accrue to the privileged, ignoring environmental degradation, this failure is likely to lead to social and political instability.

Research at the IMF found that the likelihood of economic growth being derailed is higher in countries with high and rising economic inequality.[131] In fact, noted economist and former governor of the Reserve Bank of India, Raghuram Rajan, and Nobel laureate Joseph Stiglitz found that growing inequality in many countries was the primary cause of the 2008 financial crisis. Other researchers have argued that 'policymakers' faith in their ability to get growth going through supply-side measures and deal with distributional issues later is a dangerous gamble. They should instead focus simultaneously on the size of the pie and its distribution.'[132]

---

[131]   Andrew Berg and Jonathan D. Ostry, 'Inequality and Unsustainable Growth: Two Sides of the Same Coin?' *IMF Economic Review*, Vol. 65, No. 4, pp. 792–815.

[132]   'Are New Economic Policy Rules Needed to Mitigate Rising National Inequalities?' in Jose Antonio Ocampo (ed.), *Global Rules and Inequality: Implications for Global Economic Governance* (New York: Columbia University Press).

16

The Ticking Time Bomb

Like millions before him, Anil Gujjar, the son of a farmer, arrived in Delhi from a small village in Rajasthan in the hope of finding work. With little money in his pocket, and a lot of hope in his heart, he slept the night on a sheet he spread on the railway platform. The next day he was to appear for a written exam for a menial position in the Indian Railways. Little did he know that there were nineteen million applicants for the Railways' 63,000 'Group D' positions that required little or no skills. These were jobs such as helper, porter, cleaner, gateman, track maintainer and assistant switchman.[133]

Anil knew that finding a job in today's India was very difficult and extremely frustrating. But he did not know all the depressing details. Between 2011 and 2016, unemployment increased in nearly all Indian states. Among the educated youth, unemployment more than doubled during this period from 4.1 per cent to 8.4 per cent.

According to the Centre for Monitoring Indian Economy (CMIE), nearly thirty-one million Indians are unemployed and looking for jobs.[134] While economic growth has been humming along

---

[133] Joanna Slater, '63,000 job openings—and 19 million applicants', *The Washington Post*, 5 January 2019.

[134] 'Unemployment Rate in India: Nearly 31 million Indians are jobless', *The Times of India*, 6 March 2018, https://bit.ly/2oKz6PI. Other data have been taken from the Centre for Monitoring Indian Economy website: https://bit.ly/2P0SYhk.

around 7–8 per cent per annum recently, the pace of job creation has been poor. The CMIE has noted that there was no growth in employment in the fiscal year 2017–18.

Modi's government faces a serious challenge in not only generating enough jobs to absorb the 6–8 million new entrants to the job market every year, but also to find work for others who have been looking for them. While the lack of employment data since 2016 has clouded the present jobs situation, there is no doubt that the dismal state of India's job market represents a political liability to any government. By 2021, the number of job-seekers between the ages of fifteen and thirty-four is expected to reach 480 million.

Various surveys, in the run-up to the 2019 general elections, reveal that the jobs situation was perhaps uppermost in the minds of many voters, particularly young adults in both urban and rural areas. The opposition parties sensed that Modi's attempts to boost employment in manufacturing and entrepreneurship has thus far not been successful. An official report supposedly places unemployment at an all-time high of 6.1 per cent, most of them unemployed young. The government has denied the report's existence.[135] However, in retrospect, given the BJP's resounding win in the 2019 elections, the opposition failed to get traction among voters that Modi should be blamed for the employment situation. Voters were not convinced that the Congress had any particular edge over the BJP when it came to job creation.

While unemployment is naturally an emotive issue in a country of 1.3 billion people with a young workforce, the capacity to generate jobs is not in the hands of any politician, regardless of their promises. Politicians can only adopt economic policies that would create an enabling environment for private investment, whether domestic or

---

[135]   Malini Goyal, et al., 'Will jobs actually be top of mind when India casts its vote in this Lok Sabha elections?' *The Economic Times*, 31 March 2019, https://bit.ly/2NcEJTY

foreign. But economic policies themselves, least of all politicians, cannot compel private companies to actually hire.

The hiring of workers is based on business decisions which are driven by a host of factors. As we explain below, there are also factors why companies may not hire as many workers regardless of the pace of economic growth. But some economists do not seem to be concerned. Arvind Panagariya, who served as vice chairman of India's policy-planning agency, feels that given India's high rates of economic growth, concerns about job creation are 'overblown'.[136]

I think the truth of the matter concerning job creation is the opposite. It is the confidence in growth's ability to create enough jobs that is overblown! While growth is necessary for job creation, it is not sufficient. There are many bottlenecks along the way from growth to job creation. In fact, as the article shows, economic growth has created fewer and fewer jobs in each successive spurt of growth.

For instance, during 1999–2004, when growth averaged around 6 per cent per annum, job creation surged by about 3 per cent per annum, the fastest pace of job creation in the post-liberalization period. But job creation increased by a tepid 0.6 per cent per annum in the latest period 2011–2015 when growth averaged even higher at 6.8 per cent per annum. During the first quarter of 2018-19, employment fell further to 401.9 million. The share of those working as a percentage of the working-age population fell to 42.7 per cent, lower than the same quarter in the previous fiscal year. Meanwhile, the unemployment rate in the formal sector edged up to 5.5 per cent, higher than the 4 per cent recorded in the first quarter of 2017-18, indicating a larger number of people looking for work in the formal sector but not finding them. The sharp deceleration in the rate of job creation underscores the fact that there is no correlation between higher rates of economic growth and faster rates of job creation. Why is that so?

Note that the information on employment and unemployment all refer to the formal sector, meaning companies and businesses that

---

[136]   Slater, '63,000 job openings—and 19 million applicants'.

are registered, pay taxes, and are covered by India's labour laws and regulations. They do not refer to the informal sector where people work for themselves (i.e., are self-employed). The informal sector also includes jobs that are low-skilled and do not require formal education such as rickshaw puller, domestic help, small businesses, etc. Hardly any information is available about the informal sector although it plays such as important role in the Indian workforce.

Why Economic Growth May Not Create Many New Jobs

A significant increase in job creation was one of the key promises of the BJP in the run-up to the 2014 general elections. In fact, the BJP criticized the United Progressive Alliance (UPA) government led by the Congress that it had dragged the country through ten years of jobless growth. The BJP promised to revive the economy in a significant way, according a high priority to job creation and entrepreneurial initiatives. While developments on the employment front were not good news for the BJP, it nevertheless came back and won 301 seats in the 2019 general elections—a mandate unprecedented in fifty years. The following reasons explain why voters did not hold Modi and the BJP responsible for the disappointing performance on the employment front.

Perhaps many voters realized that 'jobless growth' seems to be the new normal around the world—not just in India. By that I mean economies typically do not create as many jobs these days as they used to during past phases of economic growth. This 'jobless growth' is partly due to technological change, automation and fierce competition in a globalized world holding down profit margins. As a result, companies have been trying to squeeze out more from their existing workers rather than add to their payroll.

In fact, companies are always looking to improve their bottom line by reducing costs and seeking competitive advantage in the market. One way they do that is through mergers and acquisitions. However, there may be a net loss of jobs when companies merge. So, even if the economy is otherwise doing well, total employment can still fall. Let us consider an example.

Suppose Company B with 5000 employees takes over Company A with 1000 employees. Company B streamlines work and eliminates redundant positions that can be done by its existing staff and lays off 500 employees of Company A. In fact, through a merger, Company B may also reap economies of scale and lay off some staff as it is now able to tap into the skills of staff obtained through a merger with Company A. So, after the merger, both A and B may be able to shed some staff who had overlapping responsibilities and tasks which became entirely redundant after the merger. In most cases, successful mergers and acquisitions lead to more efficiency with which the newly formed larger company performs its main functions.

Moreover, the destruction of jobs can also result from technological advancements. For example, there was a time not long ago when both private and public sector banks had many more staff than they do now. Automatic teller machines or ATMs as well as computerized record keeping has done away with many lower-level jobs such as tellers and other clerical staff with lower-level skills. Digital security systems with automatic direct alert to the police in case of a breach has reduced, or even entirely eliminated, the need for security guards on bank premises. Assembly line production carried out by highly advanced robots dedicated to performing many repetitive tasks (for example, those involved in automobile manufacture) has reduced the need for assembly line workers in the plant.

In a recent report, the International Labour Organization (ILO) notes that India has a high potential for automation because many workers are doing low-skilled jobs such as cashiers, receptionists, legal aids, travel agents, bank tellers, etc. Low-skilled repetitive jobs have a higher potential of being automated than highly skilled jobs that require specialized or institutional knowledge. The ILO points out that in many advanced economies, fourth Industrial Revolution (4IR) technologies are expected to lead to a 'hollowing out' of labour markets, as many routine, low-skilled jobs are automated.

4IR technologies include artificial intelligence (AI), robotics, and Internet of things (IoT). Both China and the US have made huge advances in AI and its application over the past decade. The development of AI will disrupt the traditional ways industries work and employ labour. These disruptions are difficult to predict but, in enabling robots to 'learn', AI-fitted robotics may well reduce employment. For example, it is not difficult to imagine robots armed with AI to replace airport security workers and scanners to check passengers and their baggage. Such robots may also be engaged in mundane tasks of scanning all kinds of cargoes for shipment by air and sea. So, AI and robotics may well dampen the demand for security personnel in the nation's airports and shipyards. IoT involves Internet connected devices such as cameras, sensors, household appliances, cars and other things. These technologies may reduce the demand for low-skilled workers such as security guards while Internet-connected automated cars and trucks are likely to reduce the need for drivers.

According to the ILO study, as a result of potential automation of low-skilled jobs, the typical pathway for the poor (who are stuck in yet lower-skilled jobs) to move up the skills chain into better-paying jobs may dry up. But because the category of low- to medium-skilled jobs within the organized sector (e.g., those of a cashier) is still very small, India may not experience the kind of hollowing out of the labour market that advanced countries have had to face.

Nevertheless, millions of workers in the informal labour market who aspire to move into medium-skill jobs may find fewer such jobs as a result of automation. This is an additional challenge that the government has to face when formulating policies for creating better-paying jobs. That being said, India is still quite far from the adoption of 4IR technologies. Rather, 4IR is likely to be in niche markets within the organized manufacturing and service sectors.

The ILO study notes that India's under-skilled existing labour force is 'woefully underprepared' for work within the 4IR landscape. It further notes that while it would be difficult to reskill the present-day workers who are older than forty-five years, skill-based vocational training can empower the youth in working towards gainful employment. The ILO notes that in particular, 'digital skills, humanistic and interpersonal skills (especially relevant in the service sector) along with learnability (ability to adapt through lifelong learning and acquiring of new skills), will be central to accessing decent work opportunities'.[137]

The bottom line is that for unemployment to come down during any period, the number of new jobs created must be greater than the number of people entering the labour market during that period. The period can be a year or a month. Now, the number of people entering the labour market depends on the country's birth rate as well as the death rate. If more people are born than die during a year, the population will increase along with the number of new entrants into the job market. If the rate of job creation equals this net growth in population, employment will remain stagnant while if job creation falls below the net replacement rate, unemployment will increase.

Of course, people may simply give up looking for work in which case, they will no longer be counted as unemployed. The unemployment rate only includes workers who are unable to find work but are still actively looking for it. So, even if the economy is growing but there are fewer jobs around, a lot of people may give up looking for work as a result of which the unemployment rate could fall. In that case, it would be a mistake to attribute the falling unemployment rate to economic growth.

The problem of employment in India is twofold. First, India needs to invest in more education, vocational training and health. These investments cannot be expected to yield immediate results. We cannot expect greater investments in quality primary and secondary education to produce better engineers and doctors tomorrow. Similarly, we cannot expect more recent investments to increase the supply and quality of doctors, medicines and hospitals

---

[137] Tandem Research, *Emerging Technologies and the Future of Work in India* (New Delhi: International Labour Organization, June 2018), p. xv.

to start producing more productive workers shortly. By nature, such investments take a long time to bear fruit. But, they are crucial in ensuring that the benefits of economic growth are widely distributed across all income groups.

Second, there is a need to shrink the size of the informal sector by helping more workers to switch to jobs in the formal sector. This requires that the formal sector create many more jobs than it is currently doing. As we have seen, India should get ready for the coming technological revolutions which have already started to eat into job growth in many advanced countries. India needs to undertake massive investments in health, education and vocational training so that workers are better equipped to compete for the jobs of the future. While there is a lot of scope for further expanding exports, a large country such as India with the world's second-largest population has a huge potential to cater to domestic markets in many goods and services. Archaic and unnecessary labour regulations should be done away with and replaced by a minimum of government intervention to extend worker rights and ensure workplace safety.

17

India's Demographic Dividend

We will explore why enough quality jobs are not being created and its implications for India's so-called 'demographic dividend'. But, first what is meant by 'demographic dividend'? Due to the significant increase in the rate of growth of India's population since Independence, the country is now experiencing a large increase in its working-age population relative to its total population, pushing up the working age ratio. In fact, India will be the leading contributor to the global demographic transition towards a younger workforce, as the populations of the advanced countries age, along with falling, even negative, population growth.

A country with a youthful population such as India has a larger percentage of people between the ages of fifteen and sixty-four in total population than a country such as Japan. The latter has an ageing population meaning the proportion of people aged sixty-five and older in total population is high. India's youth population means that its 15–64 age group, which is the working age group, is high as a share of total population compared to a country like Japan.

Both youthful and aging societies face their own sets of problems. While a young and growing work-eligible population can be a blessing, they all need to find employment first! That means India needs to think ahead and invest in making this young population productive. Furthermore, the government needs to adopt policies that promote the private sector and job creation. If these steps are not taken the so-called demographic dividend can easily turn into a demographic curse.

An ageing society, on the other hand, has its own problems. As the old do not spend as much as the young, domestic markets for many goods tend to shrink. As a result, the economy does not grow as much. At the same time, healthcare expenditures keep increasing as the old get sick more often. Meanwhile, as most seniors are drawing pensions, they are out of the workforce and not paying taxes, straining the government budget.

If India is able to utilize this demographic dividend, meaning that the increase in the working-age population is gainfully employed, this demographic dividend could add about 2 percentage points per annum to India's per capita GDP growth over the next two decades. But the dividend is not automatic.

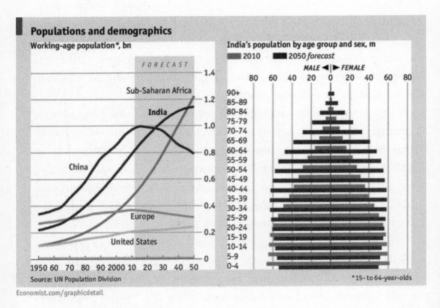

Source: 'The growth of India's working-age population', *The Economist*, 11 May 2013.

India's younger population is a double-edged sword. Properly utilized, it can boost economic growth. But, if a majority of the young workforce remains unemployed, it can easily turn into a powder keg. Anger and frustration over joblessness can explode under aggravating conditions such as the spread of fake news, the exploitation of public anger for the sake of winning elections, vote-bank politics by unscrupulous politicians and political parties, and price hikes for essential commodities.

Any number of conditions may come together to create the perfect storm, such as some perceived sense of injustice that under normal circumstances would not lead to large-scale violence. Even if such violence is mercifully avoided, a number of recent studies have found that the lack of jobs drives significant rural–urban migration which in turn leads to increasing crime such as robbery and thefts. Youth bulges are also related to an increased risk for political violence. Could India's deteriorating law and order situation and increasing fragility be early indicators of a disgruntled youth? This is quite possible, even probable.

One way governments have been able to reduce the risk is by providing its youth opportunities for education and vocational skills training. Studies have found that the level of secondary education appears to have a clearly pacifying effect on large youth bulges in low- and middle-income countries. But there is also a risk if educated youth are not able to find suitable jobs. So, while education and training can temporarily defuse anger among the youth, education is only a means to an end. Governments must still plan for and facilitate job creation schemes. Otherwise, the educated unemployed can also create future political instability and violence.

However, thus far, government initiatives for job creation such as 'Make in India', Digital India, Startup India and Smart Cities have failed to take off. For instance, under the 'Make in India' initiative, the aim was to increase the share of manufacturing in GDP to 25 per cent by 2020. The share was 15 per cent under the UPA government. But, the Parliamentary Standing Committee on Commerce (2017) noted that manufacturing sector had only grown by an average of 1.6 per cent in the last five years until 2015–16, far short of the target.

There are differing views on the reasons behind the failure of manufacturing to take off as planned. First, land acquisition laws are stringent while archaic labour regulations continue to hamper new investments in manufacturing. Second, sectors such as footwear, textiles and leather industries received no financial support from the government. Finally, there was little support from local manufacturers so that projects failed to take off.[138]

Digital India also failed because the government's stress on automation was not supported by enough spectrum or wired connectivity necessary to realize such ambitions. Moreover, major IT companies such as Wipro, Tech Mahindra, and HCL Technologies hired only a few staff since 2015–16. The IT sector is not growing as much, partly due to the uncertain international outlook for IT services. New restrictions on work permits and visas issued by the USA also put a damper on IT consulting services and related staffing needs.

Startup India, which encouraged banks to provide finance to young entrepreneurs to start their own business ventures, failed to materialize mainly due to a lack of skilled labour and lack of innovation. Twenty-five start-ups failed in two years and many employees who had left jobs to start their own companies became unemployed when their start-ups failed and they could not be reabsorbed into the labour force.

The plan to create smart cities by developing infrastructure and transportation facilities around existing towns and cities also ran into serious trouble and had to be shelved. Whereas the main aim of smart cities was to invest in technology and create more jobs for youth, the government failed to come up with a policy to encourage

---

[138] Jagriti Gangopadhyay and Wamika Kapur, 'Unemployment is Up Because "Make in India", Other Official Schemes Aren't Working', Wire, 13 June 2017, https://bit.ly/2Z7jDg5

investment in technology and define the scope and format of suitable skill-based training programmes.

Declining Female Labour Force Participation

According to an ILO study, India has one of the lowest proportion of women in the total workforce. The main reasons for low participation rates for women are low levels of education, skill sets, and sociocultural norms and belief systems. The IMF notes that gender gaps in women's economic opportunities relating to both labour market as well as entrepreneurship have remained high and persistent in India. Besides that, between 2011 and 2012, 19.6 million women have actually dropped out of the workforce for various reasons.[139]

The IMF notes that the 2016 World Economic Forum's Gender Gap Index ranked India 136th out of 144 countries on economic participation and opportunity. Apart from lower female participation rates which have been falling over time, there are also large gaps in wages and in representations in senior managerial and technical positions. Ninety per cent of total employment of females are in low-skilled, low-productivity jobs in informal sector. The wage gaps in equal work strongly suggest gender discrimination. To be sure, wage gaps against women also prevail in many countries around the world, including in advanced countries.

Women entrepreneurs (mostly in small-scale firms) make up about 10 per cent of the total number of entrepreneurs in India. About 90 per cent of these firms are operating in the informal sector. Women face major hurdles in access to formal finance (such as loans from commercial banks). This forces them to seek financing from the informal sector (typically at higher rates of interest). The lack of adequate collateral remains the major obstruction to women's access to finance. Limited financial awareness among women and social

---

[139]   Tandem Research, *Emerging Technologies and the Future of Work in India.*

restrictions on their landownership rights and inheritance also play a part in their seeking informal sources of finance.

A recent article explains some of the social and cultural reasons behind why Indian women drop out from the labour force in large numbers.[140] In fact, several studies show that the more educated a woman gets, the higher her chances of dropping out from the workforce. Even if women are trained for specific jobs, few stay in them. The most common reason for dropping out of the workforce is 'family obligations'. In the event a woman gets married, her chances of continuing to work drops significantly. If the husband has good income, the question of why the wife needs to work often arises to nip careers in the bud. Part of the reason also has to do with division of labour. Women do about 90 per cent of the housework, the highest proportion in the world. A recent study found that the engagement of girls in housework and domestic chores was the largest contributor to a gender gap in secondary education.

But this relationship does not extend to poor, illiterate women who are compelled to find work. Thus, this group typically makes up the bulk of the female workforce. Most poor and illiterate women end up in subsistence farming. In fact, over half of the women work in the agricultural sector. When incomes rise, and women obtain higher education, they opt out of work and prefer to look after the family. This is partly due to preference and partly due to social norms and expectations. Such norms and expectations arise from the fact that if a family does not need the extra income, it is better for women to simply devote themselves to raising children and taking care of their families. Hence, the likelihood of women working is inversely related to a family's income. The higher the income, the less the chances that the woman will seek employment or be encouraged to do so.

Women are also not at par with men when it comes to the skills needed to operate in a digital world. In other words, there

---

[140]   'A job of her own', *The Economist*, 7 July 2018, pp. 14–16.

is a significant 'digital gender divide' in terms of access to mobile technologies and the Internet. In 2017, less than 30 per cent of India's Internet users were women while they were 23 per cent less likely to own a mobile phone. While access to digital technologies is likely to increase in the future, access is not the same as their skilful use. Women are less likely to be digitally fluent and have the necessary skills to succeed in the digital economy. Moreover, given their low-skills base, their jobs are more vulnerable to automation.

But why do women get educated if they do not intend to make a career or if they intend to drop out of one? The reason is that educational expenses tend to act as a substitute for dowry. Families of more educated women tend to pay less dowry than those where the women are not as educated. Nevertheless, census data reveal that more women would like to work if suitable jobs were available. The *Economist* noted that a recent advertisement for 90,000 railway jobs attracted twenty-five million applicants, most of them men! So, it is not clear whether India's labour market can absorb all the able-bodied women who want to work.

There is a need to improve female workforce participation rates and skill sets because economic growth and development require the successful utilization of the entire workforce—both male and female. A growing literature finds that gender inequality can impede economic growth and the welfare of a nation. Thus, the potential gains from greater female workforce participation can be expected to be large. One empirical study found that closing the gender gap in India could boost GDP by 27 per cent.[141] But the IMF thinks that the estimated gains to GDP may be overstated given that India has a large informal sector which was not accounted for in this study.

---

[141]   D. Cuberes and M. Teignier, 'Aggregate Costs of Gender Gaps in the Labor Market: A Quantitative Estimate', *Journal of Human Capital*, Vol. 10, No. 1, 2016, pp. 1–32.

Some Proposals to Generate Employment

Proposals to generate employment have largely fallen into two categories. One addresses the need to rationalize outdated labour laws which hamper job creation. Instead, labour laws should encourage potential investors and employers to hire new workers. For instance, businesses find shedding labour quite difficult. So they remain hesitant to hire workers even when business conditions improve. Labour laws should allow the hiring and firing of workers more freely. Moreover, the costs of workers' safety, compensation, and benefits increase with the size of the firm which impede the generation of employment. For example, the Industrial Disputes Act, which covers all industrial disputes regardless of firm size, is not only unwieldy, it acts as a serious impediment to investment and job creation. The Act makes it impossible for an industrial establishment of 100 or more workers to lay off or retrench them, even if it is unprofitable. Such firms are forced to close rather than remain in business with a smaller workforce. Regulations need to be thought through to balance worker rights and safety against job creation.

Amartya Sen has suggested ways to boost employment in the informal sector rather than the organized sector which includes manufacturing. The rationale is that the lion's share of workers in India are employed in the informal sector so that an increase in employment and wages in that market holds the key to alleviating rural as well as overall poverty.

18

The Failing Grade Education System

The Modi government has been trying to implement policies to further open up the economy while investing in health, education and other areas in order to improve social indicators. The first is a recognition of the importance of growth, a nod to Bhagwati while the latter is an effort to improve social indicators and make growth more broad-based, a nod to Sen. This is the correct approach but only time can tell whether India will be successful in achieving growth with equity.

The importance of attaining high-quality growth becomes apparent when we consider the track record of the Asian Tigers of yesteryear (Hong Kong, Singapore, South Korea and Taiwan). Such growth improves the quality of life, not just income. Today, these countries are enjoying a standard of living that is broadly comparable to those in advanced countries. For sure, India's track record when compared to those of the Asian Tigers is poor.

As Nobel laureate Robert E. Lucas Jr pointed out, between 1950 and 1990, the gap in per capita incomes between India on one hand and South Korea and Taiwan on the other hand widened considerably. In terms of constant 1990 dollar value (so as to take out the effect of inflation), South Korea's and Taiwan's GDP per capita were 46.7 per cent and 54.4 per cent greater than India's in 1950. By 1992, their incomes per head increased by 742.5 per cent and 859.8 per cent over India's respectively!

That is only part of the story regarding the Asian Tigers. The other equally important part of their success story is that 'their growth is mostly explained by increased input, not by higher productivity; they saved and invested, put more people to work, and concentrated on education in order to raise human capital'.[142]

So behind every economic success story stands a broad-based government policy of providing good-quality education. The growth was not primarily due to an increase in output per worker but in investment in workers in terms of education and training (what is known as human capital). So, the question arises that if India wants to break into the ranks of advanced countries, much like the Asian Tigers, can it replicate their tried-and-tested paths to more evenly distributed prosperity?

But why is education the key to high-quality growth? This is because economic growth is driven by three factors—capital, labour and technological change. This has been the 'gold standard' in explaining economic growth since 1927 when Paul Douglas and Charles Cobb first put it forward. Beginning with an assumption of no technological change, economists were able to explain how growth happens as a result of the contributions of capital and labour. Subsequently, economists have refined the model to allow for variations in skill levels within the labour force (e.g., high-, medium- and low-skill workers as separate factors of production), and changes in technology brought on by better machines.

Here is my own take on why high rates of economic growth are themselves unlikely to propel India into the kind of human development that prevails in advanced countries. This explanation is particularly sharp and clear in the context of education.

Suppose India has managed to record 10 per cent rates of growth for ten years in a row, a stretch of consistently high rates of growth that has never been achieved since Independence. Now suppose there

---

[142]   Rudiger Dornbusch, Stanley Fischer and Richard Startz, *Macroeconomics*, 8th ed. (New York: McGraw-Hill/Irwin, 2000), pp. 75–76.

was no policy intervention to make growth more inclusive. In that case, most of the increases in income accrue to the upper 1 to 10 per cent of the income groups. These are people who went to the best schools, built the strongest networks, ate the best food, and availed of the best healthcare to keep themselves productive. So, they were best placed to take advantage of new opportunities in a growing economy.

Meanwhile, what happens to the incomes of poor households? Their incomes would also increase through the trickle-down effect. If they were earning less than, say, USD 2 a day, their incomes would increase to, say, USD 4 or USD 5 per day over ten years. Thus, millions of such families can no longer be called poor at the end of that ten-year period of high growth. Now, let us consider, what happens to the children of those previously poor families, assuming there is no policy action to improve access to more good-quality education? These children, who have 'graduated' from poverty, will nevertheless form a major segment of India's workers in the future who are not adequately educated or trained. The 10 per cent growth that happened for ten years will be increasingly at risk of petering out because an entire generation of tomorrow's workers have not been adequately prepared for the job market.

Meanwhile, India's human development indicators do not budge an inch. India can join the ranks of Saudi Arabia or Nigeria in the oil boom years but it can never aspire to join the ranks of the likes of South Korea, Singapore and Taiwan.

So can we say that growth does not matter? Of course not. But both growth as well as policy-directed development of key human indicators constitute the necessary and sufficient conditions for India to become an advanced country. This transition will not happen in ten years or perhaps even in twenty, but the foundation needs to be set now based on the right objectives and thinking.

The basic 'model' explaining growth that we discussed above yields some interesting insights when we build in some real-world complications such as varying labour skills and technological advancements. Such growth models predict that if firms cannot substitute high-skilled workers by low-skilled ones, and are forced to hire more high-skilled workers to expand production, the wages of low-skilled workers will also tend to increase. This happens because an increase in the supply of high-skilled workers in the total labour force will increase the demand for the services of low-skilled workers as well, pushing up their wages.

Education is the key to better-paying jobs, shared prosperity, higher-quality growth, and less income inequality. But, as Sen points out, India failed to invest adequately in education. While the present Modi government has been trying to play catch-up with regard to spending on education, it would take a long time to bridge the gap with more developed countries in Asia.

The fact of the matter is that governments have to pay the price for failed policies. The fallout from these policies cannot be eliminated in a few years but have long-term consequences. While India is paying the price for neglecting education and training, China is still paying the price for its one-child policy. That policy has been directly responsible for the decline in its working-age labour force and the cost of caring for an ageing population increasing rapidly.[143] The adverse effects of failed policies take a long time to be reversed.

According to the IMF, India's demographic dividend is projected to peter out over the next thirty years as its working-age labour force starts to decline.[144] In other words, India has a thirty-year window during which it needs to improve both the quantity and quality of skilled workers. It would be a shame if India should fail to capitalize on its young working-age population or demographic dividend.

The United Nations Fund for Population Activities (UNFPA) is somewhat more optimistic in noting that India can take advantage of a demographic dividend for the next fifty years. This is because the dividend varies by state. In some states such as Kerala, Tamil

---

[143] 'Three piggie wiggies notwithstanding, a younger China is not coming soon', *The Times of India*, 8 August 2018, https://bit.ly/2H9wbcG

[144] 'India's economy is an elephant that's starting to run, says IMF', *The Times of India*, 8 August 2018.

Nadu, Andhra Pradesh and West Bengal, the opportunity to take advantage of a youthful population is about to close. In other states such as Assam, Karnataka, Odisha and Maharashtra, the demographic dividend will stay open for another 10–15 years. However, in Chhattisgarh, Jharkhand and Madhya Pradesh, the dividend window is expected to stay open into the 2050s and 2060s. Such variations across states will allow India to enjoy a longer span of the demographic dividend because as the window closes in some states, it will open up in others.[145]

A number of economists, including Bhagwati and Sen, as well as the World Bank, have discussed at length about the deficiencies of the Indian education system. I will not rehash them but will present the salient points regarding the deficiencies of the current education system in India for the sake of context and clarity.

An important point underlying the arguments of almost all researchers is that when it comes to education, India's rich and poor face starkly different opportunities—both in terms of quantity and quality. The rich have access to India's finest schools, colleges and universities where graduates can not only go abroad for higher studies but seek well-paying jobs even after completion of an undergraduate degree (e.g., in engineering). The poor either cannot attend primary school or if they manage to attend one, learn almost nothing.

There are differing views as to how good are India's best institutions. Sen notes that '. . . a large number of Indians—a minority but still quite numerous—receive excellent education in India. There are elite schools, advanced centres of higher learning, and a society that values educational excellence and honours it.'

But he also notes that while institutes of higher learning such as the Indian Institutes of Technology (IITs) and Indian Institutes of Management (IIMs) offer teaching and guidance 'of the highest

---

[145]   Devender Singh, 'India's demographic dividend will play out over a longer span', Livemint, 11 January 2019, https://bit.ly/2RK4gXf

quality in the world', not a single one of them ranks in the top 200 in the world.[146]

He refers to the Times Higher Educational Supplement, noting that even if we feel that these rankings are culturally biased (as has sometimes been alleged), 'there is plenty of other evidence pointing to the same conclusion. Even the assessment by students themselves, in particular, which universities they try to get into, tend to confirm an important problem of quality deficiency. Indian students do spectacularly well once they enter any of the leading universities in the world, in a way that is hard for them to achieve within the confines of Indian universities.'[147]

Others, such as T.S.R. Subramanian, who retired as the cabinet secretary to the Government of India, feel that the IITs and IIMs have sharply declined in standards and do not compare favourably with their counterparts in the West or even in Asia (this is confirmed by the Times top twenty Asian university rankings). Subramanian points out that Indian institutes of higher learning seriously lag in terms of research output and when research is done, it is of a low quality.[148] The Western universities and even China's top-ranked institutes of higher learning receive significant funding for research from various sources. I will add that in the field of economics, not a single Indian economic journal is listed in the top 2,500 journals, ranked by impact factor.

Be that as it may, the fact remains that students graduating from any of the top twenty Indian institutes of higher learning in a technical profession such as engineering, computer science, management, medicine, etc., are literally assured of getting well-paying jobs in India today. But then, getting a job within India is one thing, but can India offer products that can stand up in foreign markets against fierce competition?

---

[146]   Drèze and Sen, *An Uncertain Glory*, p. 128.
[147]   Ibid., p. 117.
[148]   T.S.R. Subramanian, *India at Turning Point: The Road to Good Governance* (New Delhi: Rupa Publications, 2014).

Indian institutes typically do not have access to the latest technologies even as the production process in India is still trying to play catch-up with other manufacturing powerhouses. As I mentioned earlier, there is a price to pay for failed policies and it takes a long time to right the ship.

All those decades of running a closed economic model behind high tariffs has made Indian industry inefficient, even obsolete, and it will take time for them to become competitive. Meanwhile, there is also a shortfall in the quality of education being offered at India's premier institutes of higher learning. While the above provide a brief overview of the shortcomings of education for the rich, things get much worse for the poor. We will see why in the next chapter.

19

Deficiencies of the Indian Education System

As Sen and others have noted, India's investment in education has been woefully inadequate since Independence. It is only under the current government that expenditures on education have been slowly increasing. Here, the immediate problem is one of funding the investments in education. Following are the highlights of deficiencies in the Indian educational system with greater reference to primary schooling. However, many of these deficiencies also percolate up to the secondary schooling level, as is natural to expect. The problems in education fall into two broad categories—improving access and enrolment as well as the quality of education offered.

In recent years, India has been able to increase access to primary schooling for children from poor, rural families. There are now primary schools within walkable distances from most villages and rural townships. Access to schooling is primarily measured by taking the ratio of the number of students enrolled at a particular educational level as a percentage of the total number of children in that age group who should normally be studying at that grade level. By this measure, the enrolment ratios for both boys and girls have improved significantly from the early 1950s to the late noughties.[149]

---

[149] Jagdish Bhagwati and Arvind Panagariya, *Why Growth Matters: How Economic Growth in India Reduced Poverty and the Lessons for Other*

Bhagwati and Panagariya conclude that enrolments have improved across gender as well as social groups including the Scheduled Castes and Scheduled Tribes. They found that economic growth since 1991, which boosted growth, enabled the government to spend more on education. Hence, this led to an increase in enrolment ratios which had lagged behind in the pre-reform period.

While enrolment and access to primary schooling has improved in recent years, Bhagwati and Panagariya note that the Right to Education Act (RTE) of 2009 failed to set benchmarks for the quality of education provided. Instead, they argue that the RTE had ended up hurting the educational aspirations of poor children—the very group which it intended to help. Among the many deficiencies of the RTE that they discuss, the most glaring one is the setting of minimum norms and standards for physical amenities in the school and not of outcomes (such as the minimum standards for reading and writing, problem-solving, etc., expected of all students at the primary level). In fact, the RTE Act prohibits children to pass any board examinations so that it becomes 'nearly impossible to measure the progress in improving the quality of education over time'.

Sen reaches much the same conclusion and his observations are both granular and incisive.[150] He notes that 'the quality of education in Indian schools seems to be exceptionally low over a wide range of institutions. Teaching methods are quite often dominated by rote learning, including repetition—typically without comprehension—of what has been read, and endless chanting of multiplication and other tables.' That pretty much summarizes it all.

I had long felt such tendencies and practices to be the bane of the Indian educational system. Sen points out that in tests conducted in 2006 (called 'PROBE Revisited', which involved a resurvey of 200 randomly selected villages that was originally conducted in 1996),

---

Developing Countries (New York: Public Affairs, 2013), pp. 189–99.
[150]   Drèze and Sen, *An Uncertain Glory*, pp. 120–127.

nearly half of the students in classes 4 and 5 could not carry out single-digit multiplication or a simple division by 5.

The general knowledge of students was also woefully inadequate. Sen observes that the lack of quality education apparent at the primary school level also happens to be widely present in what are considered as 'top schools' in the larger Indian cities of Delhi, Mumbai, Chennai, Kolkata and Bengaluru. He provides several examples of poor quality of education attained by students at the primary level in such top schools.

The Findings and Recommendations of International Organizations

World Bank

The World Bank, based on its engagement with and financing of education systems around the developing world, has noted that schooling is not the same thing as learning. The Bank's 2018 World Development Report notes that in rural India, just under three-quarters of students in grade 3 could not solve a two-digit subtraction such as 46 minus 17, and by grade 5, half still could not do so.[151]

The problem of poor learning is not confined to rural India alone. According to the Bank, a 2015 study found that in New Delhi, the average grade 6 student could only perform at the grade 3 level in maths. In fact, the gap in learning achievement widens because by grade 9, the average student reached less than a grade 5 level with the gap growing worse over time.

It noted similar learning patterns in Kenya, Tanzania and Uganda. In Uruguay, poor children in grade 6 were assessed as 'not competent' at five times the rate of students from wealthy families. Some 260 million children in developing countries weren't even

---

[151] *World Development Report 2018: Learning to Realize Education's Promise* (Washington DC: World Bank, 2018), p. 3.

enrolled in primary or secondary school. But India is second to Malawi in the percentage of grade 2 students who could not read a single word of a short text. When it came to two-digit subtraction, India had the highest percentage of primary school students who could not perform a two-digit subtraction (among seven countries with such deficiencies including Uganda, Ghana, Nicaragua, Iraq, Kenya and Malawi).

The World Bank's conclusion is that children learn very little in many education systems around the world, and even most of those who graduate from primary school have not mastered basic competencies in reading and maths. But there is an important difference in outcomes between poor and higher-income developing countries. Whereas in poor countries, failing students are not paid extra teaching attention, in high-income developing countries, students lagging in basic competencies are singled out for remedial attention.

The World Bank notes that in its experience the learning crisis amplifies inequality by severely handicapping 'the disadvantaged youth who most need the boost that a good education can provide'. All this is not difficult to understand. In fact, the findings are pretty basic. *Children who have been left behind in education in their early formative years are bound to struggle their whole lives doing menial jobs.* These jobs demand little skills and are poorly paid, thereby perpetuating the poverty cycle, meaning their children are also likely to suffer from poverty and lack of access to education. No amount of economic growth is going to solve the problem of substandard education and unequal access to good-quality education.

Improving learning outcomes in educational systems is not an easy objective

The World Bank points out that early childhood nutrition, stimulation and care are paramount. Children must be mentally and physically prepared, alert and motivated to learn. Poor children learn the least, and this is true in nearly all countries. Students' family background such as parents' education, socio-economic status, access to books, and conditions at home remain the largest predictors of learning outcomes. We can be sure that the lack of basic infrastructure such as water and electricity as well as inadequate nutritious food, along with children being forced to work to make ends meet are also responsible for poor learning outcomes.

There is also a need to improve the management of schools. For instance, the World Bank found that good-quality school principals significantly and robustly improved student performance. Teacher absenteeism must be reduced and every effort should be expended to improve teacher quality through training and education. They must become more aware of student needs and be able to motivate students to reach higher learning curves.

Albania, Latvia, Peru, Portugal, Vietnam and some other countries have done better than most developing countries in improving learning outcomes. The World Bank notes that while it is not always possible to isolate the factors responsible for their success, a determined focus on ensuring educational quality appears to be important. For example, the World Bank notes that a major factor behind Vietnam's strong performance is its emphasis on ensuring good-quality schools throughout the country.

Finally, there needs to be a national assessment of educational progress carried out on a regular basis. The US has such a system. In order to guide an educational system, policymakers need to understand how well students are following the national curriculum, areas where the students are strong and those where they are weak, which population groups are lagging behind and to what extent, and identify the factors responsible for student achievement.

The Organization for Economic Co-operation and Development (OECD)

The OECD found that at USD 872, India's annual public expenditure on educational institutions per student is one of the lowest among

OECD member countries and partners; the corresponding G20 average expenditure is USD 6379 while the OECD and EU22 averages are more than ten times higher at USD 9120 and USD 9444 respectively. *Conclusion: India's public expenditure on education is well below its peers.*

Furthermore, the share of students undergoing vocational training in 2014 was the lowest of any G20 or OECD countries.

Surveys were carried out to measure the level of education of adult citizens of various countries. The level of upper secondary education attainment among 25–64-year-olds and 25–34-year-olds in India are one of the lowest among OECD and partner countries for which data were available. India's rank was forty-four out of forty-five countries surveyed. The level of tertiary education attainment among the above aged students is one of the lowest among OECD and partner countries with available data (forty-four out of forty-six).

As of 2014, the latest year for which cross-country data are available, the class sizes were particularly large in primary schools (average of twenty-four students in each, rank five out of forty-two) compared to other OECD member and partner countries. The larger the class size (that is student to teacher ratio), the less effective the teaching or less attention can be paid to each individual student.

The number of students per teacher in primary schools in India is the largest among OECD and partner countries. The same goes for secondary and tertiary schools. Again, this indicates that students tend to receive less attention as a result of which the quality of education is bound to suffer.

Deficiencies in the Indian Academic Assessment System

The prevalent system of assessing students in India is based on the 'final exams', which in effect judges the career prospects of students based on a few exams. These final exams (at the high school or undergraduate level) require students to demonstrate their understanding of the subject matter (such as in engineering, mathematics, physics, chemistry, etc.) within a set time limit held over a few days.

Students throughout India live in mortal fear of these 'final exams' because of their potential to ruin careers. It is clear that the concept of 'final exams' is a deeply flawed system of judging academic excellence or even the extent of learning by students. Judging a student's understanding and academic excellence based on a one-day test measures students' capacity for rote learning or sheer luck but not much else. Indeed, the education system encourages students to cram and regurgitate a standard set of questions without necessarily understanding how the concepts are actually applied in a practical manner. This is a terribly inefficient way to assess what has been learnt in class over the past year.

I find that the US system of education is much better at truly assessing student learning. What typically happens in a US school, college or university is that students are judged on a battery of tests and classroom participation throughout the year—and not on one day! So, there are no 'final exams' on which an overall grade is assigned. Rather, each teacher has the freedom to determine how the final grade in a subject will be determined. For example, some teachers may give 30 per cent weight to completion of homework (called take-home assignments), 20 per cent weight to classroom discussion or participation, 30 per cent weight to the grades obtained in tests throughout the year, and only 20 per cent to the grade obtained in the last exam. Other teachers may have an entirely different weighting scheme. But no teacher can insist that the entire grade will be determined based on one final exam. At least, I never heard of such a system of grading during the decade I spent at US universities.

A diverse set of performance criteria such as outlined above does a much better job of capturing a student's academic performance than a system based on 'final exams'. The latter simply measure the student's ability to cram and regurgitate, often without any understanding of the issues involved. In a multidimensional assessment system, if a student was to fare badly on one test or criteria, there is always hope (and therefore, the motivation) to do better next time or through some other compensating criteria. The future of the student is not condemned (sometimes for life) because he or she could not do well on one test on a particular day for whatever reason.

20

No Care about Healthcare

Any discussion of the present state of healthcare in India must start by asking whose healthcare are we talking about—the rich or the poor? There are some problems with the healthcare in place for the upper-income groups but it is reasonable and getting better. But for the vast majority of India's poor, or those in the lower-income groups with no health insurance, the healthcare system is abysmal, and not getting much better.

The healthcare system of doctors and private hospitals for the upper-income groups has improved significantly since the economic liberalization in 1991. However, there are still significant issues of reliability and consistency in quality. For instance, while the quality of doctors and hospitals in India's large cities such as Delhi, Mumbai, Kolkata and Chennai, may be satisfactory, their reliability and quality fall sharply as we move to smaller cities and towns.

Rich Indians, even those in the upper 10 per cent income group, often opt for treatment abroad particularly for serious or complicated cases. The reason is healthcare in India is still lagging behind when it comes to cutting-edge techniques, treatment protocols and experimental drugs. However, the upper-income groups do have access to good medical facilities for the treatment of most conditions.

That being said, there is a lot of variation in the standard of care even in large cities. There have been many recent cases where patients have died under mysterious circumstances leading to violent protests by the families of patients. Often, hospitals and doctors seem more interested in making the maximum profit from patients rather than treating them in the most cost-effective manner. Let me elaborate on the abject quality of doctors doing the rounds in India's cities today.

A close family friend and her husband were visiting Kolkata. During their visit, she started complaining of a loss of balance and serious weakness in her limbs. She was admitted to a well-known hospital in south Kolkata. Even after many tests such as a CT scan and MRI of her brain, they could not come up with a firm diagnosis.

As a result, her daughter in the US decided to visit Kolkata. When she visited the hospital and saw the doctor, he told her that her mother's symptoms were the signs of old age! Losing confidence in the treatment her mother was receiving, she finally got her released from that hospital. Upon arrival in the US, her mother was taken to Fairfax Hospital in Virginia directly from the airport. Within two or three days, there was a grim diagnosis—she had lymphoma of her central nervous system (CNS lymphoma). But two hospitals (she was earlier admitted to another hospital in north Kolkata before being shifted to the one in south Kolkata) and several doctors could not come up with the right diagnosis of the serious condition she was in. Given the terminal state of her cancer, her daughter had her released from the hospital and brought her home, where she passed away about six months after the diagnosis.

The other problem is that access to India's premier doctors and hospitals is strictly determined by money, and lots of it at that. Both doctors and hospitals demand payment upfront—either by an insurance company that will cover the major portion of the charges (with the balance to be paid by the patient) or outright payment by the patient. Only the rich can afford the charges. The insistence that patients without an acceptable insurance plan pay upfront typically leads to the financial destitution of families. Often, doctors and hospitals refuse to treat patients if they cannot prove their source of funds to meet the expenses.

I recount an episode that happened about ten years back. I am not sure whether hospital regulations have evolved enough since then to admit patients on an emergency basis but I will leave that for the readers to decide.

When my mother suffered a stroke, she was admitted to a rehabilitation centre in Virginia for a few weeks. During one of my visits to her at that centre, I came across an Indian gentleman who was sitting at a table along with my mother and some other patients. His head, face and arms had all been bandaged.

I was a bit taken aback seeing him in that condition. Although he had obviously suffered a life-threatening accident, he had struck up a conversation at the table. Feeling somewhat at ease, I asked him what had happened.

He said that he and his wife had recently gone to India to attend the wedding of a family member in Gurgaon. While returning from the wedding, a truck had crashed into the car in which he, his wife, and his brother-in-law were travelling. The force of the impact was so hard that he lost consciousness at the instance of impact. When he came to, he learnt that his wife and his brother-in-law were killed instantly in that accident. He was at a hospital just about a mile away from the scene of the accident. Apparently, the traffic was so bad that it took the ambulance nearly an hour to get to the hospital.

He remembered that the first question the admitting assistant asked him was how he was going to pay for the many serious operations and the months of recovery time at the hospital? When he asked about the charges, he was told it would be at least USD 40,000 to be paid upfront! He was barely able to utter that he did not have that much cash on him. She then wanted to know whether he could pay the bill using his credit card to which he said none of his credit cards have such a high line of credit. How many of us carry a card with a USD 40,000 credit line?

After this ridiculous questioning, he was told that the hospital could not admit him until there was a written assurance from someone guaranteeing that the estimated charges would be paid.

This assurance needs to be supported by documentary evidence of the source of funds! He asked a relative to call his son in the US to come immediately to India after making arrangements for the necessary funds. Finally, his son arrived in India with the funds to get him shifted into the hospital bed. For three or four days, he was kept in another room under heavy sedation after a relative put up the funds for that as well.

He was operated on and a pin was inserted into his broken leg. I said, 'If you have been treated and released, how come you are here now?' He said, 'I have to undergo a series of operations to correct the ones that were done in India because I could not even stand up straight, let alone walk. The doctors here told me that the pin that was inserted in India was off-kilter by 7 degrees. They said, "If we leave this in there, you will not be able to walk for the rest of your life."'

Apparently, the doctor who operated on him had received a number of awards for his work in India. I said, 'All this sounds like the Wild West', to which he said, 'It is worse than the Wild West.' Incidentally, he had to be evacuated from India to the US by a small medical evacuation plane (called medevac) lying flat on a stretcher for the 36-hour hopping flight.

The point is that the quality of doctors and hospitals in India is still erratic, even for the upper-income groups. Often, patients do not have any idea of how good or bad a doctor is because they have very little information on the doctor's academic background and experience. Patients mostly rely on word-of-mouth references by others in order to gain access to reliable doctors. This is due to a lack of standardization and a lack of penalties for medical malpractice. At least as of 2016, there were no regulatory bodies in India overseeing the accreditation of hospitals, monitoring the professional qualifications and work experience of doctors in private practice, or collecting and disseminating independent reviews of doctors and hospitals.[152] As a

---

[152] Anant Phadke, 'Regulation of Doctors and Private Hospitals in India', *Economic and Political Weekly*, Vol. 51, No. 6, 6 February 2016.

result, people have little faith in the medical system. Hospitals have been ransacked and doctors have been attacked by aggrieved family members. Doctors fear their lack of security and have been protesting against this atmosphere of intimidation and violence for decades.[153]

In contrast, doctors in the US live in constant fear of getting sued and so they have to be covered by insurance against malpractice lawsuits. Once a doctor is successfully sued for negligence and the patient awarded millions of dollars in damages, his medical career goes into a tailspin. As malpractice insurance to cover such doctors gets very expensive, hospitals become wary of hiring them because of the premiums involved.

I am convinced that India needs a vigorous medical malpractice culture as in the US. This system of lawsuits and malpractice insurance pre-empts the type of violence and vigilante actions by patients and their aggrieved families. It is an excellent system to ensure accountability from the profession and helps weed out negligent and incompetent doctors and nurses.

In India, patients have placed doctors on a pedestal and doctors have become used to the high perch. A system of checks and balances needs to be implemented in order to ensure better quality and consistency of healthcare. Moreover, given that many doctors graduate from poor-quality 'universities' and medical 'colleges', or graduate after cheating in final exams, there is a greater need for a system that weeds them out. Such doctors represent a clear and present danger to patients.

The government also needs to crack down on tantriks, faith healers and unlicensed doctors with questionable educational backgrounds. There needs to be mass education on the dangers posed by all kinds of quacks, magicians and voodoo scam artists who take patients for a ride and inflict additional suffering on them. Serious jail time is required for those who prey on suffering patients to make money.

---

[153] Sumati Yengkhom, 'Kolkata: Doctors protest against hospital violence', *The Times of India*, 11 May 2018, https://bit.ly/2P3pzmC

The problem is that in India the value of a human life seems to be far less than in many other countries in the world. Moreover, the courts are clogged and the quality of lawyers so shoddy, that it is difficult to obtain fair and timely decisions on medical malpractice cases. Otherwise, it is difficult to understand why a system of suing for medical malpractice cannot be introduced and implemented in the country.

That said, it is not as if the upper 10 per cent income groups in India are also facing healthcare deficits the way the rest of the population is. They can literally check out of the country in order to get the best healthcare that money can buy. They would not subject themselves to a shoddy healthcare system in dire need of major improvements.

The question can be raised that if the healthcare system in India is so shoddy, why do foreigners sometimes come to India for treatments? There are two main reasons for this 'reverse flow of patients'. First, foreign patients mostly come for relatively minor or routine procedures such as knee replacements, heart bypass operations, and dental procedures. These treatments have a lower risk of complications and a high rate of success in India's best hospitals. The latter are also eager to earn foreign exchange and market the 'medical tourism'.

Second, foreign patients often come to India due to cost considerations, particularly if they do not have insurance to cover the high cost of medical care in their own countries. Third, non-urgent medical treatments are sometimes subject to long waiting periods in countries such as the UK. While patients are covered by national insurance schemes, some would rather not wait. Moreover, in the US, there are millions of Americans without medical insurance. Most of them cannot afford to pay for the high cost of medical treatments and procedures. Faced with these kinds of costs or perhaps longer waiting times, some foreign patients find it convenient to opt for treatment in India. This does not mean that most Indians in the lower-income groups can have access to similar healthcare at a cost that *they* can afford.

Healthcare in India still has a long way to go in terms of access to good facilities and reliable doctors, particularly in smaller towns and villages. While the rich in India can afford to get reasonable treatment at a price they can afford, the poor can't. The quality of public hospitals is extremely poor and they pose serious risks to the life and well-being of patients. Moreover, the credentials of many doctors are suspect. To make matters worse, there are no independent regulatory bodies to accredit, monitor and disseminate reviews of medical providers. The BJP should renew its efforts to extend good-quality healthcare at a reasonable cost for all Indians now that the party has received the largest mandate in recent memory.

21

The Abysmal State of Healthcare
for the Poor

If this is the shoddy state of healthcare for India's relatively well-heeled, what about the system available for the low-income and the poor? In a word, abysmal. The Indian economy may be chalking up impressive rates of growth but the poor are yet to be impressed. They should not be. For one, as we have seen earlier, the increase in income have been mainly accruing to the upper-income groups with a trickle-down effect on the poor. The public healthcare system, meaning government-run hospitals staffed with government-employed doctors, are also improving at a snail's pace—if they are at all. In fact, in most cases, the public healthcare system for the poor is either crumbling or comatose.

In India, two children younger than five, die every minute. In August 2017, more than 400 children died in Gorakhpur, Uttar Pradesh, due to many reasons. The hospitals did not even have adequate oxygen cylinders to help the sick children breathe. The private supplier of oxygen cylinders had cut the supply over unpaid bills. No wonder UP ranks at the bottom of India's twenty-nine states. The scandal shook the UP government for a short while before officials made excuses and found scapegoats. This terrible tragedy has since been forgotten.

There is one government doctor for every 10,189 people, one hospital bed for every 2046 people, and one government-run hospital for every 90,343 people. Therefore, it is painfully obvious that there is a shortage of good medical schools graduating well-qualified doctors and other medical care providers to attend to poor patients.[154] Deaths in government hospitals happen with appalling regularity. The reason is lack of hygiene and the abnormally high rates of infections, lack of qualified doctors, lack of medicines and medical equipment, and a shortage of skilled nursing care. In general, the quality of healthcare for the poor is abysmal.

More than seven out of ten Indians are not covered by health insurance. Due to the lack of health insurance, patients and their families have to pay out of pocket. As a result, some 52.5 million Indians were impoverished in 2011. However, thus far, government-sponsored healthcare schemes and other publicly funded medical insurance schemes have failed to provide effective insurance coverage. In fact, nine out of thirteen studies showed that there was no reduction in out-of-pocket expenses by patients covered by such insurance.[155]

At 1.15 per cent of the GDP, going up to 1.4 per cent of the GDP taking account of the contributions by states, India has one of the lowest spending on healthcare in the world. This is projected to increase to 2.5 per cent of the GDP by 2025. But that is still inadequate and the pace is not fast enough given the crisis in healthcare.

What are some of the consequences of poor healthcare? India has the world's largest number of stunted (or low height for age) children (48.2 million) partly due to the lack of prenatal and early childhood healthcare. The stunting of children is mainly due to malnutrition. According to the World Bank, a 1 per cent loss in adult height due to childhood stunting is associated with a 1.4 per cent loss in economic productivity. The Bill and Melinda Gates Foundation noted that stunted children will not only be less healthy and productive for the

[154]   Suparna Dutt D'Cunha, 'Despite a Booming Economy, India's Public Health System Is Still Failing Its Poor', *Forbes*, 12 September 2017.
[155]   Soutik Biswas, 'India healthcare: Will the "world's largest" public scheme work?' BBC News, 4 February 2018, https://bbc.in/2MVQrOU

rest of their lives but also collectively lead to entire countries being less prosperous.[156]

India's immunization rates for children is among the lowest in the world, in most cases lower than those for sub-Saharan Africa. Even some neighbouring countries such as Bangladesh have managed to achieve higher immunization rates than India.

Most rural health centres in India lack basic infrastructure such as clean running water and electric supply, and lack of all-weather roads connecting them. Sixty-three per cent of primary health centres did not have an operation theatre and 29 per cent lack a labour room. As a result, in 2014, 58 per cent of people in rural areas and 68 per cent of those in urban areas said that they used private medical facilities for inpatient care. The public counterparts are simply not available, or if they are, they are of such poor quality that they risk the lives of patients.

India's investment in mental health is shockingly low. Expenditures have been stagnant for the last several years. It is estimated that around 10–20 million Indians suffer from severe mental disorders and nearly 50 million suffer from common mental disorders such as depression and anxiety. India is short of 66,200 psychiatrists and 269,750 psychiatrist nurses.[157]

There is an utter lack of accountability regarding India's healthcare system. India is a highly segmented country—segmented by caste, class, ethnicity, religion and language. All of these segmentations play a role in the lack of accountability regarding healthcare. Segmentation of the population into these groups, with political parties playing one group against another (that is, playing vote-bank politics), is responsible for the lack of attention to the basic needs of the poor.

As I have argued before, the upper-income groups rely on a passable healthcare system with its private hospitals and its reasonably

[156] Swagata Yadavar, 'Budget 2018: India's Healthcare Crisis Is Holding Back National Potential', IndiaSpend, 30 January 2018, https://bit.ly/2ZaBqyX

[157] Ibid.

good doctors. And if need be, they go abroad for treatment. So, they are untouched by the shoddy state of public healthcare.

As Jean Drèze notes, 'An enormous social distance separates the doctors who run public hospitals and their patients . . . In all these ways, they are far removed from the levers of power and influence. So, the system gets away with an appalling lack of accountability.'[158]

However, the Indian public is hardly aware of the serious healthcare issues that the country faces. In fact, they are often not proactive about their own healthcare as well. In fact, I think the trouble starts there. Healthcare, like charity, begins at home. For example, most Indians are not even aware of the need for annual physical check-ups. This is because awareness regarding preventive healthcare and wellness checks, long considered standard medical necessity in advanced countries, is almost non-existent in India. And most Indians do not seem bothered.

Note that preventive healthcare is only relevant for the middle-income groups or up. As far as the lower-income groups and the poor are considered, such regular medical check-ups are not the issue. For them, the far more relevant issue is the lack of access to reasonably good-quality, dependable healthcare when they need it. But they aren't clamouring for basic healthcare services either. The government's lackadaisical approach to healthcare since Independence can be traced to the lack of awareness and care about health issues among the people themselves.

What about the role of the media in raising awareness about healthcare and related rights? Sen points out that India's best newspapers, let alone the 'lightweight' ones, rarely discuss healthcare-related issues, including those that pertain to children's health. This lack of media coverage can be explained by the fact that the people themselves are not interested in reading about them!

---

[158]   Suparna Dutt D'Cunha, 'Despite a Booming Economy, India's Public Health System Is Still Failing Its Poor', *Forbes*, 12 September 2017.

After all, newspapers are in the business of increasing readership and they can't do that by covering topics that no one is really interested in reading. Hence, lack of public interest and awareness as well as skimpy media coverage have together given successive governments a free pass in presiding over a shoddy healthcare system since Independence.

In the US too, having affordable medical insurance has become a huge issue. In my own experience, the doctors, hospitals, insurance companies—all of them—are quite money hungry. But there are important differences. India cannot afford many of the protections extended by the US government to lower-income groups. These are explained below:

Most poor American citizens (who are at least 65 years of age and meet certain income and asset criteria that do not include the value of the home they live in, if they are owners) qualify for Medicaid. Medicaid is a central or federal government insurance programme with a low deductible (often, even zero) for all doctor's fees and hospital charges, regardless of the cost. So, the elderly poor and the vulnerable are protected from unexpected medical costs by Medicaid.

The government assesses each eligible applicant for Medicaid as an individual. Thus, the mother of a multimillionaire may qualify for Medicaid provided she meets the income and asset criteria laid down by the government.

But what if a poor person does not qualify for Medicaid? There are low-cost insurance plans available that would cover catastrophic illnesses. If they cannot afford the low-cost insurance premiums, *all they need to do is to show up in any hospital which would be compelled to treat them by law.* No hospital can turn away sick patients. The cost is passed on to other payees or is charged against profits when the hospital files for taxes. Again, these types of government financial assistance extended to low-income groups cannot be expected of the Government of India given the lack of resources and the sheer size of its population who are without any type of health insurance.

Improving India's Healthcare System

The private healthcare system in India works reasonably well. However, there is a need to ensure better quality control of doctors and hospitals. There should be a Central government agency, within the Ministry of Health and Family Welfare, whose main function is to ensure that the credentials of doctors in India's government hospitals and other primary and secondary health centres are adequate.

Moreover, there must be a system of keeping track of the performance of doctors and hospitals based on the experience of patients. For instance, how many patients, if any, have lodged serious complaints against a particular doctor or hospital? Have there been instances of gross violations of ethical standards by the doctor or hospital? Such reviews should be widely shared on government websites and the websites of NGOs. This system of tracking the work experience and performance of healthcare professionals and hospitals is almost non-existent in India. The reviews backed by key statistics (such as number of patients admitted, number of deaths, etc.) should be made publicly available to help patients make more informed decisions regarding their healthcare provider.

The government should actively promote a highly competitive market for health insurance. Sen has argued against private insurance for three main reasons. First, premiums will be high for those who are prone to be sick or have a poor health record although it is precisely this group of poor people who need insurance the most. Second, insured patients as well as healthcare providers have little incentive to limit medical costs. Any limits on the amounts payable for different treatments will encourage doctors and hospitals to use the cheapest treatment even if that treatment goes against patients' interests. They could also treat low-cost cases and turn away the rest. Finally, private insurance tends to be biased against preventive care and focused on hospitalization. Many private insurance plans do not cover surgical procedures, the cost of which is exorbitant. Poor families simply cannot afford them. Yet, in India, where ill health is mainly driven by communicable diseases, better preventive measures can help drive down the cost of healthcare in the long run by pre-empting the need for costly hospitalization later.

Every effort must be made to expand child immunizations and reduce child malnutrition and chronic diseases. Reduction in malaria, tuberculosis and other infectious diseases should be brought about through better public education. Moreover, there is a need to promote sanitary conditions and adopting preventive measures such as mosquito control and eradication. The government must also improve access to effective family planning methods.

The solution to the insurance conundrum is to create a time-bound consultative group on insurance consisting of government, private insurance, and civil society representing the urban and rural poor. The consultations should lead to actionable legislation governing the insurance market in India keeping in mind the important points raised by Sen and others. Private insurance should be regulated to ensure greater coverage of preventive measures such as annual physical check-ups for adults and children.

The government should increase its expenditure on the provision of healthcare services. While an intermediate target of 2.5 per cent of the GDP over the next five years or so is reasonable, the objective should be to gradually raise such expenditures in tandem with the growth of GDP. The main objective should be to expand the number and quality of government-run hospitals for the poor. Not only that, the hospitals should be subject to random and unannounced visits by senior health inspectors and officials of the Ministry of Health. Furthermore, the Ministry of Health should create and promote lines of communication between the ministry and the patient population that is being served by government hospitals.

Given the shortages of doctors and nurses in India, there is a dire need for the government to open up new medical colleges and universities as well as nursing institutes. The medical universities should aim to attract top students into medicine akin to the admission standards for the Indian Institute of Technology and other top-ranked

Indian universities. In other words, the admission criteria for these premier medical universities should be on a highly selective basis. The pay scales for graduating doctors working in government hospitals should be competitive with those in private hospitals.

Additionally, doctors posted in rural areas should be granted a 'rural hardship allowance' to attract good doctors to serve the rural poor. The flip side of such government medical jobs is that doctors who do not meet the high standards should be dropped from its ranks. Promotions should be based strictly on merit, experience and performance on the job.

22

Farmers' Despair

The woes of India's agricultural sector were captured early on by landmark Bollywood movies such as *Do Bigha Zamin* (1953) and *Mother India* (1957). The theme of these movies revolved around the plight of India's poor farmers. Burdened by huge debt to rich zamindars and moneylenders, they faced rampant discrimination based on caste, creed and gender. Illiteracy limited their employment opportunities while harvest failures due to drought led to impoverishment and malnourishment.

More than sixty years later, the story has remained much the same for the vast majority of India's farmers. In some ways, their lives are harder now. There is more land fragmentation and soil degradation through over-farming and overgrazing. Severe weather patterns due to climate change, and lesser availability of water and electricity have made life more difficult. India may be shining for the upper-income groups but for the nearly three-quarters of Indian families that depend on rural incomes, the shine is off.

Who are the rural poor? They include subsistence farmers who farm to feed themselves and their families with not many grains or vegetables to sell. Others include landless agricultural workers, and other workers who are related to fishing, pastoral lands and forests. Such rural families have little or no access to credit and eke out a living without basic services such as healthcare and education for their children. As a result, the rural poor are among the most vulnerable segments of the population. The women face discrimination in acquiring or inheriting land, accessing education and training, and securing gainful employment at par with men.

Sen makes the same point noting that poverty has declined much slower in India than in developing countries in the last twenty years or so, even though economic growth has been much faster.[159] This is because most of the increase in income due to growth went mostly to the already rich (i.e., those in the top 1–10 per cent income groups). In other words, the rich got much richer while income increases became less and less for the middle class, lower middle class, and the poor. In fact, the incomes of the rural poor have barely increased. The World Bank therefore recommends that rural communities be empowered to become self-reliant. They need to form self-help groups in order to increase community savings and promote local initiatives to increase incomes and employment.

The fact that the share of agriculture in the economy has declined over time is not necessarily a cause for worry. A maturing economy naturally undergoes a change in the pattern of production. Typically, production shifts from agriculture to manufacturing and finally to the service sector like consulting and IT. At Independence, India's agricultural sector accounted for close to 50 per cent of the country's GDP. In 1960, the share of agriculture to GDP declined to 41.8 per cent, falling further to just around 15 per cent of GDP in 2017.

This decline in agriculture's share is offset by the corresponding rise of the industrial and services sectors. In advanced countries, the share of agriculture is typically low, which does not mean that they do not grow enough food to feed their own people. For instance, the service sector accounted for about 79 per cent of the US economy in 2015, while industry and agriculture accounted for about 20 per cent and 1 per cent respectively.[160]

---

[159]   Drèze and Sen, *An Uncertain Glory*, p. 32.
[160]   Refer Eric Duffin, 'Distribution of gross domestic product (GDP) across economic sectors in the United States from 2000 to 2016', Statista, 29 April 2019.

The decline in the share of agricultural production in the overall economy does not mean that the total volume of crop production has fallen. In fact, according to the Food and Agricultural Organization (FAO) of the United Nations there has been more than a fivefold increase in foodgrains in India from 50 million tonnes in 1950-51 to 272 million tonnes in 2016-17.[161] However, even though total crop production has increased, the share of agriculture in the overall economy has declined.

This increase in agricultural production in India is mainly due to its large and medium-scale farmers who have employed better fertilizers, irrigation and other farming techniques, higher crop-yield varieties, etc. The resulting increase in agricultural output has enabled India to move away from a net food importer to a net food exporter (net meaning exports of food minus imports of food). However, agricultural yields are low by international standards.

Total crop production would have been much higher had agricultural productivity been better. The main reason for low productivity is land fragmentation and archaic state laws restricting the area of farmland each farmer can own. In fact, the average size of landholdings has declined from 2.3 hectares (5.7 acres) in 1970 to under 1.2 hectares (3 acres) today.[162]

One of the main obstacles to raising agricultural productivity has been land fragmentation. At Independence, large areas of agricultural land were mainly held by zamindars. In order to reduce inequality in landholdings and to provide poor farmers a means of livelihood, land was redistributed from zamindars to the smallholders.

But, as the size of landholdings declines, for example, when a 5-acre farm owned by a single farmer is inherited by his three sons upon his passing, their size of landholdings will decline along with

---

[161] *India and FAO: Promoting food security and sustainable development in India and around the world* (Rome: FAO, 2018).
[162] 'Farming in India: In a time warp', *The Economist*, 25 June 2015.

productivity. This is because it is not possible to use mechanized means of farming on small parcels of land. In America, the largest farmers use the most mechanized techniques thereby boosting their productivity or yield. Small farmers cannot compete with them in efficiency of production. In India, land fragmentation and the smaller number of large landowners has made it very difficult to raise agricultural productivity through mechanization and other techniques.

The issue of land fragmentation can only be addressed in the long run. Smaller lands can be consolidated over time as the younger generation of the rural population migrates to urban areas in search of better-paying jobs and the small farmers retire. Richer farmers holding more land can then buy these smaller farms to consolidate them into one. As land area under cultivation increases through consolidation, more mechanized means of cultivation can be used to boost agricultural productivity.

Another possible solution is to enable small and subsistence farmers to be able to lease out their lands to larger farms against a guaranteed payment from the additional agricultural production. In most states, the regulations governing land lease have not been relaxed and are, in any case, not well understood by farmers. They fear loss of control over their land and would therefore suffer declining production rather than lease their land to larger farmers. Moreover, given India's weak laws and enforcement of property rights, it is understandable why small farmers have little faith or trust in land-lease agreements.

Yet, most of the difficulties in agriculture are faced by India's small and marginal farmers who tend to fall into debt traps faster and in greater numbers. Take the case of Kunti Devi, a mother of four children who lives in Shekhwara village in Gaya district, Bihar. Her family of five farms on less than an acre of land just to feed themselves. Faced with frequent droughts and lack of irrigation facilities, she was forced to mortgage her land to the local moneylender. Survival required that the family work as labourers on other farms. Kunti Devi had to take out loans from the local moneylender.[163]

Manna Devi, another poor farmer in Bihar with three children, found it difficult to even feed her family. With scarcity of food being a huge issue, she could not send any of her children to school. The land she owned barely yielded 30 kg of wheat which lasted the family just four months. She had to take out loans and her husband also had to take a second job as a rickshaw puller to make ends meet.[164] The lives of Kunti Devi and Manna Devi, like the lives of millions of India's poor farmers, seem like a real-life replay of *Mother India*.

Baijanti Devi, a class 8 dropout in Bhusia village in Bihar, was somewhat more forceful and activist-like in her approach to farming. She mobilized the villagers to have a road constructed. This road made it easier for villagers to access their farmlands. However, although plans for the road were sanctioned by the district, the road eluded the villagers. She mobilized the villagers and tracked down the contractor forcing him to begin the construction. But then she realized that the contractor did not provide the mandatory drainage which was part of the sanctioned plan. So, she talked to the labourers and rallied them to force the contractor to complete the project according to the approved plan.[165]

The three cases became part of a World Bank agriculture sector project to help poor farmers improve their livelihood. The project, which began in 2007, also involved the Bihar government, and private sector and non-profit organizations. The International Development Association, a part of the World Bank Group, contributed USD 63 million out of the total estimated project cost of USD 73 million.

The government of Bihar contributed USD 7 million and the private/non-profit organizations contributed USD 3 million. Given

---

[163] 'India: Liberating Bihar's Poor from the Debt Trap', *World Bank*, 12 April 2013, https://bit.ly/2H9woN0
[164] Ibid.
[165] Ibid.

the success of the programme, the IDA financed an additional USD 100 million starting in March 2012. The project expanded social mobilization to include 160,000 poor households in three districts affected by the 2010 flooding of the River Kosi.

The project helped introduce better farming methods (among other beneficial contributions to key livelihood sectors and job creation for migrant youths) as a result of which the agricultural productivity of marginal farmers improved. The three cases recounted above provide a glimpse into how well-crafted programmes with financing from key international organizations, in partnership with domestic stakeholders, can significantly improve the lives of poor farmers.

Such World Bank projects focus on the reduction of rural poverty through a socially inclusive strategy—rural development that benefits the poor, the landless, women and Scheduled Castes and Tribes. The World Bank notes that there are significant regional disparities, and reaching some of these groups is not easy. It also notes that while rural poverty has fallen from 40 per cent in the early 1990s to below 30 per cent by around 2005, there is clearly a need for a faster pace of reduction. This shows that the rapid economic growth in the post-reform period has not led to a faster reduction in rural poverty, which has only been falling at about 1 per cent per annum. This supports Sen's contention that we cannot simply rely on overall economic growth to accelerate improvements in rural livelihoods.

Lack of education is a common problem among poor farmers. Illiteracy remains a significant obstacle to improving agricultural productivity, restricting the livelihood of small and marginal farmers. Poor farmers, due to a lack of basic education, find it difficult to understand or trust modern farming methods and techniques. Moreover, the Central and state governments have invested little by way of improving the flow of information to them in a way they can understand, use and implement. Poor and illiterate farmers do not appreciate the value of soil testing, the factors behind land degradation, and how to improve its productivity through proper use of pesticides and fertilizers. Poverty also precludes them from investing in mechanized farm equipment such as tractors and tillers. At the same time, their illiteracy makes them vulnerable to exploitation by moneylenders and large landowners.

In India, where there is huge unemployment among the youth, few would venture to take up farming as a means of employment. One reason why educated youth are not attracted to agriculture is that farming is not as prestigious an occupation as holding a salaried job in the private or public sectors. But there are exceptions proving that properly educated and motivated farmers can make a decent profit selling crops and other produce.

Take the case of Harish Dhandev, a twenty-four-year-old engineer who resigned from a government job in 2013 to start aloe vera farming. He now owns a company with a turnover between Rs 1.5 and 2 crore.[166] Harish had 80 acres of ancestral land in Jaisalmer, Rajasthan. When his father retired from a government job, he took up farming. It was then that Harish decided to lend his father a helping hand on the farm. But he had no intention of being a full-time farmer. As time passed, Harish decided to give up his secure government job and apply his planning and executive skills in farming on a full-time basis.

The first thing that Harish did was to get the soil of his land tested. Based on the test results, the agriculture department suggested that Harish grow bajra, moong or gawar—crops that need little water (Jaisalmer being a rather dry area). But Harish did some research and found out that his land was also suitable for cultivating aloe vera, even though there was a lack of market for the crop in his area. He determined that there were good prospects of selling aloe vera by using online portals such as Indiamart to gain access to national and international markets.

---

[166]   Manabi Katoch, 'This Engineer Left His Government Job to Become a Farmer and Is Earning in Crores Now!', Better India, 10 August 2016, https://bit.ly/2THpIdX

Initially, Harish planted 15–20 acres of land for which the cost was high mainly due to the cost of aloe vera saplings. But soon, the saplings gave rise to several baby plants around themselves, without the use of chemical fertilizers or pesticides. Harish used natural manure such as cow dung and cow urine. In this way, his company emphasized the organic nature of the aloe vera it marketed and sold.

Today, Harish believes that knowledge is the key to success and guides other farmers in Jaisalmer in accessing and understanding government booklets and loan schemes suited to their needs. Says Harish, 'Exposure to new resources, planning, optimization and execution—these things have helped me and I believe every farmer can benefit from such knowledge. But farmers too have to leave their fears behind and come out of their comfort zones.'

One does not need to be an engineer to do well in agriculture but basic education in reading and writing is critical. Harish's experience provides ample proof of what education can do to turn a decent profit in farming. The other important factor is ownership of sizeable land—80 acres is a pretty big plot of land.

But even if one only has 1 acre or less, education can go a long way to improving farming methods, accessing as well as understanding free government information on latest farming methods, and tapping loans on the most favourable terms available. But the education of poor farmers is a long-term project—it will probably take many years for India's farmers to catch up on their basic education.

23

Should We Worry about Farmer Suicides?

First, a Problem of Good Data

Some say that farmer suicides are increasing while others say they are declining. The reason for this confusion is the lack of reliable statistics on farmer suicides. It seems there is no agreement on the definition of a farmer! There is obviously a need for a consistent definition of a farmer. We can then better understand the issue of farmer suicides.

Among all suicide cases on the farm that are lodged with the police, only those of farmers with a land title to their name are recorded as farmer suicides. But, if a farmer working on his family farm or if a woman working on her husband's farm commits suicide, they are not counted as farmer suicides as they have no title to the land. Hence, official data on farmer suicides tend to understate the actual number of suicides among farmers with and without land titles.

In general, suicide statistics tend to be understated while statistics on the total number of farmers vary widely. So, estimates of the suicide *rate* among farmers (that is the number of farmer suicides divided by the total number of farmers) vary widely. Apart from the sheer number of farmer suicides, the rate provides an idea of the severity of the problem and changes over time.

Moreover, the total number of farmers is falling. In fact, the farmer count has fallen by nine million since 2001. The increases in suicide among farmers are all the more alarming given the declining number of farmers nationwide. More than 80 per cent of farm suicides are by male farmers. This probably has to do with the fact that as men are traditionally the breadwinners, the inability to support their families causes great mental strain.

Farmers' Debt Burden and Other Problems

Naturally, researchers and activists differ on the nature and seriousness of the problem of farmer suicides. For instance, Bhagwati and Panagariya say that farmers commit suicide at a much lower rate than the general population.[167] However, it would be misleading to simply focus on the lower suicide rates among farmers, even if they were true, to think that perhaps the issue is not so serious. We certainly cannot ignore the reasons underlying farmer suicides.

There are experts who have exclusively focused on the issue of farmer suicides for many years. The government has to seriously consider what they have to say and take remedial policy measures in order to improve the lives of farmers.

The debt burdens of farmers are high because of the lack of credit either from commercial banks or from the government under an established scheme to help farmers. Moreover, loans from these sources require the completion of a lot of paperwork and often require guarantees of collateral. Unable to obtain loans from these formal channels, poor farmers take loans from moneylenders who charge anywhere from 24 to 60 per cent interest per annum. There are no government regulations that prohibit the charging of usurious rates of interest. Farmers also lack government safety nets like food-for-work schemes, access to fair price shops where they can purchase food at subsidized rates, etc.

---

[167]   Bhagwati and Panagariya, *Why Growth Matters*, p. 83; M.S. Sriram, 'An attempt to understand and contextualise farmer suicides', Livemint, 28 December 2018, https://bit.ly/2CAYizx

The plight of the small farmer in rural India is captured by what happened to fifty-year-old Arun Namder Talele, who owns a 5-acre land about 70 miles north of Aurangabad.[168] He knew from experience that the torrential rains that pounded his land throughout September were bound to ruin his onion crop. The plot of land he owned does not have adequate drainage trenches and he had no dry place to store the onions. As a result, he lost 70 per cent of his crop.

About 10 miles from Arun Talele's farm in the village of Pahur, Sandeep Ram Karshanbakr was able to take advantage of drip irrigation. He purchased this system from Jain Irrigation through a government programme that paid half of its cost (USD 2800). The drip irrigation system allowed Sandeep Ram to cut his water and electricity usage by half. At the same time, the yields on his crop of chillies, cauliflower, eggplants, tomatoes, and cotton increased by two- to fivefold over the yields before he installed the system. While he is now planning to acquire or lease more land, many farmers like Arun Talele say they cannot afford the drip system even after the government's 50 per cent subsidy. The government should help the small farmers improve their methods and techniques including irrigation in order to raise the productivity of agriculture.

Arun Talele and millions of farmers like him across India illustrate why, far from joining the Asian Tigers, the country's thwarted potential can be likened to that of a shackled giant. Four decades after the green revolution, India still struggles to feed a growing population that is set to overtake China's in the next decade. Nearly half of the children under the age of five are malnourished. While agriculture employs well over half the working-age population, it accounts for around 15 per cent of the economy, growing only at around 3 per cent a year.

The government has failed to modernize agriculture and infrastructure to support modern methods such as adequate

---

[168] Vikas Bajaj, 'Galloping Growth, and Hunger in India', *The New York Times*, 11 February 2011.

irrigation and electric supply, water reservoirs and drainage systems, and methods to arrest and reverse soil degradation. To make matters worse, laws governing agriculture are archaic, barring corporations from farming land for food crops or facilitating the consolidation of landholdings through leasing agreements. Due to illiteracy, farmers are not able to appreciate the advantages of modern farming techniques or even to protect themselves from unscrupulous moneylenders and other middlemen.

Some Suggestions to Improve the Lives of Farmers

Various international organizations have suggested ways to improve the lives of farmers in India. For example, the Food and Agriculture Organization (FAO) suggested that the government develop employment opportunities on and off the farm. The government could promote entrepreneurship and develop the occupational skills of the rural poor. The FAO also suggested ways to improve the access of the rural poor to credit and natural resources (such as water, seeds and fertilizers) in order to improve the productivity of their farms. Moreover, the FAO strongly supported government extension of a basic level of income and social protection afforded through a direct cash transfer programme. India has since started such a cash transfer to poor families as one of the policy instruments for alleviating poverty in both urban and rural areas.

24

Descent into Environmental Disaster

While relatively rapid economic growth has lifted millions of people out of poverty and into the lower- and middle-income classes, the sustainability of this growth in the long run has increasingly come into question in relation to the serious deterioration of the country's environment. The World Bank has noted that the poorest parts of the country also happen to be the most environmentally stressed regions with land degradation, polluted waterways and degraded forests.

The traditional approach to accounting for the gross value of all goods and services produced in an economy (known as the gross domestic product, GDP) does not take into account the role of the environment in sustaining the economy. GDP is a flow which measures the size of an economy by estimating the contributions of each sector (such as agriculture, manufacturing, telecommunications, retail trade, transportation, etc.).

But the generation of the flow of goods and services uses a stock of natural resources such as land, water, forests, minerals, etc., that is scarce and getting more so over time. Yet, those who are using these natural resources in the process of producing the goods and services that go into the GDP and drive its growth do not pay for the use of these scarce resources. For instance, coal is typically used in steel and cement production or to generate electricity. Yet, neither the steel and cement industries nor the electric companies are paying for 'using' natural resources such as air and water. They are depleting these resources without paying for their renewal or clean-up.

Likewise, traditional accounting methods used to estimate the GDP also do not net out the depletion of natural resources in the production process. On one hand, these 'free goods' tend to get overused and over-exploited because nobody pays for them, nor are there any consequences for their abuse. On the other, policymakers typically do not question whether their quest for ever higher rates of growth is sustainable. But how long can we go on depleting and polluting the environment without any consequence?

The current state of the environment reflects these sad truths. The result of the neglect of the environmental dimension of economic growth is evident in the form of climate change and the steady rise in environment-related chronic diseases. We did not come to this sorry state of affairs over a few years but over many decades. Partha Dasgupta, professor emeritus of economics at the University of Cambridge, argues that our quality of life is invariably linked to the quality of the natural environment and not just on economic progress alone.[169]

The main offenders of the global environment have mainly been, and continue to be, the advanced countries. In fact, the US is the world's leading contributor of industrial pollution, greenhouse gases and other effluents, followed by China. However, while the advanced countries have now embarked on a serious effort to curb pollution, developing countries, led by China and India, are now emerging as the biggest polluters of the planet.

Economists have increasingly begun to talk about 'inclusive growth' and 'sustainable growth'. Often, there is a tendency to use these terms interchangeably. But, there are shades of difference between the two. Inclusive growth typically refers to growth with equity, whereby the benefits of economic growth are more widely

---

[169] Partha Dasgupta, *Human Well-being and the Natural Environment* (Oxford: Oxford University Press, 2001), p. xi.

shared between the low-, medium- and high-income groups. In recent years, the need for inclusive growth has gained currency among development economists and policymakers around the world—away from a focus to only reduce extreme poverty.[170] The opposite of inclusive growth is lopsided growth, where the incomes of the rich 1 per cent rise much faster than the incomes of the other 99 per cent of the population or where the rise in incomes falls off precipitously as one goes down the income slabs.

Sustainable growth is a much wider concept than inclusive growth. In other words, sustainability implies inclusivity but not vice versa. Moreover, governments may attain high rates of growth that are inclusive but they still may not be sustainable in the long run.

The factors that sustain high rates of growth are complex and involve both macroeconomic as well as environmental factors. Typically, economists, barring a few exceptions such as Dasgupta, have tended to focus on macroeconomic factors but have not explicitly considered the environmental impact and constraints to growth.[171]

In sustainable growth strategies, the government fully considers the value of the environment that is being consumed. Few countries in the world (such as the Nordic countries) have attained such environmentally friendly approach to growth. But for growth to be sustainable in the long run, economists and policymakers have to explicitly take into account the cost of environmental monitoring, clean-up and renewal. If depletion cannot be continued indefinitely, the growth strategy is not sustainable.

Environmental sustainability requires that: (i) renewable resources not be depleted (or 'harvested') at a rate higher than the rate at which they could be regenerated or renewed, (ii) the rate of waste generation

---

[170] *UNDP's Strategy for Inclusive and Sustainable Growth* (New York: United Nations Development Programme, 2017).

[171] See, for example, Scott Barrett, Karl-Göran Mäler and Eric S. Maskin (eds), *Environment and Development Economics: Essays in Honour of Sir Partha Dasgupta* (Oxford: Oxford University Press, 2014).

is confined to a level where they can be disposed of in a sustainable way, which raises questions about the capacity of the environment to safely assimilate the waste, and (iii) comparable substitutes for the non-renewable resources that are being depleted be developed.

The Current State of India's Environment

Ever since the economic reforms of 1991, as growth ratcheted upwards, India's environment started deteriorating at a faster pace. The present state of the environment can truly be called a disaster. According to the 2018 Environmental Performance Index (EPI), compiled at Yale University, India ranked 177 out of 180 countries. The three countries that had a more polluted environment than India were the Democratic Republic of Congo, Bangladesh and Burundi (last).[172] The aggregate EPI consists of twenty-four performance indicators across ten areas which cover environmental health and ecosystem vitality.

India ranks 178 out of 180 countries in air quality, which through exposure to particulate matter, presents one of the main threats to public health. In water and sanitation, the country ranks 145 while Indians suffer one of the highest exposure to carcinogenic lead in the world (ranked 175 out of 180 countries). Given the high levels of pollution and environmental degradation, its ecosystem is fragile as reflected in a vitality rank of 140. India's present state of the environment and how to go about improving it over the medium to long run can best be discussed with reference to the EPI and the component scores that ranked poorly.

Air Pollution

Air pollution killed more than a million Indians in 2017, outpacing deaths due to tobacco use. In fact, a recent nationwide study by

---

[172] Complete rankings are available at Environmental Performance Index, Yale University, https://epi.envirocenter.yale.edu

the India State-Level Disease Burden Initiative found that one in eight deaths in India can be attributed to pollution. A whopping 77 per cent of India's population is exposed to harmful particulate matter.[173]

The first order of business is to consider the key factors driving the poisonous quality of air that most Indians breathe. Unless one goes into some remote village with no industry, scanty population and vehicular traffic, the air quality in most Indian cities and towns fall far behind most, if not all, countries in the world.

The worst offenders of air quality are poor households, industrial emissions, car exhaust, construction dust and burning of crop residue, which is an archaic practice of getting rid of agricultural waste. While governments, international aid agencies and NGOs have been trying for decades to wean off the poor from the use of wood-, charcoal- and coal-fired ovens, all these efforts have thus far failed to get them to use cleaner fuels like liquefied petroleum gas (LPG) and electricity. The main problem with cleaner fuels is that they are relatively more expensive and their supply as well as distribution is much more limited. Yet, reliance on wood, charcoal, coal and cow dung is contributing to denuding of forests and a sharp increase in air pollution. The solution, to be implemented over the medium to long run, would be to tax coal and wood and offer subsidies for the use of LPG and electricity to poor households.

Since 2016, the government has made LPG available to some thirty-four million households (with a cash payment to the poor), giving them gas stoves and their first LPG cylinder free of charge. On average, households buy around four gas cylinders a year, which means they continue to use wood, dung, coal and the like to meet half their cooking needs. Still, this is a 50 per cent reduction in air pollution from the pre-2016 levels that was due to those cooking

---

[173] Joanna Slater, 'Study: India's air pollution killed a million-plus in 2017', *The Washington Post*, 8 December 2018.

methods. Further improvements in household cooking methods will take time.

India needs to increase its manufacturing industry to create more good-quality, higher-paying jobs for its qualified youth. So, even as the developed countries are cutting pollution by shifting to green, environment-friendly production processes, India's industrialization, based on coal-fired power plants and lack of proper regulation, is expected to increase air pollution. But India's toxic air is already killing more than a million people every year.

For years, China's air pollution and number of related deaths has been much higher than in India but now the situation seems to have reversed with air pollution in India turning worse than China's. Strong government regulations in China and the use of alternative green technologies have not only arrested the deterioration in air quality but also have started to improve it. The death rate from air pollution in China has been going down perceptibly.[174] In India, the number of deaths from air pollution has been going up steadily from 957,000 in 2010 to 1.1 million in 2015.

India needs to improve publicly available information on industrial pollution and also improve their quality and timeliness. If data are patchy, outdated and unreliable, the government itself will be hamstrung in formulating better regulation, targeting them appropriately towards the worst offenders, and raising public awareness about the harmful health effects of increasing pollution.

It is not only a question of generating jobs for India's increasing labour force. It is also a question of formulating an industrial policy, rather a development strategy which is sustainable in the long run. Again, an exclusive focus on growth to the exclusion of growth's negative side effects will prove to be counterproductive. The high rates of growth can only be sustainable in the long run if the negative effects, such as environmental degradation, are effectively mitigated.

---

[174] Michael Reilly, 'India Now Has the World's Worst Air Pollution', *The New York Times*, 14 February 2017.

The public is gradually becoming more aware of the environmental consequences of development without oversight. In May 2018, there were violent protests against Vedanta's proposed copper plant in Thoothukudi, Tamil Nadu, leading to thirteen deaths.[175] Such mayhem can be pre-empted by making more information available to the public in a transparent manner and announcing in advance how, when and where the information would be made available by the appropriate regulator. Transparency of government policies and operations should become a regular part of industrial policy. With rapid industrialization, it would be necessary to bring discipline in industry to exercise greater self-reporting, self-monitoring and compliance, and all of this information should be made available publicly.

However, a lack of confidence in the data has thus far hampered greater willingness on the part of industry to share the information publicly. *The best way is to require industry to install high-quality, certified air pollution equipment backed up by well-qualified pollution regulators in the appropriate government regulatory agencies.* Every plant should be required to post the results of annual inspections by the regulator on its website as well as onsite at the plant. In general, there is a dire need to improve environmental regulation in India through a combination of high-quality data from the Continuous Emissions Monitoring System (CEMS) introduced in 2014 (which tracks pollutants from seventeen categories of grossly polluting industries in real time) and a system of incentives and penalties based on high-quality, verifiable data.

It is not simply a matter of better regulation or even better data. A regulatory system is only as good as the means to ensure compliance and penalize violators. If regulatory agencies are weak with a lack of qualified staff or staff that is not honest, and if clogged courts make it extremely difficult to punish violators in a timely and transparent manner, such weaknesses in governance will hamper efforts to ensure compliance with the stipulated regulations.

---

[175]   Malavika Vyawahare, 'India needs transparent industrial pollution data, regulation reforms', *Hindustan Times*, 21 August 2018, https://bit.ly/2H8vhwX

Take the case of Agra. More than two decades after an industrial ban, Agra's average air quality index (AQI) is among the five worst cities in India. The Taj Trapezium Zone Authority (TTZA) placed more than a dozen restrictions on industries in order to protect the Taj Mahal from the ravages of pollution. However, these restrictions have remained largely on paper. In fact, a polluted haze surrounds the city and it is getting worse every year. TTZA officials are not even able to prevent garbage being burnt in the city nor are they able to control the level of airborne dust.

The particulate matter in and around Agra has reached such a dangerous level that it is no longer a matter of simply protecting the Taj from environmental damage but preventing all kinds of respiratory illnesses among the populace. Agra's pollution has remained high in spite of the Ministry of Environment, Forests and Climate Change (MoEFCC) closing down several industries. A project to create a three-layer green barrier between Rajasthan and Agra was not fully implemented. As a result, the air quality deteriorates significantly in the summer months. In the winter, other pollutants like 2.5 micron (μm) particulate matter and nitrous oxide (NO_2) severely ruin the air quality.

Another factor contributing to air pollution is that a rising and affluent middle class now owns and uses many more vehicles. In the 1960s and early 1970s, when I went to school and college in India, owning a car was a luxury. My father, a government servant, could only afford a scooter. In fact, very few middle-income families could afford to own a car. But now, given the rising incomes, easy credit, and reasonable auto prices, many middle-income families own two or more cars. As a result, most city roads are clogged with vehicular traffic. To make matters worse, most cars on Indian roads are more than fifteen years old and are fitted with outdated and largely ineffective pollution control systems. The resulting exhaust fumes from trucks, buses and cars are a significant driver of poor air quality.

The government should offer an incentive to consumers to switch to electric or hybrid cars by way of a one-time tax break amounting to a certain percentage of the car's value or a certain fixed rupee amount. Older cars should be retired to the scrap heap against a one-time tax credit equal to a certain percentage (say, 10 per cent) of the car's current market value. This is not likely to be very expensive for the government given that older cars are worth little and that the rebate amount is a small fraction of that value. Similarly, older public transport buses and trucks should also be retired and the programme financed through a green transportation tax, higher transport fares, or some combination of those surcharges.

The decades-old practice of burning paddy straw by farmers in Punjab, Haryana and western Uttar Pradesh also contribute to Delhi's dangerous air quality. In a way, this is the price of success— that of the green revolution. But no one seems to have a clue how to handle the by-product of so much stubble burning. Ministers in Delhi, Punjab and Haryana have been going around in circles blaming each other. It is not simply a question of imposing penalties on farmers. They need to find a way to remove stubbles in order to prepare the fields to sow the next crop.

There have been proposals to employ root stubble digging machines that plough back the stubbles into the soil thereby acting as a fertilizer. But, in many cases stubbles are less of a problem than the paddy straw and the husk that are left over from the threshing and milling. For instance, Punjab had almost twice the weight of its paddy harvest (18 million tonnes) in leftovers of straw and husk (34 million tonnes).[176] As farmers in Punjab and Haryana no longer use paddy straw for cattle feed, that too is being burned.

Technology may offer a solution to the problem of disposing of the crop residue. There is a two-stage technique whereby the straw and stubble can be converted into a fuel gas that can be used for cooking, heating and power generation, as well as to power cleaner transportation than gasoline. This process, called gasification, involves the incomplete burning of biomass or coal in a limited

---

[176] Prem Shankar Jha, 'Easy solution to India's air pollution problem', Third Pole, 17 November 2017, https://bit.ly/2KPlehr

supply of air or oxygen yielding significant amounts of hydrogen, carbon monoxide and methane.

There are other techniques to convert the mixture of hydrogen, carbon monoxide and methane into a form of fuel for transportation— from CNG to diesel to methanol and jet fuel. There are yet other techniques to produce dimethyl ether that can potentially replace LPG used as cooking gas. These are not futuristic ideas but are currently available techniques.

Pollution taxes should be imposed on polluters and the proceeds should be supplemented by budgetary resources such as transportation, toll and road taxes to fund large-scale induction of these technologies to improve air quality. Not only that, these technologies can also improve farmer incomes and save valuable foreign exchange by reducing imports of gasoline. Green technologies will lead to better overall health outcomes and lower healthcare costs in the long run.

Conclusion

Nature is not some fixed and indestructible resource but rather it can be depleted as well as degraded. Yet, economists and economic policymakers assume that natural resources like water and air can be used freely as inputs into the development process. Consequently, governments often neglect the importance of maintaining natural resources. The process of economic development cannot be sustained if land, water and air resources are being polluted at an unprecedented rate. If polluters are not held accountable for the cost of clean-up and renewal, governments, and ultimately the taxpaying public, have to bear the cost. Hence, environmental policies must not only regulate, monitor and penalize polluters, they must also help renew natural resources in order to avoid scarcity and derailing development itself.

25

India's Water Crisis

India is one of the most water-stressed countries in the world meaning the country has one of the lowest availability of water per person. The main reason has been an expanding population. Clean water has become a scarce commodity in many Indian cities. At the same time, groundwater is being depleted, particularly in the villages, as more people extract water using tube wells and pumps. In fact, more than half of India's districts are affected by groundwater depletion or contamination.[177]

In dry and industrial Gujarat, it will take decades for the rivers and lakes to recover from all the heavy pollution due to increasing industrialization. The rivers and lakes of India continue to be heavily polluted not only due to industrial discharge but also due to gross abuse by the people themselves. Incessant municipal waste, sewage, the bathing of cattle and people, washing of clothes, frequent submersion of idols—all contribute to the ever-increasing pollution of India's waterways and other waterbodies.

Only one-third of waste water is currently being treated. Raw sewage, which makes up the rest, flows into rivers, lakes and ponds. People fall ill because they do not get enough safe drinking water. Waterborne diseases such as diarrhoea, cholera and typhoid take a toll

---

[177] 'Helping India Manage Its Complex Water Resources', World Bank, 22 March 2019, https://bit.ly/2YZFLdh

mostly on the poor who pay a price in terms of lost wages and high costs for treatment which they have to pay as they have no health insurance.

Yet, Indians cannot turn away from the rivers and lakes as they are intimately related to religious rituals and a lifestyle that is centuries old. Industrial sewage and agricultural run-off spill into the lakes and other waterways at thousands of locations around the country. Besides the obvious harmful impact of industrial sewage, agricultural run-off also severely pollute the water due to the use of chemicals and pesticides in cultivation. The question is what can the government do to alleviate water pollution in the long run?

The first step in improving water quality is to strictly monitor the chemical and industrial waste as well as domestic sewage from India's towns and cities. The second step would involve industry and households being charged a fee according to the amount of waste being dumped into the water. Currently, industries are themselves charged with cleaning up their effluents which often leads to cheating, for example, by only cleaning in the presence of inspectors. But, when inspectors leave, they continue to dump their waste into rivers and lakes at zero cost. This situation is unsustainable.

Water is getting more expensive but Sushila Devi, who lives in a slum in the Wazirpur area of Delhi, paid an unthinkable price.[178] Her husband and son died in a fight over water in March 2018, finally pressurizing the government to drill a tube well. While water quality has improved in the meantime, it is still not drinkable. Nearly half of India's population faces acute water shortage with close to 20,000 dying from waterborne diseases. Slum dwellers like Sushila have to queue up daily for water from tankers as the municipality does not supply the area. Often, the slum dwellers get into fights to collect the water.

The Supreme Court mandated in early 2013 that all polluting industries must ensure that the waste water they are discharging

---

[178] Annie Banerji, 'India's "worst water crisis in history" leaves millions thirsty', Reuters, 5 July 2018, https://reut.rs/2MtRnef

into the rivers and lakes meet certain minimum quality standards after being treated to eliminate harmful contaminants. It is not clear to what extent this decision by the highest court is being actually implemented by municipality and other regulatory bodies.

What Can be Done?

For starters, the government has to set the norm on the minimum quality of the water being released into the rivers. These standards should be checked regularly and randomly without notice. Violators of the norms should be subject to stiff penalties including closure of plant operations and possible prison sentences for repeat offenders. Charges should be set at a level that equals, at a minimum, the cost of cleaning.

Likewise, households should also be monitored by respective municipalities and water authorities on the amount of water they release and the amount of waste being discharged into the rivers. The amounts involved should be tracked by meters that cannot be accessed by the households themselves. Thus far, neither industry nor households have been charged a waste disposal tax and this 'free-rider' benefit at the cost of the environment cannot be sustained.

Today, Mumbai generates about 2100 million litres of sewage a day. The total volume of sewage generated by India's 200 cities and towns is estimated to be around 36 billion litres which can micro-irrigate 3–9 million hectares. The technology exists to treat sewage water so that it can be productively used in agriculture and replenish rivers and lakes. River pollution can be significantly reduced through a public–private collaboration on the use of latest technologies.

Singapore has shown the way. Recently, the prime minister of Singapore drank the treated water being released by the country's sewage treatment plant to demonstrate the quality of water after treatment. What is required is strong political will to improve the quality of India's environment.

Recent Initiatives to Improve India's Water Resources

There are new initiatives to monitor the water quality of rivers in India on a regular basis. The Water Resources Information System (WRIS) database was developed by the Central Water Commission in collaboration with the Indian Space Research Organization (ISRO). The database contains pertinent information on 15,615 rivers and streams in the country. Thus far, some 302 polluted river stretches have been identified on 275 rivers based on biochemical oxygen demand (BOD) level in rivers, a key indicator of organic pollution. Rivers have been identified for implementation of clean-up projects on a cost sharing basis between Central and state governments.

Effective 2014, clean-up and other water quality enhancement projects related to the Ganga and its tributaries have been transferred to the Ministry of Water Resources, River Development and Ganga Rejuvenation. The World Bank is helping to build sewer networks and treatment plants in several towns and cities along the Ganga. One of the objectives is to make sure that no untreated wastewater is allowed to flow into the Ganga.

Large amounts of budgetary resources have been allocated to clean up polluted stretches of thirty-one rivers in seventy-five towns spread over fourteen states. Funds have also been released to state governments for various pollution abatement schemes including water treatment. The National River Conservation Directorate (NRCD) in the Ministry of Environment, Forests and Climate Change (MoEFCC) is implementing the centrally sponsored schemes for the conservation of rivers, lakes and wetlands in the country.

These initiatives are welcome but a lot more needs to be done on a systematic and sustained basis over the long run in order to improve India's water quality. The aim should be to first arrest the decline in environmental conditions (as reflected, for example, in deteriorating EPI indicators). It is only after environmental indicators begin to register significant improvements that we can expect a perceptible decline in environment-related diseases and an improvement in the quality of life.

The main reason why Indian farmers experience a lot of droughts is that the annual rainfall is concentrated around a few weeks during the monsoon season. The country is a major producer of grain, which need a lot of water to grow and harvest. But, as a result of droughts and the long hot summers, river currents have ebbed while water levels in wells have dropped by as much as 85 feet (26 metres). Farmers are sometimes forced to abandon their land and move to cities. Hence, apart from a crisis of supply, India also faces a water management problem.

One of the government's primary objective is to extend, by 2030, universal access to safe drinking water at a price people can afford. However, government water experts are less sanguine. Most think that India's water demand will double the country's supply by that year.

Meanwhile, the government's plans to interlink rivers (such as the Ken with the Betwa) is meeting fierce resistance from environmentalists, farmers and locals. They are convinced that such mammoth interlinking of the rivers will have a detrimental impact on protected forest areas (such as the Panna National Park—home to endangered tigers) and waste river water that is already scarce.[179]

Part of the solution is to develop methods for rain catchment. Rather than letting the rainfall go to waste, rain harvesting could help water collection for agricultural production. Filtration methods could convert part of the rainfall into water suitable for drinking. India does not have a long window period to start developing and implementing some of these measures in order to avoid a water crisis.

---

[179] Paul Salopek, 'India is in a historic water crisis. Will diverting 30 rivers solve it?' *National Geographic*, 6 March 2019, https://on.natgeo. com/2TubBLF

PART 4

THE LONG AND WINDING ROAD
TO REDEMPTION

26

First Steps on the Road

This chapter provides a brief overview of some recent measures towards better governance. However, given India's limited fiscal space (meaning capacity for taking on extra expenditures), questions naturally arise on whether some of these programmes can be sustained. In fact, while some initiatives seem viable and have taken root, others seem to have fallen by the wayside. Readers can form their own opinions. My intention is to present a round-up of some of the cases of weak governance discussed in the rest of the book.

Aadhaar and Other Initiatives towards Digitization

The ownership and use of mobile phones has soared. This has allowed the government and the public to communicate with each other without the need for personal contact. In fact, the digitization of public and private records and the increasing reach of the Internet are beginning to reduce entrenched bureaucratic corruption. As a result, the efficiency of government services is also improving.

The ever-widening pool of mobile phone ownership has started to bridge the digital divide—such as between the rich and the poor, the educated and the illiterate, and the urban and the rural populace. In fact, the increasing reach of cellphones is raising the awareness of the poor about their right to government services.

Meanwhile, expanding access to the Internet is slowly improving their lives.

The increasing affordability of mobile phones could expand its use as a platform for the delivery of government services such as cash transfers and deposits rather than merely serve as a means of communication. By cutting out the middlemen, mobile phones are reducing opportunities for corruption by public officials in the delivery of routine government services.

The twelve-digit Aadhaar identification number assigned to every citizen has greatly helped the poor and the uneducated to establish their identity and to receive services without having to bribe public officials. However, given India's spotty electricity supply and lack of Internet access in remote areas, real-time verification of Aadhaar identification can be a problem. Moreover, weak privacy laws and use of the Aadhaar card for which it was not designed, has led to hacking and identity theft. Nevertheless, in spite of these initial drawbacks, the Aadhaar system has been the right step forward in helping to rein in corruption and improving the effectiveness of government services.

Swachh Bharat

The Swachh Bharat or Clean India mission was launched by Prime Minister Modi in 2014 in order to address issues of cleanliness and waste management that have been plaguing Indian cities and villages ever since Independence. At its heart is an effort to empower citizens to clean their surroundings including streets and neighbourhoods. This initiative was dovetailed with the objective of ending 'open defecation' across India through the construction of toilets and ensuring their easy access for households, particularly in the rural areas. In order to finance the construction of millions of toilets and improve sanitation and cleanliness, a Swachh Bharat tax of 0.5 per cent was tagged on to service tax income.

This programme has been largely successful in improving the cleanliness of Indian cities and in ending open defecation in more than half of all Indian states. The programme has also helped to spread greater awareness of these issues among the rural population. Following a recent visit to Delhi, Kolkata and other cities, my overall impression is that while Swachh Bharat represents the first steps on the road to a clean India, the country has a long way to go before it can declare victory. There is a dire need to improve waste management and disposal using the latest technologies while simultaneously improving public awareness and action to keep India clean.

'Make in India', FDI, Startup India and Mudra Yojana

While the liberalization and streamlining of rules to attract foreign direct investment (FDI) into India significantly improved India's ranking in the World Bank's 'Ease of Doing Business' index and increased such investments, they did not lead to a commensurate increase in employment. The IMF has noted that 'the surge of FDI flows to India appears to be concurrent with FDI policy reforms since 2014 that resulted in a permanent regime change to allow freer flows'.[180] While multinationals and other foreign companies set up some manufacturing units, their demand for additional skilled labour fell short of what is required to make a dent in youth unemployment. Moreover, the pool of skilled manpower available in India is also shallow placing limits on the 'Make in India' initiative.

Meanwhile, the laudable initiatives to encourage young entrepreneurs to start their own small-scale enterprises were not successful in most cases. Many who left secure jobs to launch such ventures were left in debt and without a steady source of income. Difficulties included the imposition of service taxes on fledging start-ups, inadequate financing, lack of support on technical issues, market research, and product quality control. The result? Of the nearly 7500 start-ups registered in 2016, only 1300 remained in business the very

---

[180] *India: Selected Issues,* IMF Country Report No. 18/255, August 2018, pp. 21–25.

next year.[181] Today, it is doubtful whether even a fraction of these ventures is still profitable.

Jan Dhan Yojana and Ujjwala Yojana

The Jan Dhan Yojana (JDY) introduced by the Modi government builds upon a similar scheme called the Direct Benefit Transfer for LPG (DBTL), which was initiated under the Congress government in 2013. While the DBTL was aimed at transferring fuel subsidies to eligible households for domestic cooking, the JDY was launched with the wider objective of transferring subsidies and pensions to all beneficiaries.

An empirical study found that directly transferring subsidies to households under the DBTL reduced fuel purchases in the household sector by 11–14 per cent compared to a system involving middlemen.[182] Commensurately, black market prices of LPG fell by 13–19 per cent as households were able to purchase more fuel in formal markets rather than having to go to the black market.

Similarly, under the Pradhan Mantri Ujjwala Yojana (PMUY), more than five crore Below Poverty Line (BPL) households got LPG connections for just Rs 1600. By opening the accounts in the names of women of these households, the PMUJ scheme also helped empower women. There was also a move by the government to discourage wealthy households from getting fuel subsidies they do not need. By all accounts, these schemes have helped reduce grass-roots corruption in India to some extent, and enjoy wide support among the electorate.

---

[181] Raghav Bahl, 'Why Startup India is a Big Policy Failure', Quint, 30 January 2018, https://bit.ly/2nkOYHZ

[182] Prabhat Barnwal, 'Curbing Leakage in Public Programs with Direct Benefit Transfers: Evidence from India's Fuel Subsidies and Black Markets' (Department of Economics, Michigan State University, 2016).

Goods and Services Tax

The India-wide implementation of the goods and services tax (GST), which came into effect from 1 July 2017, was a singular achievement of the Modi administration. The reform of India's complicated system of indirect taxes was started by Vishwanath Pratap Singh in 1985 when he was the minister of finance in the Rajiv Gandhi government. Others like Prime Minister P.V. Narasimha Rao and his finance minister Manmohan Singh and later in 1999, Prime Minister Atal Bihari Vajpayee along with prominent economists such as I.G. Patel and Bimal Jalan were also involved in the modification and refinement of the original 1985 version. The bill was stuck in Parliament since then. It was only after Modi and the BJP came to power with an unprecedented majority in 2014 that the bill was finally passed after intensive discussions with all stakeholders.

The GST is divided into five slabs—0, 5, 12, 18 and 28 per cent. Certain goods such as petroleum products, alcoholic drinks and electricity are not subject to the GST but taxed separately by state governments according to the previous tax scheme. The transportation sector is one of the beneficiaries of the GST. For example, trucks carrying food, perishables and other products were subject to lengthy delays to pay toll at various check points. Following implementation of the system, delays in shipment fell significantly while bribes collected by the police at the checkpoints dried up. Thus, the GST was responsible for the reduction of grass-roots corruption and improving the speed of delivery and the efficiency of interstate commerce.

Moreover, the GST has simplified India's myriad taxes into a simpler structure. However, the original drafters of the GST did not intend to have five different slabs as under the present version. The original intent was to have just three rate slabs. Hence, there is a broad consensus among economists that the present multiple rate structure and other exemptions is excessive, which would increase administrative costs to ensure compliance. So, economists typically recommended a simpler rate structure with fewer exemptions.

Nevertheless, I am certain that with increasing experience in the administration of the GST, the government would be able to improve the efficiency of the system in the collection of taxes, plug loopholes for evasion, and deny politically motivated claims for exemptions. This is not unusual. Most countries go through a steep learning curve in improving the collection of tax revenues after rolling out a new GST. Initial teething problems in improving the collection of taxes under the GST is to be expected in a vast and incredibly diverse country such as India.

Meanwhile, the imposition of the GST hit certain sectors of the economy employing hundreds of thousands of low- and medium-skill workers particularly hard. Consider Agra's footwear industry which supplies 65 per cent of India's footwear needs. These days, a visitor there would be greeted by piles of unsold footwear and shuttered stores. Gagan Das Ramani, president of the Agra Shoe Federation, notes that business has fallen by half and entire factories have shut down due to high taxes. Under the earlier VAT regime, footwear was exempt from taxes but the GST slab of 5 per cent for shoes up to Rs 500 and 12 per cent for those costing more has ruined many businesses. In addition, a 28 per cent GST on raw materials has thrown thousands out of job, says Harsh Vanjani of the Agra Shoe Federation.[183]

The initial dampening effect of new taxes on business is a standard textbook effect. However, the initial adverse impact on demand will dissipate over time as customers get used to paying the taxes and new price expectations are formed. *These are not reasons for lowering the GST on a selective basis.* In fairness, no case can be made that businesses be allowed to operate without the payment of any taxes. In fact, as demand recovers along with rising incomes, there

---

[183]   Goyal, et al., 'Will jobs actually be top of mind when India casts its vote in this Lok Sabha elections?', *The Economic Times*, 31 March 2019.

is a need to consolidate the GST into two or at most three slabs, preferably with zero exemptions.

Farm Loan Waivers and Income Support

In an earlier chapter, I shared about the deep discontent festering among farmers since Independence. While the days of food dependency of the 1960s are long gone, the woes of the farmer have continued to mount amidst ample food production. Economists call this the paradox of the plenty. Most economists feel that government policies to buy agricultural products from farmers at low prices is largely to blame for impoverishing farmers. In fact, one of Modi's top priority when he came to power in May 2014 was to fight high food price inflation, which had fuelled the anger of urban voters and led to the defeat of the Congress party. But these low government procurement prices for agricultural products have inevitably hurt farmers.

Ashok Gulati, a professor of agriculture at the Indian Council for Research on International Economic Relations, stresses that the paradox of the plenty needs to be solved.[184] Unless the government reforms the marketing of agricultural products, encourages technical innovation, and improves infrastructure to benefit farmers, loan waivers and other means of income support are not going to solve the paradox. Gulati concludes that all direct income support schemes for farmers result from a failure to implement key agricultural sector reform policies.

Anecdotal information indicates that, in the long run, loan waivers and direct income support schemes are unlikely to be effective in alleviating the hardships of farmers. Rahul Chauhan, a twenty-seven-year-old farmer in Ujjain, had big hopes riding on Modi's campaign promise to create millions of new jobs. Today, he remains dependent on his parents' 2.7-hectare farm, unable to

---

[184] 'Can India Solve Its Food Paradox?' *Knowledge@Wharton*, 28 March 2019, https://whr.tn/2z88u05

find employment elsewhere. Meanwhile, prices for the chickpeas, lentils, and other legumes that their farm produces, have fallen even as 'input' costs on labour, fertilizers and pesticides have continued to increase. Other farmers are hurt by increasing imports of pulses, curbs on exports of onions and potatoes, and periodic raids on traders suspected of hoarding fruit and vegetables.[185]

Not only are the various income support schemes inadequate in relation to farmer needs, the benefits do not always reach the intended beneficiaries. For instance, waivers typically relate to loans taken from public sector banks. However, many small farmers who were not able to qualify for such loans, were forced to get the funds from private moneylenders at exorbitant rates. The loan waiver schemes do nothing to reduce the debt burden of such farmers.

Moreover, Modi's move to demonetize certain large denomination notes in November 2016 (ostensibly to encourage digital payments, discourage cash transactions and improve tax compliance) added to farmers' woes. After all, cash is king in the farmers' world.

In the run-up to the 2019 general elections, both the Congress and the BJP courted farmers with new handouts. But most economists feel that neither Modi's income support schemes nor the Congress's loan waivers really address the conflict between a liveable farm income and affordable food prices for the urban masses. For instance, in February this year, the Modi government announced that it would provide Rs 6000 a year in three equal instalments to an estimated 120 million farmers with less than 2 hectares of land. Modi aimed to help shore up rural support for the BJP which accounts for almost two-thirds of the electorate. But apart from the huge problem of identifying eligible farmers, the cash transfer itself is quite small. Moreover, the scheme may anger the 30 per cent of farmers holding more than 2 hectares of land who do not qualify. No wonder many farmers remain disgruntled.

---

[185] Amy Kazmin, 'Left behind in the fields', *Financial Times*, 12 March 2019.

Questions can also be raised about the long-term viability of these well-intentioned but wrong-headed income support and loan waiver schemes. Needless to say, both schemes are incredibly expensive and the extent of support they actually provide is suspect. The question is whether India can afford to undertake additional expenditures given the limited capacity of the government. For instance, the Central and state governments are already facing large deficits in recent years, although the deficit has declined slightly over the last few years. Moreover, the finances of the states have deteriorated further squeezing the fiscal space.

Given the states' large and rising share of fiscal deficits and debt, they can ill-afford additional spending due to farm loan waivers, income support schemes, and the UDAY scheme (under which states take over the debt of electric companies). The long-term viability of these schemes is suspect without new sources of revenues. Considering the lack of fiscal space, it would be far better for the government to progressively loosen controls on agricultural prices so that they reflect, more fully, the free market prices. Any adverse impact on the poor should be mitigated through a direct transfer of subsidies to eligible families to be financed in part through new taxes on rising incomes of farmers with larger landholdings and taxes on informal sector workers based on a capacity to pay. This goes to the heart of the free-rider problem which is responsible for India's poor tax performance.

27

Outline of an Agenda for Reform

This book covered a lot of ground in providing an overview of the state of India's governance and the price Indians are paying for related weaknesses. Along with a worsening in five out of the six aspects of governance from 1996 to 2017, the fragility of India's democracy also increased from the ninety-third position in 2006 to the seventy-second position in 2018. Here, we briefly recapitulate the recommendations to improve governance made throughout this book followed by a discussion on the need to *develop the capacity* to implement such policies.

Law and Order

The current abysmal state of law and order (or rather disorder) is due to a rotten system that starts at the top—the dirty politics that gets 'leaders' elected, a culture that sees no finality in the Supreme Court's orders, a CBI that is in the pocket of the ruling party, and a police force that is in the pocket of the chief ministers. So, with senior police personnel making their careers by buttering up politicians and feeding their egos, their commitment to ensure the public's security takes a back seat.

The application of the rule of law must begin with politicians. 'Do as I say, not as I do' is not a credible prescription for a reform agenda. It never was; it never will be. As a start, candidates running for an election, whether at the panchayat, local, municipal, state or Central government level must not have any criminal convictions or cases pending against them. Any violations of the law should automatically bar the person from running for any elected office. The current political system where criminals are allowed to run for elected office on the possible but rare chance that the charges against them could have been trumped up by an opposition party, simply ends up promoting a goonda raj, not a democracy.

The rule of law should require elections to be held in a transparent manner using public and private donations, as well as government funds earmarked for that purpose. Funding information must be widely disseminated in a fully transparent manner. That means, political parties should be required to publicly share information on their campaign financing. They must be compelled to share a full accounting of what they spent at each election and the source of their funds. The objective would be to cut the use of black money in elections so that such funds become irrelevant in running them. Accordingly, the limit on donations for elections should be raised sharply and adjusted annually to reflect the current cost of holding them given the size of the electorate.

Finally, the VIP and VVIP perks and benefits that are currently provided to cabinet ministers, members of Parliament, and state representatives should be reduced to a bare minimum, preferably zero. Their salaries should be increased to offset some of the loss in benefits. Every minister and national leader, except the prime minister and the president, should be required to go through security checks and line up with ordinary citizens with no recourse to 'VIP lounges' or any other privileges. No pampering of ministers should be allowed and any existing VIP/VVIP privileges should be revoked by the Supreme Court, and the order implemented under penalty of law.

The rule of law should also be strengthened by building a strong legal infrastructure over the medium to long run. Legal infrastructure includes the establishment of excellent colleges and universities devoted to the study of law. Foreign legal academics should be regularly invited by these institutions of higher learning in order to encourage an interchange of ideas and impart lessons in comparative jurisprudence. The objective would be to develop high-quality lawyers and judges in order to strengthen the legal system. Upgrading the legal infrastructure would also require an increase in the number of lower- and higher-level courts commensurate with an increase in legal professionals. Meanwhile, the backlog in court cases must be cleared in an expeditious and time-bound manner.

The government also needs to devote sufficient resources for the development of world-class forensic laboratories specializing in the scientific examination of evidence collected at crime scenes. Court decisions must be based on hard evidence collected by a modern, well-trained and efficient police force, and the decisions themselves must be transparent, fair and timely without regard to any political consideration or interference. Vigilante justice and riots will automatically start to decline once justice is delivered swiftly and fairly based on irrefutable forensic evidence. Evidence-based trials would foster the perception that justice will be carried out without fail.

All measures should be taken to ensure a truly independent police force. It is a very bad idea to politicize investigative and enforcement agencies such as the CBI and the police forces. These should report to a special panel within the Supreme Court or the Parliament and not to any individual politician or political party. *Chief ministers should have no say in police decisions.* Moreover, the police and intelligence personnel across the country need to be given high-quality training in order to modernize them in their investigative methods.

Need for Strong and Independent Institutions

Other institutions also need to be strengthened in order to improve enforcement of rules and regulations. For instance, the Reserve Bank of India should be strengthened and made much more independent from the Ministry of Finance and other departments of the government. Independence of the RBI and progressive privatization of public sector banks are two important steps the government can take to encourage prudential lending standards and spare citizens the pain of serial banking scams.

The customs and tax departments must be strengthened to curtail tax evasion and improve the collection of taxes. The revenue department, customs and other regulatory agencies would need to collaborate on curtailing tax evasion and boosting revenue performance. The government should consider reforming the customs in order to improve its efficiency and tax collections. However, a strengthening of overall governance is necessary in order for customs reform to be effective in the long run.

Measures to Curb Corruption

Corruption can only be curbed by tackling it on many fronts. Widespread corruption has led to weak revenue collections causing India to lag behind the revenue performances of developing countries in general and China in particular. India would need to develop policies to expand its narrow tax base to include workers in the informal sector (based on verified income levels) as well as agricultural incomes that are above the minimum taxable income.

The design of a good tax system should start from the assumption that every worker in the informal sector is subject to tax, unless proven otherwise. Enforcement mechanisms need to be strengthened and modernized in order to rope in the millions of tax cheats hiding in plain sight in the informal sector. Lack of enforcement due to corruption and weaknesses in tax administration have helped to convert the informal sector into a formal sector for tax evasion.

The onerous burden of proving ownership of black money, the huge backlog in Indian courts, along with the uphill task of tracing long-lost funds in foreign accounts that can be shifted instantly, make it almost impossible to get the money back. Instead of fanning these pipe dreams, the government should come clean with the legal challenges as they really stand and discuss realistic policies to stop the drain of black money.

Developing Stronger Voice and Greater Accountability

The media must be bred to become full-time attack dogs, ready to go for the jugular of the unlawful. In order to ensure that the media is as unbiased as possible, their financing by political parties must be outlawed, unless a newspaper or TV channel clearly declares itself to be the mouthpiece of a party. Financing of the media by business houses must be declared and conform to clear guidelines. The government must invest time and effort to develop appropriate policies to make the media truly independent and of high quality.

The quality and depth of investigative journalism must be improved. *Violence against journalists should attract maximum sentences especially set aside for that purpose.*

Towards Sustainable and Equitable Development

I do not subscribe to the idea that India's development strategy should stress pro-growth policies first in order to generate enough revenues to finance larger investments in health and education. Rather, given a large informal sector, narrow tax base and widespread tax evasion, I believe that India's revenue performance can only improve gradually as these drawbacks are redressed. In fact, I find that past revenue performance was not very responsive to economic growth. Over a twelve-year non-contiguous period of high growth averaging 8.5 per cent per annum, the revenue to GDP ratio only increased by 0.4 per cent.

Moreover, India can do better even with the revenues it raises. We find that there are at least four countries in Asia (Bangladesh, Indonesia, the Philippines and Sri Lanka) which have attained better human development outcomes with a lower revenue performance compared to India.

Sustainable growth requires that the benefits of growth are not only widely distributed but that the impact on the environment be mitigated using green technologies, levying appropriate penalties on polluters and financing clean-up to reverse environmental degradation. Unless the government tightens its environmental policies towards stricter monitoring and control of pollution with a system of incentives and penalties, rapidly increasing air and water pollution will soon start to constrain economic growth.

Health and Education

India needs to make much larger investments in health and education in order to build a productive workforce. By their very nature, health and education investments have long gestation periods of two or three decades before they can start to make decent returns. The reason is obvious. We cannot expect today's investments in primary and secondary schooling to produce better-trained workers tomorrow. Similarly, the acute shortage of qualified medical professionals and good hospitals in the rural areas would require a long time to be reversed. Such investments today cannot be expected to produce more healthy workers tomorrow. More education with a focus on high-quality vocational training will be necessary to bring Indian workers up to par with their peers in China and other competitors such as South Korea, Singapore and Malaysia. Otherwise, the 'Make in India' initiative will be dead in the water and the demographic dividend may turn into a ticking time bomb. Thus, while the immediate returns on higher investments in health and education may not be visible, such investments ensure that the benefits of growth are widely shared in the long run. In the absence of such investments, economic growth is likely to create more inequality, thereby risking the sustainability of growth.

Capacity Development for Better Governance

India's institutions need to be strengthened to improve their capacity for implementing reform. Institutions must work across the states and the Centre to design, formulate and integrate their policies so that they are consistent throughout the country. At the same time, they would need to take local conditions into account. The lack of good governance can derail the best laid plans for economic development.

Sustainable development cannot be achieved in an environment of poor governance. It is a mistake for policymakers to simply focus on generating ever higher rates of growth in order to reduce poverty. Therefore, for India to realize inclusive development, the Central and state governments would need to collaborate on strengthening public institutions and building their capacities to bring about better governance. These institutions must be held accountable to the public. Improving public services such as municipalities and public works requires that they take the opinions of all stakeholders into account. Their performance also needs to be monitored on a regular basis. Hence, the first step to capacity development involves the *compilation of governance measures.* These measures will allow Central and state governments to monitor the effectiveness of public institutions charged with the responsibility of delivering government services.

For example, in primary and secondary education, public and private schools could provide data on student achievement in various areas of competence at specific grade levels as notified by the education department on a periodic basis. Now, such a system of ensuring better educational outcomes may be difficult to realize if schools falsify their data to reflect higher levels of student achievement. The incentive for falsification of outcome indicators would be higher the more teacher bonuses are tied to them.

That is why self-reporting has to be supplemented by random audits. The Central government should develop such an information system but its implementation and management should be the responsibility of state governments. For transparency, the public should have access to the information so that they can monitor the effectiveness of various projects and programmes.

Currently there are a few institutions in India providing training in public administration. Even these are narrowly focused on catering to a small segment of officials in limited areas. Enlarging these programmes to cover more sectors and officials at all levels of the Central and state governments will require significant institution-building effort. The government should consider tapping private sector involvement as well as partnerships with international organizations to design and carry out these programmes. We illustrate the need for institutional strengthening in the area of city administration.

Consider the urban sector. A few large metropolitan cities have some planning and development capacity but large secondary cities such as Kanpur, Patna and Siliguri have little or no planning and development capacity. They are also saddled with very inefficient administrations.

As a result, cities have grown in a haphazard manner with extremely poor infrastructure. In fact, international rankings show that Indian cities are among the least desirable places to live in in the world. Furthermore, because of inadequate investment in job creation in secondary cities, the metropolitan cities have attracted enormous flows of rural migrants leading to intense pressures on civic facilities and infrastructure, unplanned expansion of urban limits and a rapid rise in serious crime. The living conditions in the sprawling slums of India's flagship cities such as Delhi, Kolkata and Mumbai are abysmal. Municipal services are extremely erratic and limited, particularly concerning water supply and sewerage, solid waste disposal and public health facilities. Such shortcomings have resulted in serious and chronic public health issues.

New policies, regulations and extensive strengthening of administrative capacity in urban management and development are urgently needed. There are a few institutions in India providing training in urban planning and development and municipal management. To address this on a long-term basis, the Government of India should establish a network of educational and training institutions similar to the IIMs. These institutions would provide specialized training to public officials and individuals in urban infrastructure planning and development and municipal finance and administration. Multilateral development banks such as the World Bank and the Asian Development Bank have specialized experience in these areas and can be requested to assist in designing and setting up such institutions.

Waiting for Light at the End of the Tunnel

When the supine electorate gets sick of corruption and begins to yearn for integrity, when the grievances of the poor and the marginalized can no longer be assuaged through vacuous political speeches, there will arise a nationwide clamour for better governance. I am hopeful that a new generation of Indians, more educated and aware of their rights than their parents, will lead the push for a better life in ways large and small. Shorn of the shackles of fragility and poor governance, a resurgent India will reclaim its rightful place as one of the world's leading powers.

In closing, I am reminded of the late US president John F. Kennedy's words:

> All this will not be finished in the first 100 days. Nor will it be finished in the first 1,000 days, nor in the life of this Administration, nor even perhaps in our lifetime on this planet. But let us begin.[186]

---

[186]   John F. Kennedy, Inaugural address, 20 January 1961.

Appendix

Fragile States Index (FSI)[187]

The FSI is based on both quantitative and qualitative information on the following pressure points in order to establish broad trends in fragility. Qualitative information includes those gleaned from media articles, research reports and other qualitative data points while quantitative indicators are based on data published by international organizations such as the United Nations and the World Bank. Millions of pieces of information are gathered from diverse sources under each class of indicators into a form that can track developments in a country's fragility. Ultimately, the FSI determines the quality of life of the residents of a country.

Demographic Pressures

The demographic pressures indicator considers pressures upon the state deriving from the population itself or the environment around it. For example, the indicator measures population pressures related to food supply, access to safe water and other life-sustaining

---

[187] The Fund for Peace (FFP), a reputed non-profit think tank based in Washington DC, compiles the widely peer-reviewed fragile states index for 178 countries (reference, https://fundforpeace.org/). The FFP was originally founded in San Francisco in 1957.

resources, or health, such as prevalence of disease and epidemics. The indicator considers demographic characteristics, such as pressures from high population growth rates or skewed population distributions, such as a 'youth or age bulge', or sharply divergent rates of population growth among competing communal groups, recognizing that such effects can have profound social, economic and political effects. Beyond the population, the indicator also takes into account pressures stemming from natural disasters (hurricanes, earthquakes, floods or drought), and pressures upon the population from environmental hazards.

Factionalized Elites

The factionalized elites indicator considers the fragmentation of state institutions along ethnic, class, clan, racial or religious lines, as well as brinkmanship and gridlock between ruling elites. It also factors the use of nationalistic political rhetoric by ruling elites, often in terms of nationalism, xenophobia, communal irredentism (e.g., a 'greater Serbia') or of communal solidarity (e.g., 'ethnic cleansing' or 'defending the faith'). In extreme cases, it can be representative of the absence of legitimate leadership widely accepted as representing the entire citizenry. The factionalized elites indicator measures power struggles, political competition and political transitions, and where elections occur, factors in the credibility of electoral processes (or in their absence, the perceived legitimacy of the ruling class).

Group Grievance

The group grievance indicator focuses on divisions and schisms between different groups in society—particularly divisions based on social or political characteristics—and their role in access to services or resources, and inclusion in the political process. Group grievance may also have a historical component, where aggrieved communal groups cite injustices of the past, sometimes going back centuries, that influence and shape that group's role in society and relationships with other groups. This history may in turn be shaped by patterns of real or perceived atrocities or 'crimes' committed with apparent impunity against communal groups. Groups may also feel aggrieved because they are denied autonomy, self-determination or political independence to which they believe they are entitled. The indicator also considers where specific groups are singled out by state authorities, or by dominant groups, for persecution or repression, or where there is public scapegoating of groups believed to have acquired wealth, status or power 'illegitimately', which may manifest itself in the emergence of fiery rhetoric, such as through 'hate' radio, pamphleteering, and stereotypical or nationalistic political speech.

In a country with a diverse population such as India, fragility of state can increase if schisms between different groups of people develop along caste, clan, class, ethnicity, nationality or religious lines. These divisions may develop due to internal strife or external exploitation to cultivate a vote bank. The FFP notes that even less diverse states have erupted into mass unrest due to 'a variety of circumstances, such as competition over resources, predatory or fractured leadership, corruption, or unresolved group grievances. The reasons for state fragility are complex but not unpredictable.'

Public Services

The public services indicator refers to the presence of basic state functions that serve the people. On one hand, this may include the provision of essential services such as health, education, water and sanitation, transport infrastructure, electricity and power, and Internet connectivity. On the other, it may include the state's ability to protect its citizens, such as from terrorism and violence, through effective policing. Further, even where basic state functions and services are provided, the indicator considers to whom these are provided. For example, does the state narrowly serve the ruling elites, such as security agencies, presidential staff, the central bank, or the diplomatic service, but fail to provide comparable levels of service to the general populace? A typical distinction in the provision of services in many developing countries is between rural versus urban populations. The indicator also considers the level and maintenance of general infrastructure to the extent that its absence would negatively affect the country's actual or potential development.

Security Apparatus

The security apparatus indicator considers the security threats to a state, such as bombings, attacks and battle-related deaths, rebel movements, mutinies, coups or terrorism. The security apparatus also takes into account serious criminal factors, such as organized crime and homicides, and perceived trust of citizens in domestic security. In some instances, the security apparatus may extend beyond traditional military or police forces to include state-sponsored or state-supported private militias that terrorize political opponents, suspected 'enemies' or civilians seen to be sympathetic to the opposition. In other instances, the security apparatus of a state can include a 'deep state', which may consist of secret intelligence units, or other irregular security forces, that serve the interests of a political leader or clique. As a counter example, the indicator will also take into account armed resistance to a governing authority (such as the Naxalites in India), particularly the manifestation of violent uprisings and insurgencies, proliferation of independent militias, vigilantes or mercenary groups that challenge the state's monopoly of the use of force.

Worldwide Governance Indicators (WGI)[188] (Compiled by the World Bank)

Following is a brief description of the six dimensions of governance as described on the website of the World Bank:

Voice and accountability dimension captures the perceptions of citizens in the fairness of the process of selecting their government, freedom of association, and a free media. A diverse range of concepts are assessed such as accountability of public officials, respect for human rights, extent of political and civil rights, transparency and fairness of the electoral process, press freedom, transparency of government policy-making, etc.

The dimension of political stability and absence of violence/terrorism measures the perceptions of the likelihood of political instability and/or politically motivated violence, including terrorism. Hence, it captures such concepts as violent demonstrations, armed conflict, security risks, government stability, internal and external conflict, ethnic tensions, etc.

Government effectiveness dimension captures perceptions of the quality of public services, the quality of the civil service, the degree of independence from political pressures, the quality of policy formulation and the credibility of the government's commitment to such policies. Specifically, this dimension of governance includes concepts such as quality of infrastructure like primary education, satisfaction with public transportation systems, satisfaction with

[188] The Worldwide Governance Indicators is a research project of the World Bank. The WGI summarizes the views on the quality of governance provided by a large number of enterprises and citizens in industrial and developing countries. These data are gathered from a number of survey institutes, think tanks, non-governmental organizations, international organizations and private sector firms. The indicators do not reflect the official views of the World Bank and neither are they used by the Bank to allocate resources; reference link: https://bit.ly/31LVwRT

roads and highways, satisfaction with education system, quality of public administration, efficiency of raising tax revenues, integrity of government officials, etc.

Regulatory quality captures perceptions of the ability of the government to formulate and implement sound policies and regulations that permit and promote private sector development. Thus, it measures and collates such information as nature, range and extent of price controls, discriminatory tariffs, discriminatory taxes, burden of government regulations, effectiveness of anti-trust policy, ease of starting a new business, investment and financial freedom, stringency of environmental policy, etc.

Rule of law captures perceptions of the extent to which citizens have confidence in, and abide by, the rules of society, and in particular, the quality of contract enforcement, property rights, the professionalism, reliability and effectiveness of the police force, extent of violent crime, extent of organized crime and criminal gangs, fairness of the judicial process, timeliness of the judicial process, intellectual property right protection, gender rights and laws protecting the rights of women.

Control of corruption captures perceptions of the extent to which public power is exercised for private gain, including both petty and grand forms of corruption. Hence, it captures concepts such as corruption among public officials, public trust in politicians, diversion of public funds, fraud in export and import payments, fraud involving public utilities, irregular payments in judicial decisions, transparency and accountability in the public sector, etc.

Table. FSI and Its Component Indices, 2018

Country	Rank	Total	C1: Security Apparatus	C2: Factionalized Elites	C3: Group Grievance	E1: Economy
South Sudan	1st	113.4	10.0	9.7	9.7	10.0
Somalia	2nd	113.2	9.7	10.0	9.0	8.9
Yemen	3rd	112.7	9.9	10.0	9.5	9.6
Syria	4th	111.4	9.9	9.9	9.9	8.5
Central African Republic	5th	111.1	9.1	9.7	8.8	8.8
Congo Democratic Republic	6th	110.7	9.1	9.8	10.0	8.1
Sudan	7th	108.7	8.7	9.7	10.0	8.0
Chad	8th	108.3	9.5	9.5	7.7	9.0
Afghanistan	9th	106.6	10.0	8.6	8.1	8.3
Zimbabwe	10th	102.3	9.1	10.0	7.0	8.6
Iraq	11th	102.2	9.0	9.6	9.3	6.3
Haiti	12th	102.0	7.4	9.6	6.2	8.4
Guinea	13th	101.6	8.9	9.6	8.9	8.9
Nigeria	14th	99.9	8.9	9.6	9.3	8.0
Ethiopia	15th	99.6	8.7	8.4	8.8	6.7
Guinea Bissau	16th	98.1	8.6	9.6	5.2	8.0
Kenya	17th	97.4	8.4	9.6	8.9	7.0
Burundi	17th	97.4	8.5	7.9	7.6	8.1
Eritrea	19th	97.2	6.9	8.1	7.4	7.8
Pakistan	20th	96.3	8.8	8.9	9.7	6.6
Niger	21st	96.2	8.4	8.9	7.7	7.3
Myanmar	22nd	96.1	9.0	8.3	9.8	5.6
Cameroon	23rd	95.3	8.0	9.1	8.4	6.7
Uganda	24th	95.1	7.1	8.6	8.6	6.0
Libya	25th	94.6	9.3	9.4	7.8	8.0
Cote d'Ivoire	25th	94.6	7.7	9.1	7.8	6.8
Mali	27th	93.6	9.3	5.4	7.9	7.6
North Korea	28th	93.2	8.3	8.8	5.8	8.9
Congo Republic	29th	93.1	7.0	6.7	7.5	7.3
Liberia	30th	92.6	6.7	8.6	5.5	8.0
Mauritania	31st	92.2	6.6	8.8	6.7	7.4
Bangladesh	32nd	90.3	7.9	9.3	8.4	5.8
Angola	33rd	89.4	6.8	7.2	7.2	6.3
Rwanda	34th	89.3	6.0	8.0	9.7	6.3
Sierra Leone	35th	89.1	4.3	7.8	6.5	8.4
Egypt	36th	88.7	8.2	8.8	8.9	7.9
Mozambique	36th	88.7	6.7	6.6	5.1	8.3
Timor-Leste	38th	88.3	6.9	8.3	6.2	7.6
Nepal	39th	87.9	6.2	8.8	9.6	6.1
Swaziland	40th	87.5	6.0	6.8	3.1	9.8
Zambia	41st	87.2	4.9	5.9	5.6	7.8
Djibouti	42nd	87.1	6.2	7.3	6.2	6.7
Gambia	42nd	87.1	6.6	7.7	3.5	8.7
Lebanon	44th	86.8	8.4	9.6	8.2	6.1

E2: Economic Inequality	E3: Human Flight and Brain Drain	P1: State Legitimacy	P2: Public Services	P3: Human Rights	S1: Demographic Pressures	S2: Refugees and IDPs	X1: External Intervention
8.9	6.3	10.0	9.9	9.2	10.0	10.0	9.6
9.3	9.5	9.1	9.3	9.6	10.0	9.7	9.1
8.2	7.2	9.7	9.7	9.8	9.6	9.5	10.0
7.8	8.1	9.9	9.3	9.9	8.2	10.0	10.0
9.8	7.4	9.4	10.0	9.4	9.3	10.0	9.5
8.5	7.0	9.6	9.5	9.8	9.6	10.0	9.7
7.7	8.6	9.7	8.9	9.3	9.3	9.5	9.2
9.3	8.6	8.8	9.7	8.8	10.0	9.3	8.0
7.8	8.1	9.1	10.0	8.2	9.2	9.9	9.4
8.2	7.6	9.7	8.9	8.5	8.9	8.2	7.6
7.0	7.4	9.2	8.3	8.4	8.7	9.6	9.4
9.5	8.7	8.7	9.4	7.4	9.0	7.7	9.9
7.6	7.4	9.7	9.4	7.4	8.8	7.9	7.1
8.3	7.2	8.3	8.9	8.6	9.1	7.5	6.2
6.8	7.6	8.5	8.5	8.7	9.5	9.0	8.4
8.9	7.8	9.2	9.2	7.5	8.8	7.0	8.3
7.6	7.5	8.1	8.3	7.3	8.9	8.0	7.8
7.0	6.0	8.9	7.7	8.9	9.4	8.7	8.7
8.1	8.6	9.4	8.1	8.7	8.7	8.0	7.4
6.2	7.1	7.8	7.9	7.7	8.1	8.4	9.1
8.2	7.6	7.0	9.4	6.8	9.1	8.0	7.8
7.4	6.9	8.6	8.6	9.0	6.3	9.2	7.4
7.5	7.5	8.5	8.4	7.6	8.1	8.0	7.5
7.3	7.6	8.3	8.0	7.9	8.9	9.0	7.8
5.3	6.3	9.8	6.7	9.4	4.6	8.0	10.0
7.7	7.3	7.6	8.5	7.6	8.2	7.5	8.7
7.3	8.6	6.1	8.5	7.3	8.0	8.2	9.5
7.5	4.4	10.0	8.6	9.4	7.2	4.4	9.9
7.8	7.7	9.0	9.2	8.5	8.2	7.5	6.8
8.1	7.5	7.1	9.0	6.2	8.5	8.4	9.0
6.5	7.2	8.2	8.8	7.8	8.8	7.7	7.7
6.4	7.9	7.5	7.8	7.6	7.8	7.8	6.1
9.6	6.9	8.5	8.8	7.0	9.2	6.8	5.1
8.0	7.4	7.0	7.1	6.9	7.7	8.0	7.2
8.6	8.3	6.6	9.1	5.1	9.1	7.7	7.6
5.7	5.2	8.3	4.6	9.9	6.6	7.0	7.6
9.1	8.0	6.5	9.4	5.3	9.8	6.1	7.7
7.1	7.9	6.4	8.2	5.0	9.5	6.0	9.2
6.4	6.4	7.1	6.9	7.4	8.7	7.5	6.8
8.1	7.3	8.6	7.8	8.8	9.1	4.6	7.6
9.3	7.6	8.0	7.6	7.7	9.5	6.4	6.9
7.9	5.5	8.1	7.8	7.7	8.1	7.0	8.7
6.6	8.2	8.3	7.5	8.9	8.1	6.3	6.7
5.5	5.3	7.3	5.4	7.3	5.3	9.0	9.4

Country	Rank	Total	C1: Security Apparatus	C2: Factionalized Elites	C3: Group Grievance	E1: Economy
Burkina Faso	45th	86.5	8.5	7.8	4.2	6.6
Venezuela	46th	86.2	7.4	8.5	7.3	8.3
Philippines	47th	85.5	9.8	8.0	8.2	5.2
Malawi	47th	85.5	4.5	8.1	5.6	8.1
Togo	49th	85.2	6.8	7.6	4.9	6.7
Sri Lanka	50th	84.9	7.1	8.8	8.7	5.5
Papua New Guinea	51st	84.8	6.9	7.1	6.0	6.1
Iran	52nd	84.3	7.2	9.6	9.3	6.4
Cambodia	53rd	84.0	6.5	8.6	6.6	5.5
Madagascar	54th	83.6	7.2	7.8	3.8	7.6
Equatorial Guinea	55th	83.4	6.2	8.2	6.0	6.2
Solomon Islands	56th	83.1	5.9	8.2	6.2	7.4
Comoros	57th	82.6	6.4	8.0	5.1	7.9
Turkey	58th	82.2	8.0	9.1	10.0	4.5
Guatemala	59th	81.8	7.3	7.1	8.8	5.4
Laos	60th	80.7	5.2	8.3	6.4	5.5
Lesotho	61st	80.1	6.2	7.3	3.6	8.4
Senegal	62nd	79.6	5.9	6.9	6.1	7.2
Tajikistan	63rd	79.5	6.4	8.4	7.1	7.0
Tanzania	64th	79.4	5.4	5.7	4.9	6.3
Uzbekistan	67th	79.1	7.1	8.8	6.9	6.1
Kyrgyz Republic	65th	78.6	6.8	8.0	8.1	6.7
Israel and West Bank	66th	78.5	6.6	8.1	10.0	4.1
Honduras	68th	77.3	7.1	6.8	5.6	6.4
Russia	69th	77.2	8.6	8.1	8.5	4.9
Jordan	70th	76.8	5.6	6.9	8.3	6.7
Colombia	71st	76.6	6.6	7.6	7.0	4.5
India	72nd	76.3	7.1	7.3	8.3	5.0
Algeria	73rd	75.8	6.9	7.1	7.3	6.3
Benin	74th	75.7	6.2	6.7	3.1	6.5
Nicaragua	75th	75.3	5.3	7.1	6.2	5.6
Bolivia	76th	75.2	6.2	8.0	5.7	5.4
Thailand	77th	75.0	8.7	9.4	8.2	3.4
Azerbaijan	78th	74.6	6.1	7.9	6.2	4.1
Fiji	79th	74.5	7.1	7.9	6.6	6.2
Micronesia	80th	74.4	4.3	5.6	3.7	8.5
Bhutan	81st	74.3	4.2	7.5	8.2	5.0
Ecuador	82nd	74.2	6.5	8.2	7.0	6.0
Morocco	83rd	74.0	5.5	6.6	8.2	5.1
Georgia	83rd	74.0	6.5	9.1	7.6	5.8
South Africa	85th	72.9	6.4	6.6	6.4	7.1
Turkmenistan	86th	72.6	6.0	7.8	6.3	4.8
Ukraine	86th	72.6	7.4	8.0	6.4	6.6
Gabon	88th	72.5	4.7	7.9	3.5	5.8
Maldives	89th	72.4	6.1	8.3	4.5	5.6
China	89th	72.4	5.9	7.2	7.6	4.1

E2: Economic Inequality	E3: Human Flight and Brain Drain	P1: State Legitimacy	P2: Public Services	P3: Human Rights	S1: Demographic Pressures	S2: Refugees and IDPs	X1: External Intervention
7.9	7.5	6.8	8.4	5.9	8.8	6.3	7.8
6.6	6.0	9.0	7.8	9.0	5.7	5.1	5.5
5.4	6.3	7.5	6.4	7.1	7.5	7.2	6.9
8.0	7.7	6.4	8.3	6.2	9.4	5.5	7.7
8.2	7.5	8.1	8.5	6.8	7.5	6.9	5.7
6.8	7.4	6.6	4.8	8.4	6.7	8.1	6.0
9.1	7.4	6.5	9.1	7.3	7.8	4.9	6.5
5.6	6.2	9.2	4.2	9.2	5.0	6.2	6.2
6.5	7.5	8.5	7.5	7.8	6.5	5.4	7.1
9.1	7.0	6.8	8.9	5.8	9.0	4.2	6.5
8.4	5.2	9.8	8.0	8.9	7.6	4.2	4.7
8.7	7.2	6.5	7.5	4.9	8.0	4.1	8.5
7.2	7.1	7.0	7.9	6.0	7.3	5.0	7.7
5.4	4.9	7.7	4.9	7.8	5.2	9.3	5.4
7.8	7.2	6.6	7.2	7.1	7.1	5.3	4.9
6.2	7.7	8.9	6.7	7.6	7.0	5.4	5.8
7.8	8.3	5.6	7.8	4.9	8.0	4.7	7.5
7.1	8.0	4.4	7.3	5.7	7.7	7.0	6.4
4.5	6.1	9.1	5.3	8.3	7.6	4.1	5.6
7.4	7.6	5.8	8.7	6.0	8.3	6.4	6.9
6.7	5.8	9.5	4.7	8.7	5.4	5.3	4.1
5.6	6.7	7.4	4.8	7.2	5.6	5.0	6.7
6.5	4.1	6.5	4.5	7.2	5.7	7.5	7.8
7.4	6.1	6.9	6.6	6.8	5.8	4.6	7.2
5.9	3.7	8.5	3.9	9.2	4.7	5.5	5.7
5.1	4.0	6.1	3.9	7.7	6.2	9.1	7.1
7.3	5.9	6.0	5.6	6.7	6.3	7.4	5.7
6.7	6.4	4.4	7.1	5.8	8.0	5.0	5.2
6.3	6.0	7.2	5.7	6.3	4.9	7.1	4.6
7.9	7.4	5.1	8.4	4.9	8.0	5.2	6.3
7.7	7.8	7.6	6.5	4.9	5.4	3.8	7.4
8.3	7.1	6.6	6.5	6.0	6.3	3.7	5.5
5.0	5.0	7.6	4.1	8.0	6.5	5.6	3.5
5.6	4.0	8.8	5.1	8.6	4.3	7.4	6.5
6.0	8.5	6.6	4.7	6.6	4.4	3.0	6.9
8.0	9.9	5.2	5.7	3.6	6.6	3.6	9.8
5.6	7.2	4.0	5.8	6.3	5.8	6.7	8.0
6.7	5.5	6.2	6.2	4.5	6.0	5.4	6.0
5.9	8.0	6.9	4.9	6.5	4.9	5.8	5.7
5.2	4.6	8.0	4.0	5.3	3.4	7.2	7.3
7.2	5.8	6.8	7.0	4.3	6.9	5.1	3.3
6.7	5.0	9.7	5.3	8.7	5.4	3.2	3.8
3.9	4.9	7.9	3.9	6.5	3.9	4.9	8.3
6.2	6.1	7.9	6.6	7.5	6.6	4.2	5.4
3.3	6.5	8.3	5.5	8.0	5.7	4.4	6.2
7.0	4.9	8.6	5.4	8.5	6.2	4.6	2.4

Country	Rank	Total	C1: Security Apparatus	C2: Factionalized Elites	C3: Group Grievance	E1: Economy
Indonesia	91st	72.3	6.2	7.0	7.2	4.8
Sao Tome and Principe	92nd	72.1	5.0	6.3	4.2	8.5
Tunisia	92nd	72.1	8.0	7.8	7.4	6.6
Mexico	94th	71.5	8.5	5.4	6.9	4.7
Bosnia and Herzegovina	95th	71.3	5.4	8.7	6.9	6.0
El Salvador	96th	71.2	7.2	4.3	6.4	5.3
Belarus	97th	70.5	5.8	8.3	6.8	5.5
Guyana	98th	70.4	6.6	5.1	7.0	6.1
Saudi Arabia	99th	70.2	6.0	8.5	8.1	4.4
Peru	100th	70.1	6.8	6.9	7.7	3.5
Paraguay	101st	69.8	6.3	7.8	5.5	5.0
Moldova	102nd	69.5	5.8	8.3	7.3	6.1
Armenia	102nd	69.5	5.2	7.4	5.8	6.6
Dominican Republic	104th	69.2	6.1	6.2	5.5	5.2
Namibia	105th	68.8	5.2	3.5	5.5	7.1
Brazil	106th	68.7	6.8	5.2	6.5	4.5
Vietnam	107th	68.4	4.3	6.9	5.7	4.8
Ghana	108th	68.1	4.3	4.9	4.1	6.0
Serbia	108th	68.1	5.2	8.3	7.3	6.4
Cape Verde	110th	68.0	5.1	5.5	3.8	5.5
Samoa	111th	65.5	4.4	5.1	4.2	6.6
Macedonia	112th	64.8	5.3	7.3	6.6	6.1
Bahrain	113th	64.4	6.6	7.6	8.7	3.8
Suriname	114th	64.0	4.6	5.8	5.5	7.2
Belize	115th	63.7	6.7	4.3	3.8	6.6
Malaysia	116th	63.6	6.0	6.8	6.2	3.4
Kazakhstan	117th	63.4	4.9	7.6	7.9	5.9
Jamaica	118th	63.1	6.8	3.7	3.1	6.7
Cuba	119th	62.9	4.9	7.0	3.7	4.0
Botswana	120th	62.0	4.1	3.3	4.6	5.7
Cyprus	121st	60.3	4.4	7.9	6.0	5.7
Albania	122nd	60.1	4.8	6.5	4.2	5.7
Grenada	123rd	59.9	5.5	5.6	3.6	5.8
Brunei Darussalam	124th	59.8	4.8	7.4	5.6	3.8
Seychelles	125th	56.8	6.1	6.0	4.2	3.8
Kuwait	126th	55.9	3.9	7.5	4.4	2.7
Antigua and Barbuda	127th	55.6	5.7	3.7	3.6	4.8
Montenegro	128th	55.3	4.3	6.5	8.2	5.5
Greece	128th	55.3	4.4	4.1	5.1	6.2
Mongolia	130th	54.9	3.3	5.5	3.5	4.9
Trinidad and Tobago	131st	54.6	6.5	5.6	3.9	4.5
Oman	132nd	52.6	3.9	6.6	2.6	4.6
Bulgaria	133rd	51.7	4.6	5.3	5.1	5.5
Hungary	134th	50.2	3.0	5.3	4.5	5.1
Bahamas	135th	50.0	4.6	4.5	3.8	4.5
Panama	136th	49.5	5.5	2.2	5.6	2.9

E2: Economic Inequality	E3: Human Flight and Brain Drain	P1: State Legitimacy	P2: Public Services	P3: Human Rights	S1: Demographic Pressures	S2: Refugees and IDPs	X1: External Intervention
5.5	7.2	4.8	5.6	7.3	6.7	5.1	4.9
6.3	8.8	5.3	5.6	3.0	6.3	4.7	8.2
5.0	6.0	6.6	4.1	6.2	3.9	4.4	6.1
5.8	5.5	6.2	6.5	6.2	5.8	4.8	5.2
5.0	5.4	6.2	3.3	5.3	3.7	7.5	7.9
6.1	7.9	4.5	6.1	6.0	6.9	4.8	5.6
4.6	3.1	8.7	3.9	8.0	5.2	3.3	7.3
5.4	9.1	5.1	5.9	3.4	5.9	3.8	7.0
4.7	3.9	8.3	3.5	9.0	5.0	4.4	4.4
7.1	7.1	6.9	6.4	4.0	6.5	4.0	3.2
7.6	5.9	7.1	5.9	5.6	5.4	3.2	4.5
4.5	6.4	6.6	4.7	4.6	4.5	3.6	7.1
4.2	6.1	8.1	3.4	6.9	2.8	6.7	6.4
5.6	6.8	6.5	6.6	5.6	7.0	3.0	5.1
7.9	7.1	3.0	7.1	3.5	8.1	4.7	6.1
7.7	4.8	6.7	6.1	6.7	7.6	2.7	3.4
4.7	6.2	8.3	4.4	7.7	5.8	4.4	5.2
6.3	8.1	3.9	7.5	5.0	6.7	4.7	6.6
4.5	5.0	5.2	3.9	4.1	4.0	7.9	6.3
6.8	7.7	5.0	5.7	3.7	6.9	3.9	8.4
4.6	9.4	5.2	4.6	4.0	5.4	2.6	9.5
4.9	4.9	5.5	3.8	3.5	2.8	7.8	6.3
4.3	3.7	8.4	1.8	8.9	3.8	2.3	4.5
6.1	6.5	4.7	5.3	4.6	5.4	2.7	5.6
5.1	6.6	4.9	5.6	5.0	4.6	3.3	7.2
4.7	5.3	7.4	3.9	7.7	5.0	3.7	3.5
3.9	3.3	8.4	3.7	7.0	4.2	2.7	3.9
4.8	8.4	4.5	6.1	5.8	4.7	3.0	5.5
5.1	4.9	7.6	4.4	7.2	5.6	3.7	4.8
7.5	5.8	3.0	6.8	5.0	8.2	4.2	3.8
5.6	3.7	4.5	2.4	3.0	3.5	5.0	8.7
3.3	7.5	6.0	3.8	4.5	3.4	3.3	7.0
4.6	8.2	5.2	3.6	3.0	4.5	2.9	7.4
7.8	4.7	8.0	1.7	7.4	3.4	1.9	3.3
5.2	6.0	5.2	2.4	3.5	4.8	2.9	6.7
3.9	3.9	7.3	2.3	7.6	4.7	3.2	4.5
4.2	6.7	5.1	3.8	4.4	4.6	3.2	5.8
2.1	3.8	4.3	3.2	3.9	2.5	4.3	6.8
3.4	3.0	6.4	3.5	3.2	4.2	6.0	5.8
6.1	3.5	4.0	5.1	4.4	4.8	2.7	7.0
4.6	7.9	4.2	4.0	3.8	4.2	2.6	2.8
4.5	2.8	7.1	3.2	7.8	4.5	2.4	2.6
4.1	3.9	4.2	4.1	3.2	3.4	4.2	4.0
3.5	3.0	6.1	2.9	5.2	1.5	6.2	3.9
4.2	4.6	3.3	4.3	3.7	6.6	2.5	3.4
7.1	4.9	3.0	4.6	4.0	4.4	2.8	2.4

Country	Rank	Total	C1: Security Apparatus	C2: Factionalized Elites	C3: Group Grievance	E1: Economy
Romania	137th	49.4	2.7	5.7	6.5	4.6
Croatia	138th	48.7	3.2	4.4	5.5	5.6
Barbados	139th	48.2	4.4	4.2	3.8	5.6
Qatar	140th	48.1	2.3	5.0	4.3	1.8
Argentina	141st	46.1	4.6	2.8	4.7	4.2
Latvia	142nd	44.9	2.7	4.3	8.3	3.8
Italy	143rd	43.8	4.8	4.9	4.8	5.1
Costa Rica	144th	43.2	3.5	3.8	3.9	4.3
Estonia	145th	43.0	3.0	5.9	7.5	3.4
United Arab Emirates	146th	42.8	3.4	3.6	3.1	2.5
Slovak Republic	147th	42.5	2.1	5.0	6.6	4.3
Poland	148th	41.5	2.1	4.2	5.9	3.9
Spain	149th	41.4	3.1	7.2	5.8	4.9
Chile	150th	40.7	3.5	2.2	3.3	3.5
Mauritius	151st	40.5	2.0	3.2	3.5	4.3
Lithuania	152nd	39.4	2.9	3.0	4.1	4.2
Czech Republic	153rd	39.0	2.9	5.3	5.1	4.3
United States	154th	37.7	3.5	5.8	6.1	2.3
Malta	155th	36.2	3.3	2.0	3.6	4.0
South Korea	156th	35.7	2.4	3.9	2.6	2.0
Uruguay	157th	35.4	4.1	2.7	2.3	3.5
Japan	158th	34.5	1.9	2.6	3.4	3.8
United Kingdom	159th	34.3	3.2	5.0	6.4	3.6
France	160th	32.2	3.2	1.9	7.0	4.0
Singapore	161st	30.4	1.3	4.0	2.3	1.7
Slovenia	162nd	30.3	1.3	2.0	4.5	3.5
Belgium	163rd	29.7	2.3	4.4	4.6	4.5
Portugal	164th	27.3	1.0	2.5	2.2	4.8
Austria	165th	26.2	1.3	3.2	4.8	1.9
Netherlands	165th	26.2	1.8	3.4	4.5	2.4
Germany	167th	25.8	2.0	2.6	4.9	1.9
Canada	168th	21.5	2.5	2.5	3.1	1.8
New Zealand	169th	20.9	1.5	1.4	3.3	3.3
Sweden	170th	20.8	2.4	1.8	1.8	1.6
Australia	170th	20.8	2.4	1.7	3.6	1.9
Luxembourg	170th	20.8	1.4	3.4	2.8	1.3
Ireland	173rd	20.7	2.4	1.5	1.1	3.1
Iceland	174th	20.3	0.8	1.8	1.1	3.2
Denmark	175th	19.8	1.4	1.4	4.4	1.7
Switzerland	176th	19.2	1.4	1.0	3.6	2.0
Norway	177th	18.3	1.8	1.1	3.4	2.0
Finland	178th	17.9	2.2	1.4	1.5	3.2

Source: Fund for Peace, Washington DC.

E2: Economic Inequality	E3: Human Flight and Brain Drain	P1: State Legitimacy	P2: Public Services	P3: Human Rights	S1: Demographic Pressures	S2: Refugees and IDPs	X1: External Intervention
3.9	4.2	5.5	3.7	3.8	2.9	2.6	3.3
3.0	4.4	2.6	2.5	3.3	3.2	6.7	4.3
4.3	5.3	2.2	2.4	3.2	4.9	2.2	5.7
4.6	2.4	6.3	1.3	6.2	3.5	1.7	8.6
5.1	2.8	4.5	3.5	3.8	3.5	2.2	4.3
3.8	4.8	3.1	2.6	2.8	2.6	2.5	3.6
2.6	1.7	3.7	3.0	1.7	3.8	5.2	2.5
5.0	4.4	2.1	3.7	1.6	3.0	3.6	4.2
2.9	4.0	2.4	2.6	1.9	2.5	2.8	4.0
3.1	2.8	6.6	1.9	7.9	3.7	2.1	2.1
3.2	3.9	4.3	2.1	2.5	2.0	3.5	3.0
2.7	4.5	3.6	2.0	3.7	2.7	3.3	2.9
3.2	1.6	6.8	1.9	1.5	1.7	1.9	1.7
5.4	4.1	3.0	3.7	3.1	5.0	2.1	1.8
3.2	4.6	2.7	3.0	3.7	3.3	2.6	4.4
4.2	4.3	2.4	3.2	2.2	2.5	2.2	4.3
2.4	2.5	5.0	2.3	2.2	1.1	3.5	2.4
4.0	2.2	2.4	1.3	3.3	3.3	2.1	1.5
2.3	3.4	3.6	1.7	3.0	2.2	4.1	3.0
2.7	3.7	3.9	1.6	3.2	2.6	1.9	5.3
3.8	4.1	0.7	2.8	3.1	3.5	2.4	2.5
1.3	3.5	0.9	1.9	3.1	4.5	4.1	3.5
3.7	2.4	1.8	1.3	1.8	2.1	1.9	1.0
2.9	2.5	1.0	1.1	1.9	2.5	2.5	1.8
3.5	3.0	3.9	1.0	4.9	2.2	1.4	1.2
3.1	3.3	2.4	1.3	1.2	2.0	3.7	2.0
2.4	1.7	1.7	2.0	1.2	1.7	2.5	0.7
2.2	1.9	1.3	2.5	1.5	2.6	2.1	2.6
2.6	1.2	1.4	1.0	1.0	1.6	5.3	0.9
1.9	2.5	1.0	0.8	1.0	2.2	3.5	1.2
2.7	2.0	0.7	0.9	0.8	1.7	4.9	0.7
2.2	2.0	0.7	1.2	1.3	1.6	1.9	0.7
2.0	2.4	0.6	1.1	0.8	1.8	1.8	0.9
1.6	1.2	0.8	0.9	0.9	1.7	5.2	0.9
1.9	1.3	0.7	1.2	2.0	1.4	2.0	0.7
1.3	1.8	0.7	1.8	1.0	1.3	3.2	0.8
1.9	2.6	0.7	1.4	1.7	1.5	1.7	1.1
0.9	2.6	1.0	1.0	0.8	1.4	1.8	3.9
1.3	2.0	0.9	0.9	1.2	1.7	2.1	0.7
1.9	1.8	0.7	0.9	1.5	1.2	2.5	0.7
1.0	1.4	0.6	0.8	0.9	1.3	2.9	1.1
0.7	2.3	0.9	0.7	0.7	1.1	2.2	1.0